Illustration from the Souvenir Album for *The Marriage Circle* (1924)

Ernst
LUBITSCH

a guide to
references and resources

A
Reference
Publication
in
Film

Ronald Gottesman
Editor

Ernst
LUBITSCH

a guide to
references and resources

ROBERT CARRINGER
BARRY SABATH

G.K.HALL&CO.

70 LINCOLN STREET, BOSTON, MASS.

Copyright © by Robert Carringer and Barry Sabath

Library of Congress Cataloging in Publication Data
Carringer, Robert
  Ernst Lubitsch: a guide to references and resources.

  (A Reference publication in film)
  Bibliography: p.
  Includes indexes.
  1. Lubitsch, Ernst, 1892-1947.   I. Sabath, Barry,
joint author.   II. Series.
PN1998.A3L832   791.43'0233'0924   78-1639
ISBN 0-8161-7895-X

This publication is printed on permanent/durable acid-free paper
MANUFACTURED IN THE UNITED STATES OF AMERICA

for Sonia

*

for Gladys *and* Herman Lazar

Contents

Preface

The following work is a guide to research on the films and career of Ernst Lubitsch. It attempts to provide a record of all the important critical, historical, and biographical information that is available about the director. It begins with a biographical and a critical essay which furnish background and give a general overview of Lubitsch's life and films. These essays are followed by an annotated filmography (Section III); an annotated bibliography of writings about Lubitsch (Section IV); descriptions of Lubitsch's stage performances, writings, and other significant film·related activity (Section V); a guide to archival resources for further research (Section VI); and a list of Lubitsch films available for rental and purchase (Section VII). Author and film title indexes for Sections III through VII are also included.

These general procedures and policies have been followed:

Each item has been assigned an entry number, beginning with 1 for the first item in the filmography and continuing for each entry through all the remaining sections, and these entry numbers are the basis of the index.

The information within each section is arranged chronologically. In the filmography, the year of each film's release is given after its title. In the other sections, a year heading is given under which the individual items for that year are grouped (alphabetically within the year for bibliography entries, chronologically for film or stage projects). The year designation is not repeated through the entries, so that all dates given in an entry refer to the year heading unless otherwise indicated.

In a small number of cases an asterisk (*) appears before a film title or bibliographical entry. This designates an item the authors have not seen.

Whenever a reference gives only a name and a date, such as Weinberg (1968), that item will be found in the bibliography (Section IV). (The example given would be Herman G. Weinberg's book The Lubitsch Touch, published in 1968.)

If no English-language version of a foreign film was ever prepared, an English translation of the original title is given in quotation marks in parentheses following the title. These translations are not indexed.

Names were a special source of difficulty. Many of Lubitsch's collaborators (like Lubitsch himself) had bi- or international careers, and in Hollywood their names were usually Americanized. Our usual policy has been to adopt the most frequent American usage. For instance, Ernest Vajda designates the Hungarian playwright Vajda Ernö, who emigrated to the United States in the 1920s and was screenwriter on several Lubitsch films (and who was also often called Ernst Vajda in the American press). Similarly for figures whose collaboration with Lubitsch began in Germany and continued in America: for instance, for Lubitsch's perennial screenwriter in the silent era we have used the form Hans Kraly (he was also called Hanns and also Kraely in America) except where the name appears as official credit on a German film, in which case it is Hans Kräly. When citing players, whose foreign-looking names were sometimes changed more than once, we have also followed the policy of citing the most frequent American usage.

We have normalized capitalization in the titles of books, articles, and films in accord with prevailing contemporary usage.

The following guidelines have been observed in the individual sections:

The Films: Synopsis, Credits and Notes (Section III). Each entry includes (where the information is available) a plot synopsis, extensive credit lists, notes on significant production and distribution matters, a list of major reviews, and citations of published items of importance about that particular film. (Sometimes an item written about a single film may have special significance, in which case we include it separately with an annotation in the bibliography section. Such instances can easily be found by checking the film title index.)

Almost all of the synopses are based on screenings of the films themselves. In the few instances where we were unable to screen a print of an extant film, or where we added special information to our own synopsis, we have derived the synopsis or the additional information from such sources as copyright records, retrospective booklets, and contemporary reviews; these circumstances are so indicated. [There are eight Lubitsch films or fragments of films known to be extant that we have not seen; seven German titles--Fräulein Piccolo and Hans Trutz im Schlaraffenland, two early comedies he acted in; Wenn vier dasselbe tun, an early comedy he acted in and also directed; Ein fideles Gefängnis, an early comedy he directed; Kohlhiesels Töchter, a later comedy he directed; Das Weib des Pharao, the last of his German costume spectacles; and Die Flamme (fragment), his last German feature--and Eternal Love, an American silent feature with added synchronized sound.]

Information on Lubitsch's films in Germany (especially the first
five years) is very scant. In establishing the titles and chronology
of the German canon we have followed Gerhard Lamprecht, Deutsche
Stummfilme [1903-1931], 9 vols., Berlin: Deutsche Kinemathek e.V.,
1967-1969. There is one set of exceptions: we have included in the
filmography five items which are not listed by Lamprecht but which
have been listed in major Lubitsch filmographies such as Huff (1947),
Verdone (1964), Brion (1968), and Weinberg (1968) and about which no
additional information is available: Meyer auf der Alm (1913), Meyer
als Soldat (1914), Aufs Eis geführt (1915), Wo ist mein Schatz?
(1916), and Der Schwarze Moritz (1916). (All other items which have
been attributed to Lubitsch but which do not appear in Lamprecht are
included and explained in Section V under "Apocryphal and Unverified
Film Credits.") Occasionally we have been able to supplement the
credit and production information in Lamprecht with material from
retrospective festival programs, and booklets and press sheets, published memoirs and biographies, specialized studies such as Horak
(1975), and other sources such as unpublished research information
furnished to us by Jay Leyda. But the historical record on many of
these films is still very fragmentary, and in some cases the chronological order we have assigned is conjectural. The amount of information on the German films increases significantly after 1918 (because Lubitsch's features began then to draw considerable attention
and also because most of the films after 1918 survive) and again
after December 1920 (when his films began to be shown in the United
States).

Plot synopses for the American films are based on actual screenings in all but three cases: Kiss Me Again and The Patriot (both
apparently lost) and Eternal Love (inaccessible). The principal
credits for the American films are almost always taken from the
prints themselves if original English-language release prints were
available (though corrections were sometimes necessary, as when there
were inconsistencies between what appears in the credits and what
appears in the film itself). Additional credits and information are
based on extensive research in studio records, newspapers and trade
papers, publicity materials, memoirs and biographies (published and
unpublished), interviews, and archival records. An attempt has been
made to verify every credit in the American films independently of
previously published filmographies. New credits or production details which turned up in the process of this research have been included in the filmography proper if there was sufficient verification (usually the documentation is provided elsewhere in the entry,
as in the notes or the "also see" citations at the end of most entries). Material for which there was insufficient verification
(whether or not it has appeared in previous filmographies) is usually
included in the notes following the filmography.

The date after a source work is the date of first performance or
publication; if not given it is not known. The dates of shooting
have usually been reconstructed from contemporary trade papers.

Lengths of silent films, both German and American, are given in both
feet and meters. Published lengths or running times of films often
vary considerably (trade reviewers listed conflicting information,
there was recutting between preview and release, and so on); whenever
we were unable to resolve such discrepancies we indicated the vari-
ances.

One note of special interest: once Lubitsch started directing he
inevitably played an active role in the scripting of his films as
well. Though he probably deserves a co-writer credit on almost every
film he directed, beginning with his first American film, Rosita, we
have included such a credit only in those very rare cases (such as
The Smiling Lieutenant) when he took the credit himself.

We have included for every Lubitsch film shown in America a citation to the reviews in the New York Times, Variety, and Film Daily
(called Wid's Daily in the early years). (The Times weekday reviews
are readily accessible in the collected New York Times Film Reviews.
We have also included the Sunday followup reviews, which are not included in this collection but are available on microfilm--as are Variety and Film Daily.) Next we have included other American trade
reviews: Moving Picture World for the silent era, its successor
publication Motion Picture Herald for the sound years, and Daily
Variety and Hollywood Reporter from 1933 on. Then come reviews
from American magazines (all items listed in general and specialized
periodical indexes plus numerous others uncovered in the process of
research), followed by the London Times, then by British and foreign-
language items. Notes: Several publications occasionally ran articles of excerpts from reviews in big city newspapers; we have also
cited and identified these when we have them. We have also cited
Carl Sandburg's film reviews which appeared in the Chicago Daily News
from 1921 to 1927. No page numbers are given for New Yorker reviews
because that magazine was published in two editions with separate
pagination during much of the period covered.

The "also see" citations in each entry indicate highlights of the
inception, production, and exhibition of the film, mainly as they
were reported in the trade press, plus other items such as published
notes and study guides, articles on performers, sections of memoirs
and biographies, and brief critical or historical writings which ap-
ply specifically to that one film.

Writings about Ernst Lubitsch, 1920-1977 (Section IV). This
section describes items of significance that have been published in
English, French, German, and Italian. Also included are descriptions
of a monograph in Russian (99) and a special Lubitsch periodical issue in Danish (197), as well as bibliographical citations of a small
number of items the authors have not seen (designated by an asterisk). Only items we considered to be of real importance are listed.
(Numerous items of lesser importance pertaining to an individual film
have been included in the "also see" entries in the filmography.

Some items we judged of very little importance have not been included
at all. Material on Lubitsch in general film surveys and histories
is not included unless it has special significance.) A number of the
entries are actually groupings of related items on the same person or
topic, such as Mary Pickford (149), the press interviews on Lubitsch's first American visit (85), the 1968 Museum of Modern Art Lubitsch retrospective (161), or the several analytic subject entries
involving topics of special importance in Lubitsch's career--the
"German invasion" (84), Paramount's Astoria studios venture (102),
the Motion Picture Production Code (123), Lubitsch's term as head of
production at Paramount (124), his independent production venture
with Sol Lesser (133), and so on. Note: Often, more than one article on a topic appears in the same issue of a newspaper or trade magazine. In such cases the citation is given as follows: Variety,
Dec. 17, 1920, pp. 1, 45, p. 41 (indicating that one article begins
on page 1 and is continued on page 45, and a second article appears
on page 41).

Among the bibliographical entries are several extended studies of
Lubitsch's films: two books (162, 205), two monographs (155, 160),
six special features or issues of magazines and journals (143, 144,
152, 158, 159, 197), an unpublished M.A. thesis (189), and an unpublished Ph.D. dissertation (199).

Writings, Performances, and Other Film Related Activity
(Section V). Lubitsch's "Stage Performances" are given in three
separate lists. The basic list, "Productions for Max Reinhardt (Verified)," was established from Die Spielpläne Max Reinhardts 1905-
1930, ed. Franz Horch (Munich: R. Piper, 1930). Verifications and
additional information were found in programs or photographs in the
Max-Reinhardt-Forschungs-und Gedenkstätte, Salzburg; the Leo Baeck
Institute, New York City; and the Max Reinhardt Archive, Center for
Modern Theatre Research, State University of New York, Binghamton. A
second list includes Max Reinhardt productions in which Lubitsch is
reported to have appeared but for which verification is lacking. A
third (brief) list includes reported non-Reinhardt stage performances
by Lubitsch.

The twenty-one separate items listed as "Writings" are all signed
by Lubitsch or carry his byline. (Undoubtedly many of them are ghost
written.) The list of "Miscellaneous Film Credits" includes Lubitsch's minor involvement in three projects by other directors and
one previously unreported minor project of his own. "Unrealized
Projects" is a lengthy list of film and stage activities which Lubitsch planned and participated in but never saw to fruition. The
information is derived principally from trade papers (in many cases
there is additional corroboration in other sources). While some of
these projects actually reached the stage of active preparation, others are undoubtedly not much more than trial balloons. In any case,
in each instance we have tried to indicate the extent of Lubitsch's
involvement. At the end of this section is a single list in one entry of unrealized projects about which very little is known.

Preface

"Apocryphal or Unverified Film Credits" is a single list combining
three categories: films or film credits once incorrectly attributed
to Lubitsch but later corrected; films or film credits attributed to
Lubitsch but not yet either verified or discounted; and possible additional film credits for Lubitsch mentioned in this work for the first
time but for which information on the precise nature of Lubitsch's
role is still lacking.

Archival Sources (Section VI). This section includes a detailed
description of prints of films, scripts, production stills, clipping
files, and other special material on Lubitsch and his films in principal libraries and archives throughout the United States and abroad.
The descriptions of the American collections are based on our own
examination of the materials. The entries on foreign archives are
based on descriptions provided by the archives themselves. Note:
Script designations varied from studio to studio in Hollywood. For
clarity, we have adopted a uniform generic naming system for scripts:
any script used in the preparation for or making of a film we call a
production script (and then give the precise designation--"first
draft continuity," "final," and so on--that appears on the script
itself); the full release script of a sound film we call a scene and
dialogue continuity; a release script without dialogue (whether silent or sound) we call a scene continuity; and a release script with
dialogue alone we call a dialogue continuity.

Film Distributors (Section VII). This section lists Lubitsch
films currently available for purchase or non-theatrical rental in
the United States, followed by a list of the rental sources. For
various reasons, the availability of films is in constant flux; for
up-to-date information consult the current edition of Feature Films
on 8mm and 16mm, compiled by James L. Limbacher. Note: Only two of
Lubitsch's German films are currently available for rental, Carmen
and Madame Dubarry, and only four of his American silents, The Marriage Circle, Lady Windermere's Fan, So This Is Paris, and The Student Prince. Among his sound films, The Smiling Lieutenant, Heaven
Can Wait, and That Lady in Ermine are not currently available.

This work contains a considerable amount of new information about
Lubitsch. The record of his life and career after 1920 has been
carefully reconstructed from specialized sources, many of which have
not been used in previous writing. There is new information too on
his early years, such as the calendar of his acting performances with
the Max Reinhardt company. But there is a vast amount yet to be done
before the record about Lubitsch will be reasonably complete, and the
present effort is intended as a base for further research. The
largest gap in the Lubitsch record concerns his early life and career. So far as we know, no serious, systematic, full-scale effort
to study any facet of his professional activity in the German period
has ever been undertaken. A number of the original participants in
Lubitsch's early stage and film projects are still alive, several of
them living in the United States. A good portion of the newspaper

and trade press records for the period survive in libraries and archives in Germany. Some of the rare early German trade periodicals
have recently become available on microfilm (see entry 351). One of
the major priorities in Lubitsch studies ought to be a careful inves-
tigation into his biography and career before 1920. If this volume
helps to stimulate such efforts, it will have accomplished one of its
goals.

Acknowledgments

We are very grateful to the following institutions and their staffs, and especially to the individuals and departments named, for their generous cooperation and assistance in the preparation of this work: Reference Department, University Library, University of Illinois at Urbana-Champaign; Mildred Simpson and Sam Gill of the Margaret Herrick Library, and Tony Slide of the National Film Information Service, Academy of Motion Picture Arts and Sciences; Jim Powers and Anne Schlosser, American Film Institute, Beverly Hills; the Leo Baeck Institute; James Card and Marshall Deutelbaum, International Museum of Photography, George Eastman House; Henry Marx, Goethe House; Patrick Sheehan and Barbara Humphrys, Motion Picture Section, Library of Congress; Eileen Bowser, Charles Silver, and Emily Sieger, Film Study Center, Museum of Modern Art; Edward J. Reese, Modern Military Branch, Military Archives Division, National Archives; Theatre Collection, Library of the Performing Arts at Lincoln Center, New York Public Library; Department of Cinema Studies, and Elmer Holmes Bobst Library, New York University; Alfred G. Brooks, Max Reinhardt Archive, State University of New York at Binghamton; Robert Epstein of the UCLA Film Archive, Audree Malkin of the Theater Arts Library, and Brooke Whiting of the Special Collections Library, University of California at Los Angeles; English Department, and Unit for Cinema Studies, University of Illinois at Urbana-Champaign; Robert Knutson, Department of Special Collections, Doheny Library, University of Southern California; and Susan Dalton and Steve Masar, Wisconsin Center for Film and Theatre Research. We also thank the members of Fédération Internationale des Archives du Film (FIAF) outside the United States who provided information for the archival survey in Section VI, and especially Slavoj Ondrousek and Myrtil Frida of the Czechoslovak Film Institute; Heinz Rathsack of the Stiftung Deutsche Kinemathek; and Eberhard Spiess of the Deutsches Institut für Filmkunde.

Those who study Lubitsch will always owe a special debt to the pioneering work of Herman G. Weinberg. We give warm thanks to Samson Raphaelson for providing us with detailed recollections of his close association with Lubitsch and to Jay Leyda for sharing with us his vast professional knowledge and experience. For unstinting service above and beyond the call of friendship we are grateful to Betty

Acknowledgments

Kepley and George Scheetz. The assistance of the following persons
was indispensable: Nancy Allen, Monty Arnold, Helene Berger, David
Culbert, Lotte H. Eisner, Allen Estrin, William K. Everson, Christian
Gollub, Harold Grieve, David Hamrin, Steven P. Hill, Henry Kahane,
Anna Koretz, Richard Koszarski, Lisa Lewis, Mary Loos, Herbert G.
Luft, Constance Markey, George Marton, Marta Mierendorff, P. M.
Mitchell, Gary Osterbach, Gene Ringgold, and Donald Staples.

We acknowledge with deep appreciation the financial assistance
provided by the Research Board, Graduate Collete, University of Illinois at Urbana-Champaign.

I. Biographical Background

Ernst Lubitsch was born on January 28, 1892, in Berlin. His ancestry may have included Polish and Hungarian elements. He was brought up in the predominantly Jewish garment district around Hausvogtei Square where his father, Simon Lubitsch, operated a small clothing store. One of Lubitsch's earliest memories, he later recalled, was of deciding at age six he wanted to be an actor. But like many parents, Simon expected his son to go into the family business. When Lubitsch left high school, the Sophien Gymnasium, at sixteen, he served for a time as an apprentice in his father's shop. According to reports, he was a bumbling clerk and was soon shunted off to the back room out of sight to keep books. Not very long after, Lubitsch devised a way so that he could study acting at night while working for his father during the day. At nineteen Lubitsch was short and slight, clumsy and gawky, with a crooked nose and pronounced facial features, and already looked like a much older man-- not a very promising appearance for a would-be actor. Soon he began to appear in low comedy roles in music halls. Eventually Victor Arnold, a member of the Max Reinhardt theater company and a renowned Shakespearean comedian, arranged an introduction for Lubitsch to Reinhardt, the driving force behind the contemporary German theater.

Reinhardt possessed a rare gift for discovering talent. Many of the major actors, directors, and designers who were to become famous in the ensuing heyday of the German film industry, such as Paul Wegener, Paul Leni, F. W. Murnau, and Emil Jannings, served their apprenticeships in Reinhardt's theater company. Reinhardt saw promise in Lubitsch and took him into the company, where he continued to work and appear for seven years, beginning in 1911. His early roles were as extras or walk-ons. Later he began to specialize in old-age roles such as Wagner in Faust, Part I. He also played numerous small Shakespearean roles and occasionally had much larger parts, such as the female witch in the pantomime The Green Flute and the villain Kostylev in Gorki's Lower Depths.

Although his roles were gradually enlarged, Lubitsch never achieved major status in the Reinhardt company. Nevertheless, his seven years with Reinhardt laid a solid foundation for his future career. He received a full education in the mechanics and skills of staging comedy. Years later, he recalled of this experience:

1

> ...when I was a young man in Max Reinhardt's company in
> Germany I was Shakespearean straight man to one of the
> greatest Shakespearean clowns. If so much as one
> snicker still could be heard in the balcony, I had to
> keep my mouth shut. 'Ride the laugh!' he would yell
> when we came off the stage. 'Say nothing until the
> house is ready to listen again!' He would kill me
> every time I forgot (New York Times Magazine, Mar. 3,
> 1940, p. 13).

He learned all the rudiments of acting, and though he was never to be
an actor of consequence himself, one of his strongest skills as a
film director was in handling actors. He also gained a broad range
of experience with a wide variety of dramatic works, from classics
old and new to offbeat romance spectacles, and like Reinhardt himself
was later able to move freely among the various types--for instance,
making a small, quiet, intimate adaptation of a stage comedy like So
This Is Paris (1926) and immediately following it up with an ambitious big-budget spectacle like The Student Prince (1927). Finally,
he learned the staging of spectacle from Reinhardt, the acknowledged
modern master of the craft, an influence which was to be quite evident when he shortly began to make film costume romances.

In 1913, Lubitsch began appearing in short films to supplement
his small salary from the theater. He was able to earn twenty marks
for a day's work in front of the camera and was still able to continue with his theater work at night. He drew from his own experience in his earliest films, the "department store romances." In
these slapstick comedies he usually played an uncoordinated and
bungling but ambitious Jewish apprentice who makes good in the end.
Soon Lubitsch began directing his own films. He has described how
he made the leap from acting to directing:

> Although being starred in...DER STOLZ DER FIRMA [1914],
> and despite its success, my picture career came to a
> standstill. I was typed, and no one seemed to write
> any part which would have fitted me. After two suc-
> cesses, I found myself completely left out of pictures,
> and as I was unwilling to give up I found it necessary
> that I had to create parts for myself. Together with
> an actor friend of mine, the late Erich Schoenfelder, I
> wrote a series of one-reelers which I sold to the Union
> Company. I directed and starred in them. And that is
> how I became a director. If my acting career had pro-
> gressed more smoothly I wonder if I ever would have be-
> come a director (Entry 269).

At this point began Lubitsch's prolonged association with producer Paul Davidson, founder of the Union Film Company and later to
be one of the guiding forces in the Ufa studios. For a short period
he divided his time between writing, directing, and appearing in his

own short comedies and acting in comedies directed by others. After making several successful films for Union, Lubitsch formed a short-lived independent production company with some friends, but according to Davidson, the one film he made "was so bad that no one wanted to buy it" and soon after he returned to the Union fold. Lubitsch made one non-comedic film in this period. In his opinion, it was a total flop because he departed from his popular screen persona:

> Like every comedian, I longed to play a straight leading man, a sort of 'bonvivant' role. So together with my collaborators I wrote a screenplay, called ALS ICH TOT WAR ("When I Was Dead"). This picture was a complete failure as the audiences were unwilling to accept me as a straight leading man (Entry 269).

So Lubitsch returned to the kinds of roles audiences expected him to play in Schuhpalast Pinkus (1916), another ethnic slapstick comedy about a store clerk who makes good. According to Lubitsch, it was so successful it got him a new contract with Union to make more pictures of the same sort. Gradually a small repertory company began to form around Lubitsch the director. It included photographer Theodor Spar-kuhl, set designer Kurt Richter, and writer Hans Kraly (who continued writing scenarios for Lubitsch throughout the silent era). In 1916 they were joined by an energetic and impudent young blonde and former film extra. Lubitsch had discovered her, christened her Ossi Os-walda, and featured her opposite himself in Leutnant auf Befehl. Her mischievous charm and effervescence scored an immediate hit with au-diences, and the following year Lubitsch featured her in a film built around her talents, Ossis Tagebuch (1917). This was the first of Lubitsch's films in which he did not appear himself. After Ossis Tagebuch he concentrated more and more on directing and appeared in fewer films. Altogether he made more than a dozen films with Ossi, who became known as "the German Mary Pickford."

In November 1917, a merger of German film companies, including Davidson's Union company, produced the Universum Film A. G. (Ufa). One of the early projects of the new company was to introduce Pola Negri, an eminent Polish actress who had been brought to Berlin under the aegis of Reinhardt, to the German public in a vehicle worthy of her talents. Davidson, Lubitsch, and Negri all later claimed credit for initiating the project, but in any case Lubitsch's first dramatic feature, Die Augen der Mumie Mâ (1918), starred Negri and was a phe-nomenal success. With deep-set brooding eyes, jet-black hair, and an alluring but hard sensuality, Negri was a Middle European Theda Bara. Her second film with Lubitsch was Carmen (1918), the well-known story of a gypsy femme fatale which Bara had made a version of in 1915. Carmen was an unprecedented success. With this film, one critic wrote at the time, "The effectiveness of the German film industry and its indisputable capability to compete successfully on the world mar-ket has been unequivocally proven" (in Licht-Bild-Bühne, quoted in Horak [1975], p. 74).

By this time Lubitsch had given up his theater work and was de-
voting full time to films. He continued to direct slapstick comedies
such as <u>Meyer aus Berlin</u> (1918) and he also ventured in new directions in comedy, such as with his spoof of the American bourgeoisie
in <u>Die Austernprinzessin</u> (1919) and his Bavarian adaptations of
Shakespeare, <u>Kohlhiesels Töchter</u> (1920) and <u>Romeo und Julia im Schnee</u>
(1920). But Ufa officials knew that it was the costume films that
were truly capable of reaching an international market. After <u>Carmen</u>
Lubitsch went on to make a series of super-spectacular costume films
with Negri (or in one case a Negri substitute)--<u>Madame Dubarry</u> (1919),
<u>Sumurun</u> (1920, in which Lubitsch made his last acting appearance in a
featured role), and <u>Anna Boleyn</u> (1920). These films had huge budgets
and unusually high production values for the times, including mammoth
sets erected on the backlot instead of painted backdrops, lavish costumes, and masses of extras. Well-scripted, ostentatiously staged,
and directed with meticulous attention to detail, they performed so
well at the box office that Ufa was able to show a profit for the
fiscal year 1920, just one year after the Armistice.

One of the Lubitsch costume films, <u>Madame Dubarry</u>, retitled <u>Pas-</u>
<u>sion</u> for U.S. release, was the film that broke the blockade in effect
from World War I against American importation of German films and
launched the so-called "German invasion." Popular sentiment against
things German was so strong in this country at the time that <u>Passion</u>
was originally announced as "imported from Italy," and later much was
made of the fact that Pola Negri was not German. Lubitsch was described as "apparently Teutonic," and one American reviewer wondered
if he had "ever worked in Paris, or under French influence," since
<u>Passion</u> did not seem the work of a "heavy-handed German director, of
the kind indigenous to Germany." Cautious backers carefully tested
the film in selected locations before its New York premiere on December 12, 1920, and it was received enthusiastically everywhere. Its
phenomenal success with American audiences opened the way for other
Lubitsch films--<u>Anna Boleyn</u> (retitled <u>Deception</u>) opened in April 1921,
<u>Carmen</u> (retitled <u>Gypsy Blood</u>) in May, <u>Sumurun</u> (retitled <u>One Arabian</u>
<u>Night</u>) in October--and other previously unseen German films such as
Wiene's <u>The Cabinet of Dr. Caligari</u> (opened April 1921) and Wegener's
<u>Der Golem</u> (opened June 1921). The American release of these films
ultimately led to the importation of German directors and stars.

With the tremendous success of German films in America, American
producers quickly realized that Germany was an advantageous center
for film activity. In the spring of 1921 Adolph Zukor's Famous Players Corporation invested in the establishment of the Europeaischen
Film-Allianz (Efa), a coalition of producing units that included
(among others) the Max Reinhardt and the Ernst Lubitsch companies.
Lubitsch recruited many of his former associates to join his Efa company, and his first Efa production, <u>Das Weib des Pharao</u> (1922), starring Emil Jannings, was a grand costume film in the tradition of
<u>Madame Dubarry</u>. One aspect of the Famous Players program was to pro-
vide for an interchange and cross-fertilization of talent between

European and American directors. Consequently Lubitsch left Germany for America on December 12, 1921, to study film producing conditions in this country, and it was understood that he might direct one film at the New York studios of Famous Players. His first American visit had a triumphant beginning. The arrival was covered with great enthusiasm by the American press, and the 29 year old Lubitsch was hailed as "the Griffith of Europe." While in New York, Lubitsch attended the premieres of von Stroheim's Foolish Wives and Griffith's Orphans of the Storm. He had been expected to visit Hollywood and also to be in attendance for the American premiere of The Loves of Pharaoh on February 21, 1922, but instead he abruptly cut his visit short and sailed for Berlin on January 17. According to Variety, Lubitsch had received unpleasant telephone calls and letters, and he gave as the reason for his sudden departure the belief that "he was regarded here as an unfriendly person and an enemy of the American actor" (Variety, Feb. 3, 1922, p. 46). Famous Players urged him to disregard these troublemakers and tried to persuade him to go to Hollywood to film an elaborate spectacle. But Lubitsch would not be dissuaded. Once back in Germany he made Die Flamme (1923), with Pola Negri as a Parisian strumpet who temporarily reforms, a period film on a smaller, more intimate level than the costume spectacles.*

Despite a few successes, the majority of German films shown in America had not been hugely profitable. Efa was disbanded, and Famous Players decided to recoup their investments by importing their European talent to work in the United States. Pola Negri left for America in September 1922. Lubitsch was hesitant to accept Famous Players' offer, but when Mary Pickford cabled him an invitation in November to come and direct her in Dorothy Vernon of Haddon Hall, a

---

*At the end of the production of Die Flamme, in August 1922, Lubitsch was married to Irni (Helene) Kraus, the widow of a German soldier and mother of two plump boys, Ernst, age nine, and Edmund, age six. Lubitsch's new wife had acted in several small roles in German films and stage productions, but had never appeared in a film directed by her husband. Several years later, in 1925, it was reported that she had repeatedly tried to coax her husband into allowing her to appear in his films. It was also reported that Mrs. Lubitsch would appear in films by Warner Brothers (the studio that employed her husband at the time), but her acting career never resumed.

Lubitsch's domestic life did not keep up with the successful pace of his professional career. On June 23, 1930, his wife sued for divorce. She charged that her husband was "99% in love with his work and had no time for home" (New York Times, June 24, 1930, p. 23). He was also accused of insulting her friends and of scolding and nagging her. Several months later, a further reason for the divorce became known. At a Saturday night benefit ball given by Mary Pickford and Douglas Fairbanks at the Embassy Club, Lubitsch got into a fist fight with Hans Kraly, his veteran scenarist. Kraly had escorted the former Mrs. Lubitsch to the affair. When the fight broke out, Mrs. Lubitsch responded by hitting her ex-husband. Two hours after the fracas, Kraly and Mrs. Lubitsch announced their plans to wed. Although the two never did marry, Lubitsch declared at the time that his former friend had broken up the Lubitsch marriage. The irony was all too apparent. A genuine Lubitsch plot situation had apparently been played out under the master's own roof. Kraly never worked for Lubitsch again.

5

departure from her usual "Little Mary" pictures, he quickly accepted
and a loan-out arrangement with Famous Players was worked out.

Lubitsch arrived in America in mid-December. His association
with Pickford was a case of one strong-willed and independent personality in conflict with another. First Lubitsch rejected the script
of Dorothy Vernon of Haddon Hall and suggested Faust instead, with
Mary as Marguerite. Preparations got under way but soon this project
was abandoned too. Finally they settled on Rosita (1923), a story
Lubitsch had brought with him from Germany, with fair-haired Mary as
a Spanish street singer. (Ironically, Pola Negri was simultaneously
filming another version of the same story just across town.) Practically everyone who has seen Rosita has been impressed with it but
Mary Pickford detests the film and has conspired over the years to
keep it out of circulation.

After Rosita Lubitsch's plans were indefinite. His Famous Players contract was cancelled by mutual agreement in mid-June 1923, and
he was said to be considering a permanent return to Germany. However, Warner Brothers persuaded him to accept a four-year term contract. Warner Brothers was a small but expanding studio that had
mainly turned out competent action films. The Warners felt that ac-
quiring an internationally-famed director would lend prestige to the
studio. The proven record of Lubitsch's German films at the box office was another big incentive. Curiously, in view of her distaste
for Rosita, Mary Pickford also signed Lubitsch to a three-year contract later the same year, but despite several announcements of impending projects, nothing ever came out of the new contract with
Pickford.

Around the beginning of this affiliation with Warners, Lubitsch
was invited to a preview of Charlie Chaplin's A Woman of Paris (1923).
Chaplin's film was a sentimental melodrama with a cynical tinge about
a kept woman, the rich playboy who supports her, and the former
sweetheart who eventually commits suicide over her. Lubitsch claimed
that this film had a tremendous influence on him. A major part of
this influence must have been the encouragement A Woman of Paris gave
him to start making the kinds of films he wanted to. He said at the
time:

> ...in my first [American] picture, I had to make all
> kinds of concessions to what they told me the American
> people wanted. I made my first one that way. This one
> I am going to make to please Lubitsch (Motion Picture
> Classic, Feb. 1924, p. 38).

Because of his artistic reputation, Lubitsch was able to win a contract with Warner Brothers that practically gave him carte blanche.
It guaranteed him prerogatives he had been accustomed to in Germany,
such as having his own continuing production staff, selecting his own
story properties, working closely with writers of his choice, and

shooting and cutting his films in relative freedom from front office
interference. In fact, the contract was even said to include a
stipulation that the Warners would not appear on a Lubitsch set unless they made arrangements in advance. The liberality of the Warners contract was one reason why Lubitsch was able to adapt to American filmmaking with such facility. Lubitsch made five films for Warner Brothers--<u>The Marriage Circle</u> (1924), <u>Three Women</u> (1924), <u>Kiss Me
Again</u> (1925), <u>Lady Windermere's Fan</u> (1925), and <u>So This Is Paris</u>
(1926). His Warners films were small-scale, small-cast efforts that
dealt with intimate relationships between married couples, lovers, or
immediate members of a family. They openly dealt with sex outside of
marriage, refused to conform to conventional moral judgments, and
treated delicate sexual matters with good-natured humor. Reviewers
at the time were especially impressed with how they used editing and
functional details to develop the characters and advance the narrative line.

During his Warners tenure Lubitsch was also loaned out to direct
one film for Paramount, <u>Forbidden Paradise</u> (1924), starring Pola
Negri. This comic treatment of the amorous passions of Catherine the
Great of Russia was in the tradition of Lubitsch's German costume
films. With this film Paramount hoped to duplicate the popularity
Miss Negri had achieved under Lubitsch's direction in Germany but
that had been missing from her American films. Warners agreed to the
loan-out because they felt a Lubitsch-Negri reunion would further Lubitsch's American reputation and would therefore increase his value
to them. <u>Forbidden Paradise</u> was an enormous critical and box office
success.

Shooting on Lubitsch's fifth Warners feature was completed at the
end of May 1926. The Warner brothers felt that by this time Lubitsch
was well enough acquainted with American customs to undertake American subjects, so his next project was to be an elaborate American
spectacle on the scale of <u>Madame Dubarry</u>. Lubitsch was eager to undertake the project and he was also interested in directing a film
version of Samson Raphaelson's play <u>The Jazz Singer</u>, which he had
seen on Broadway. Both projects came to an abrupt halt, however,
when he left Warner Brothers in August 1926, a year and a half before
his contract was due to expire.

The events leading to Lubitsch's departure from Warners are very
tangled. Under his Warners contract he was receiving $60,000 a pic-
ture plus percentage, on a two-picture-a-year basis. In February
1926, while still under contract to Warners, he conducted negotiations with United Artists. Warner Brothers threatened to go to court
to hold him to his contract. At about the same time Lubitsch received several offers at around $100,000 a picture. In mid-April
Warners discussed a new five-year contract which would guarantee Lubitsch $150,000 per picture, according to <u>Variety</u> the highest per-
film price ever guaranteed a director. But in August Lubitsch tenta-
tively accepted an offer from the Paramount group to make five films

over a three-year period at $125,000 a film, to begin immediately.
Signing of this contract was held up, however, because Warners demanded that Lubitsch finish his pending commitment to them. When MGM
asked to borrow Lubitsch from Warners for one film, negotiations between the three studios ensued and Paramount and MGM agreed jointly
to buy the balance of Lubitsch's Warners contract for $150,000. Lu-
bitsch would make the film for MGM and then begin his three-year contract with Paramount. When they released Lubitsch from his contract,
Warners used the excuse that the recent success of Vitaphone and the
studio's decision to devote exclusive attention to sound, was responsible for a shifting of their priorities.

In less than four years in America Lubitsch was already recognized as one of Hollywood's top directors and all the major studios
were clamoring for his exclusive services. His personal life had
also undergone an equally radical transformation in the same short
period. When he first visited America he spoke no English. Even on
Rosita in 1923 his English had been halting and he sometimes needed
an interpreter. He wore on the set what he had worn in Germany,
knickers, bow tie, and large cap. By 1927 he had altered his attire,
shed many of his Teutonic mannerisms, and learned to speak a confi-
dent (though heavily accented) English. He had also developed an un-
canny understanding of the subliminal needs of American audiences.

After directing a silent version of Sigmund Romberg's operetta
The Student Prince (1927) for Irving Thalberg at MGM, Lubitsch began
his association with Paramount on The Patriot (1928), a historical
depiction of the life of mad Czar Paul I starring Emil Jannings. Lubitsch was then loaned to United Artists to direct John Barrymore in
Eternal Love (1929), a revenge romance set in the Swiss Alps. The
years 1927 and 1928 were a transitional period for the American film
industry. The Patriot and Eternal Love, silent films made during the
changeover to sound, were both released with added synchronized sound
tracks.

Lubitsch's career flourished at Paramount once sound came in.
Since the time of the "German invasion" Paramount had continued to
build up its European connections, and there was a strong European
contingent at the studio. Lubitsch's films in this period helped to
establish Paramount's reputation as the most "Continental" of the
studios and the home of sophistication and polish. In the first
years of talking pictures, he was preeminently a director of musicals.
These films are clearly of a piece with his other American work.
They are invariably marriage comedies with witty interpolated music
that advances the intricate plots, and totally unlike the Warners ex-
travaganzas in which simplistic boy-girl plots were a pretext for
stringing together costly production numbers. In his first musical,
The Love Parade (1929), a witty domestic romance set in a mythical
Central European kingdom, Lubitsch brought together Jeanette Mac-
Donald and Maurice Chevalier for the first time. Chevalier had previously made one Hollywood talking film, the mediocre Innocents of

8

Paris. MacDonald was appearing in stage musicals at the time. They immediately became the top musical film stars in America, and Lubitsch was established as one of the leading directors of musicals. Through editing, a moving camera, and off-screen business Lubitsch was able in this film to eliminate much of the staginess that had been characteristic of early sound musicals. These advances were further developed in Lubitsch's subsequent musicals, which were highly influential.

After The Love Parade Lubitsch directed Chevalier in musical sequences in the all-studio revue, Paramount on Parade (1930). Then he directed MacDonald in another "naughty" musical, Monte Carlo (1930), which suffered from the presence of Jack Buchanan instead of Chevalier as her co-star. The transition to sound caused many Hollywood careers to falter, but Lubitsch remained on top. In 1930, he made the Film Daily fifth annual list of "Ten Best Directors." He was the only director who had appeared on all five lists.

In August 1930 Paramount announced an ambitious venture to transfer a major portion of its production schedule to its Astoria Studios in Long Island City, New York. According to Variety (Sept. 3, 1930, p. 1) "accessibility to Broadway plays and players" was the chief motive for the move. Most of the studio's sophisticated product would be made in the East, while its outdoor action material would continue to be produced on the West Coast. Lubitsch was appointed supervising director of the Astoria operation, and his duties included deciding what stories were to be filmed. Among the studio contingent who went East were two writers who would work with Lubitsch on his upcoming projects--Ernest Vajda, a transplanted Hungarian playwright who had worked on The Love Parade and Monte Carlo, and Samson Raphaelson, the Broadway playwright who had just recently signed with Paramount. Lubitsch's next film was to be an adaptation of Maurice Rostand's French anti-war play, The Man I Killed, and Lubitsch had chosen Raphaelson to co-author the script because he regarded the writer of The Jazz Singer, a play he highly admired, as a specialist in tragedy. (Ironically, the "serious" dramatist went on to author eight of Lubitsch's most witty comedies.) After they had written the script for The Man I Killed, Lubitsch, Vajda, and Raphaelson then wrote The Smiling Lieutenant (1931), an adaptation of an Oscar Straus operetta, a vehicle for Chevalier which was shot at Astoria. Two months after principal photography had been completed on this film, Paramount decided to close the Astoria studio. Though Variety headlines had originally billed the move as the beginning of the end to Hollywood's predominance, the Eastern studio operation had been a disappointment and the venture was abandoned.

After his return to Hollywood, Lubitsch became involved in the production of The Man I Killed (1932), a pacifist tract set after World War I and his only fully "serious" sound film. Studio executives were wary that The Man I Killed might be mistaken for a gangster film, so after the New York opening the title was changed to Broken Lullaby. Although most critics still had high praise for the

"Lubitsch touch" even in a more somber context, The Man I Killed was
a commercial failure and after it Lubitsch never again risked unpopu-
larity by departing from the comic vein in which he was most comfor-
table.

Late in 1931 Jeanette MacDonald and Maurice Chevalier were teamed
again for One Hour with You (1932), a sound remake of Lubitsch's The
Marriage Circle. George Cukor was named director, under Lubitsch's
supervision. (Lubitsch's contract called for him occasionally to
supervise the productions of other directors.) After shooting had
begun in December from a script prepared by Lubitsch and Raphaelson,
Lubitsch felt that Cukor was incorrectly interpreting the comic values
of the script and he gradually took over the direction, though Cukor
remained on the set. At a preview, Lubitsch demanded that either his
name or Cukor's be removed. Cukor's credit was eliminated and he re-
taliated by filing an injunction against the exhibition of the film.
Eventually, however, a compromise was worked out whereby Cukor was
billed as dialogue director and was also allowed to go to RKO to direct Constance Bennett in her next film.

Lubitsch's contract with Paramount was scheduled to expire in
March 1932 and the studio did not hold an option on him. He had been
receiving $125,000 for each film he directed. Early in the year
Paramount began discussing possible terms for a new contract, such as
eliminating his supervising duties or expanding them by making him an
associate producer or giving him his own production unit. Columbia
and United Artists also made bids for his services. Lubitsch was un-
decided. For one thing, he was considering the possibility of making
his debut as a Broadway director. He was in New York for a time
reading scripts and making preliminary plans. Several different
projects were discussed, including the possibility of starring Maria
Jeritza in an operetta version of The Czarina, which had been the
source play for Forbidden Paradise and would be again later for A
Royal Scandal. Finally in March he signed a new contract with Paramount to direct three pictures in the coming year.

Lubitsch's first film under his new contract was Trouble in Paradise (1932), his first non-musical sound comedy. It was in this
genre that he excelled during his remaining years at Paramount. Lubitsch's sound comedies typified the elegance usually associated with
that studio. They were high-society domestic farces set in European
capitals, and they had sparkling dialogue, well-constructed plots,
shimmering sets and costumes, and an air of Continental suavity. Lubitsch always regarded Trouble in Paradise as his most stylish film.
Most critics have agreed with him. After Trouble in Paradise he
quickly prepared an added sequence for the multi-director Paramount
studio omnibus, If I Had a Million (1932). Lubitsch's sequence featured Charles Laughton as a clerk taking unceremonious leave of his
boss after he receives a check for a million dollars, and it was
singled out by most reviewers for its terse comic effect. Then in
April 1933 Lubitsch went to New York to work with Ben Hecht on the

screenplay for <u>Design for Living</u> (1933), from Noel Coward's Broadway hit about a free-living ménage à trois in Paris. For the second time in his Hollywood career Lubitsch was working from a well-known play. In both cases he stamped his own personality on the screen adaptations by dispensing with most of the original dialogue. Just as he had eliminated most of the famous Wilde epigrams from the intertitles in <u>Lady Windermere's Fan</u>, in <u>Design for Living</u> he retained only one line from the stage play--"good for our immortal souls."

Lubitsch's Paramount contract permitted him to direct one outside picture. After <u>Design for Living</u> he went to MGM to make his last musical of the thirties--<u>The Merry Widow</u> (1934), Franz Lehár's risque operetta featuring a hero who is a sexual favorite of all the girls at Maxim's. As early as 1930 MGM had wanted to reunite the <u>Love Parade</u> trio of Lubitsch, MacDonald, and Chevalier in a lavish sound production of the operetta. After years of complex legal negotiations, numerous draftings of treatments and scripts, and a prolonged and well-publicized search for a star, MGM finally settled on its original choice of director and stars in mid-February 1934. Producer Irving Thalberg intended for his <u>Merry Widow</u> to be one of MGM's most lavish productions in its history. Four versions were filmed simultaneously, for domestic, English, French, and Belgian audiences. The total projected budget was $1,640,000. Lubitsch was not able to exercise complete control over the production of <u>The Merry Widow</u>. He had not been involved in the film's inception and although a final script was shaped by him with Raphaelson and Vajda, it had been developed by the MGM assembly line of writers and script doctors. He was forced to work under Thalberg, who almost always had his own way in the end even with the most strong-willed of directors. In addition, a drive toward more strict enforcement of the Motion Picture Production Code began in the late stages of production of <u>The Merry Widow</u>. There were Hays Office objections to certain parts of the film, and accommodations had to be made. For instance, Jeanette MacDonald told of one particular scene that had to be reshot because of the Code's rule that it could not be played with her in a horizontal position. Finally Lubitsch was permitted to shoot the scene by having her keep both feet planted firmly on the floor while she was lying on the couch. (He got around the censors by showing her feet only in establishing the scene.) After thirteen weeks of shooting, <u>The Merry Widow</u> was completed on July 17, 1934. Although it met with acclaim from the critics, audiences found <u>The Merry Widow</u> very disappointing.

Lubitsch returned to Paramount and began to make plans for a new film. Then, on February 4, 1935, Hollywood was astonished to learn that Lubitsch, at the height of his career as a director, had been named head of production at Paramount. The studio was in the throes of reorganization. Emanuel Cohen, production chief since 1932, was suddenly relieved of his duties, and Henry Herzbrun, the studio attorney, and Lubitsch were jointly named to replace him. Under this arrangement Lubitsch was to have full creative control over all

Paramount pictures, while Herzbrun was placed in charge of studio operations. Most people felt that this would be a temporary measure, and that Lubitsch would very soon return to directing. But he quickly convinced skeptics otherwise. On February 8, he and Herzbrun held a conference of Paramount directors and writers at which Lubitsch expressed surprise at the furor that had followed in the wake of his appointment and assured the directors there would be no interference in their work and no imposition of the Lubitsch touch.

During his tenure as production head Lubitsch adopted the "retake and remake" process, whereby a film would be put back into production after principal photography had been completed if there were clear possibilities for improving it. He also centralized all decision-making concerning story purchases and director, writer, and actor contracts in his office. He rescinded the policy of allowing directors to withdraw from projects and decreed (perhaps under orders from the home office) that directors would either go through with their assigned films or have their contracts terminated. He signed King Vidor and Lewis Milestone as directors and renewed Wesley Ruggles' contract. During this period, Lubitsch had one well-publicized fracas. While Klondike Annie was being made, there was constant friction between Lubitsch and the film's star, Mae West, who felt she ought to be playing opposite younger men. Their arguments grew so heated that Lubitsch in desperation turned over all studio matters relating to Miss West to Herzbrun and William LeBaron, the film's producer. When Lubitsch was later accused of having treated the actress dictatorially, he retorted, "Try to push her around, did I? She's much too heavy" (New York Post, Feb. 25, 1936, p. 2).

While he was production head Lubitsch found time to personally supervise one film, Desire (1936), directed by Frank Borzage. The story material was characteristic Lubitsch--a Hungarian source play, European capitals, international jewel thieves, phony royalty--and his direct influence can be felt throughout the film, such as in the witty transitions involving automobiles and Dietrich's black-and-white costumes. Lubitsch made plans to supervise two other productions which never came off--The Chocolate Princess, an all-black musical, and a remake of Hotel Imperial to star Marlene Dietrich in Pola Negri's original role.

In February 1936 William LeBaron was installed in Lubitsch's place as Paramount production head and Lubitsch left for a three-month vacation in Europe.* During Lubitsch's term in the post,

---

*The vacation was also a belated honeymoon. Lubitsch had married Sania Bezencenet (Vivian Gaye) in a small ceremony in Phoenix, Arizona, on July 27, 1935. It was Miss Gaye's first marriage. An artists' agent in London, she had come to Hollywood in the early thirties when one of her clients, Sari Maritza, had obtained a Hollywood contract. In 1934, Miss Gaye took charge of the story department of a large agency and she met her future husband when she sold him the play

production had lagged, costs had soared, and profits dwindled. For instance, The Big Broadcast of 1936, made under Lubitsch, cost $1,200,000 and lost $337,000. The following year The Big Broadcast of 1937, made under LeBaron, cost $847,000 and showed a profit of $450,000.

Lubitsch returned to Paramount on June 1 and took up new responsibilities as head of his own unit. (As production head he had had two contracts, an arrangement which allowed him to take over an independent production unit whenever he left the other post.) His unit was to turn out four films, one of which he was to direct himself. Paramount had high hopes for the Lubitsch unit and announced the following month that it would be in charge of all films featuring Marlene Dietrich and Claudette Colbert, two of the top stars on the studio roster. The Lubitsch unit began the preparations on his next two films, Angel and Bluebeard's Eighth Wife, but apparently never really functioned beyond that stage. One of the things Lubitsch had detested about his year as production head was having to supervise over sixty different films. He worked best by fully concentrating on one film at a time, and he realized that he had to give up his own creative work when he became creative supervisor of the work of others. His work on Angel, for instance, from selection of story, to detailed preparation of the script, through principal photography and down to final editing, occupied almost a full year of his time. Obviously, a production unit could not be run by giving such precise attention to each individual feature.

Angel (1937), with Dietrich as a British society woman with a past who is forced to choose between her husband and another man, and Bluebeard's Eighth Wife (1938), from Alfred Savoir's play, an American Taming of the Shrew with the roles reversed (and the first Charles Brackett-Billy Wilder collaboration), were the last of Lubitsch's vintage "Continental comedies." Lubitsch has said it was a review of Bluebeard's Eighth Wife that first spurred him into reassessing his career. The reviewer had enjoyed the farcical comedy, but had questioned whether audiences of those days were really interested in such light-hearted subjects. Lubitsch confessed to an interviewer:

Desire was based on. Miss Gaye was twenty-seven at the time of their marriage, sixteen years younger than her husband. The marriage lasted until 1943 and produced one child, Nicola, born October 27, 1938.

Prior to his second marriage, Lubitsch had been romantically linked with several other women. In 1931, there were press reports that he and Ona Munson were seeing a lot of each other. After her divorce from Edward Buzzell, rumors circulated that Miss Munson was secretly wed to Lubitsch or the two would soon marry. Miss Munson admitted she planned to marry Lubitsch, but her comments were premature. When Lubitsch was vacationing in Berlin at the end of 1932, he met twenty-six year old Greta Koerner, reputed to be a wealthy Viennese widow. She arrived in Hollywood several months later, claiming that Lubitsch had deluged her with cables, telegrams, and phone calls, with the intent to marry her. Lubitsch reportedly paid her a great sum of money so she would not reveal the contents of the letters. She soon returned to Berlin.

We can't make pictures in a vacuum now. We must show
people living in a real world. No one used to care how
characters made their living--if the picture was amusing. Now they do care. They want their stories tied
up to life. People nowadays have to make their living
(New York Sun, Nov. 7, 1939, p. 11).

Bluebeard's Eighth Wife was Lubitsch's last film at Paramount. On
March 19, 1938, after an enormously creative eleven years, Lubitsch
ended his stay at that studio for good. Variety suggested that economic considerations were behind the move:

Banker influence in Paramount reportedly was the moti-
vating factor in departure of Ernst Lubitsch from Par
lot as producer after checkup of record showed that in
last 11 years Lubitsch has produced only two pictures
which were real money-makers.... Lubitsch is an expensive producer who always goes along on shooting, with
resultant heavy cutting in reaching final print (Variety, Apr. 6, 1938, p. 10).

Several months after Lubitsch had left Paramount, Myron Selznick,
one of Hollywood's top agents, formed an independent production company with Lubitsch on a profit-sharing basis. The initial Lubitsch-
Selznick production was to have been The Shop around the Corner, and
when the Selznick venture folded in November, MGM agreed to take over
Shop around the Corner on a two-picture deal which also included
Ninotchka (1939), a satire on Soviet communism to star Greta Garbo.
With Ninotchka Lubitsch branched out into new areas of comedy. It
was his first political satire and today it is probably Lubitsch's
most famous film. In The Shop around the Corner (1940), a gentle and
loving depiction of a family of employees in a small leather goods
store in Budapest, Lubitsch was drawing from his youthful experiences
in his father's shop in Berlin. Lubitsch said of this film:

As for human comedy, I think I never was as good as in
Shop around the Corner. Never did I make a picture in
which the atmosphere and the characters were truer than
in this picture (Entry 269).

Another attempt by Lubitsch at independent production came about
in 1939, when he and veteran independent producer Sol Lesser formed
their own company, with an arrangement for their films to be released
through United Artists. Lubitsch was scheduled to direct two films
each year, to begin after his association with MGM ended in January
1940. Only one film came out of the venture, That Uncertain Feeling
(1941), a remake of Lubitsch's Kiss Me Again (1925), with Merle Obe-
ron as a Park Avenue socialite who is attracted to a "Bohemian" concert pianist (Burgess Meredith) and Melvyn Douglas as the husband who
is trying to win her back. In March 1941, Lubitsch signed a three-
year contract as producer-director at 20th Century-Fox to begin in

the summer. He had withdrawn from the deal with Sol Lesser, but he still owed United Artists one film under the distribution arrangement. To fulfill the commitment he made To Be or Not To Be (1942), a black comedy set against the Nazi invasion of Poland with Jack Benny and Carole Lombard as husband and wife luminaries in the leading Warsaw theater company. For one of the very few times in his career Lubitsch was working from an original story idea rather than using an existing source, perhaps a suggestion of how close the material was to him. He was also drawing explicitly on his Jewish background and his early years in the Max Reinhardt company. It was an ill-fated project from beginning to end: Fox was anxious for Lubitsch to begin his term contract with them, but Walter Wanger, who was originally set to produce, withdrew in August, Alexander Korda took over, and shooting did not begin until November; Carole Lombard died in a plane crash shortly before the film's release; and at the time of the release the Nazis had been winning in Europe. It was impossible for audiences of the time to appreciate To Be or Not To Be (United Artists eventually wrote it off as a salvage operation), and only in later years did it come to be seen as one of Lubitsch's major comedies.

Lubitsch finally reported to 20th Century-Fox in mid-February 1942, almost a full year after he had signed the term contract, and he remained under contract to this studio until his death. By now one of the Hollywood majors, Fox had been built up by Darryl F. Zanuck, who kept a tight rein on the production operation. Fox was noted for unpretentious historical films, period pieces, prestige literary adaptations, and somewhat restrained musicals. Lubitsch came to the studio at a time when the war had drained Hollywood of many of its top talents. He was a highly respected director and also a prolific one. But the war had produced fundamental changes in the national mood and these had begun to be reflected in Hollywood films. Audiences had resented Lubitsch's making comedy out of so serious a subject in To Be or Not To Be, and he was lambasted for his supposed lack of sensitivity to the plight of the Poles. He was deeply hurt by the charges against him. He had a great deal of difficulty getting his next project started. He was fifty years old, and within a year he was to have the first of a series of heart attacks. He completed two films in nearly six years at Fox, and both were solid features that marked new departures for him. But overall his 20th Century-Fox period must be seen as something of a decline.

For his first six months at Fox Lubitsch remained idle. He started several projects but eventually cancelled them before they reached the cameras. In August he took time out to make a training and morale building film for the Army, under the supervision of Lt. Col. Frank Capra. The film was called Know Your Enemy Germany. Lubitsch worked on the script with his writers and then shot the film in one week in mid-October. Reportedly it was too ponderous for its purpose and was never used. (The project was later reassigned to different personnel in the Capra unit.) Lubitsch rarely mentioned this project. The Army's rejection of it must have been a bitter blow to him. He was especially sensitive about his status in America as an expatriate German during the war. He had become an American citizen only shortly before the war (the year after his German citizenship had been taken away in an anti-Semitic drive in 1935), and his German ancestry and accent were still apparent. He showed great concern about the war, and friends still recall how he served with pride and dignity as air-raid warden for his Bel Air neighborhood during the blackouts. He took his job seriously, and more than once was heard shouting at his neighbors, in his German accent, "Lights out!"

In February 1943 Lubitsch began shooting his first Fox feature and also his first film in color, Heaven Can Wait, a sentimental flashback biography relating the amorous highlights in the life of an incurable philanderer. It was an American period comedy in keeping with Fox's predilection for nineteenth-century subjects but its autobiographical dimension was also evident. The comedy in this film was more mellow than in earlier Lubitsch films and its satire more refined. With it Lubitsch won back most of the critics who had deserted him over To Be or Not To Be. He planned for his next film to be another wartime subject, All-Out Arlene, a satire on the WACs involving an engaged couple who are both in the Army. He went to Washington to confer with the head of the WACs about the project and began work on the script with newly arrived screenwriters Phoebe and Henry Ephron, but preparations came to a halt on September 1, 1943, when he suffered a massive heart attack. A long period of recuperation followed, during which Lubitsch's activities were severely restricted.

Lubitsch returned to the Fox lot on January 10, 1944, and began reading scripts under a new contract to produce three films. The last of the three he was to direct himself if his health allowed. In April Fox bid on the screen rights to Franz Werfel's Broadway hit Jacobowsky and the Colonel as an acting vehicle for Lubitsch. Lubitsch was eager to take on his first acting role in almost twenty-five years, as the Polish scapegoat Jacobowsky, but Fox was outbid for the property by Columbia. Lubitsch then served as producer and also directed rehearsals on Otto Preminger's A Royal Scandal (1945), based on the play The Czarina, which Lubitsch had filmed in 1924 as Forbidden Paradise. He was then involved in a production capacity on Dragonwyck (1946), which was directed by Joseph Mankiewicz. This brooding Gothic tale was based on a popular novel by Anya Seton; it is unlike anything else Lubitsch was ever associated with. At the end of November 1945 Lubitsch's doctor gave his consent for him to return to directing. Cluny Brown (1946), his first film in over two years, is a satire on British class consciousness with Jennifer Jones as a servant girl and plumber's niece who breaks out of the roles imposed on her by others. It was the only film directed by Lubitsch based on a best-selling novel, but he was still able to remold the material according to his own comic style. At the time Lubitsch commented on his return to directing: "Producing, but not creating a picture was frustrating. Now I feel like a dancer with a broken leg who suddenly can dance again" (New York Times, Dec. 16, 1945, II.3).

In the spring of 1947 Lubitsch began preparation of what would be his last film, That Lady in Ermine (1948). He had been interested in the operetta Die Frau im Hermelin (1919) for some time. He had planned a "straight, romantic" version to star Irene Dunne and Char Charles Boyer in 1943, and the following year had proposed to Jeanette MacDonald that she star in it. That Lady in Ermine was his first musical in thirteen years. It had Betty Grable defending her tiny kingdom against foreign invaders with the assistance of a look-alike ancestor in a painting who comes to life. Raphaelson worked on the script with Lubitsch, and has said of the experience:

> ...Lubitsch was a very sick man plodding along on for-
> mula and I couldn't fight him. What I had to do was
> deliver what a worn-out man expected and I did it as an
> act of compassion, knowing it was going to be warmed-
> over Lubitsch and a repetition of his formula (Weinberg
> [1968], p. 206).

Lubitsch had shot for thirty-six days and was over half finished with the production on November 29, 1941. The next day, Sunday, he suffered another heart attack and died instantly at the age of fifty-five. Otto Preminger shot the remaining twenty-six days but Lubitsch received sole credit as a posthumous gesture. Preminger altered Lubitsch's plans according to his own conceptions. One sequence he eliminated, Lubitsch had shot and was very pleased with--the finale, in which the barefoot lady in ermine, as she is returning to her picture frame for good, allays her ancestors' suspicions by opening her ermine coat and revealing what she has on underneath.

Hollywood paid its final respects to Lubitsch in an elaborate funeral service at Forest Lawn on December 4. Jeanette MacDonald sang "It's Always a Beautiful Day," which Lubitsch had written for his daughter Nicola, and "Beyond the Blue Horizon," one of Lubitsch's favorite songs, which she had sung in Monte Carlo. Mourning friends suspected that Lubitsch would have rolled his eyes and wondered why she never sang it with so much feeling when he could still hear it. Eight months before, Lubitsch had received a special Academy Award for his accomplishments in the industry, his only "Oscar." Mervyn LeRoy's tribute when he presented the award provides a fitting eulogy:

> He had an adult mind and a hatred of saying things the
> obvious way. Because of these qualities and a God-given
> genius he advanced the technique of screen comedy as no
> one else has ever done.
>
> Suddenly the pratfall and the double-take were left
> behind and the sources of deep inner laughter were

17

tapped. The housebroken camera learned to stop at a
closed door instead of peeking gawkily through the key
hole.

A master of innuendo had arrived (Los Angeles
Times, Apr. 6, 1947, p. 1).

With Lubitsch's death, Variety noted, the very small number of
directors whose names carried boxoffice drawing power had been cut by
one. The special lure had been the "Lubitsch touch," but those who
knew him say audiences often missed the best part of the show in not
seeing Lubitsch himself. He was physically unimposing: short and
stocky, with a dark complexion, coal black hair, crooked nose, and
wonderfully alert, twinkling brown eyes. He had a scowling face and
a broad irrepressible smile. He loved to laugh and wink and leer and
was a constant practical joker. He was impish and diminutive, a
"Puck with a cigar." A natural comedian, he relished an audience.
He would inevitably show his actors and actresses how to perform a
scene by acting out every role himself and immersing himself in the
character. He liked to dance (or "shimmie" as he called it). He
loved music. While waiting between takes he would often play the
piano or the cello, two instruments he had taught himself to play.
He was always animated, projecting nervous and excited energy. He
was a self-made man and a master of his profession. He had a wide
knowledge of film mechanics and a shrewd sense of film story. He was
gentle but demanding; eclectic but uncompromisingly original. He
cultivated his own ensemble of gifted workers who proved faithful to
him, film after film. Talented people outdid themselves under his
tutelage: actors created their best roles, screenwriters wrote their
best scripts. He was a complex personality--coarse and refined,
tough and sentimental, cynical and compassionate, obvious and subtle,
knowing and innocent--and a consummate artist.

II. Critical Survey

One of the most remarkable things about Lubitsch is the enormous range and versatility of his filmmaking career. At the time he started acting in films in 1913 the medium and the industry were still in their infancy. By the time of his death in 1947 film had become a highly developed art form and filmmaking a major international business enterprise. Lubitsch was able to adapt to the fundamental and sometimes rapid changes in the technologies and circumstances of filmmaking over these years with a steadiness and consistency that are no less than astonishing. A profile of his career reads like a summary of landmarks in thirty-five years of film history. When Lubitsch started in films (at about the same time as Chaplin and De Mille) Griffith had been directing films for five years, Thomas Ince for three. Like Griffith, Lubitsch went into films to supplement his income as a stage actor, served his apprenticeship making shorts, and only gradually worked his way up to making features. Also like Griffith, he first achieved international recognition with a series of ambitious historical costume spectacles. The tremendous success of these films outside Germany helped to open an international market for The Cabinet of Dr. Caligari (1919) and the other classics of German Expressionism that followed, as well as to pave the way for the emigration of German filmmakers to Hollywood in the 1920s. When Lubitsch left Germany for America in 1922 he was widely recognized as the leading film director in Europe. Within five years he had made eight films in America and had earned a new reputation for himself as one of the leading American directors. In the years following, Lubitsch proved to be one of the pioneering geniuses in Hollywood's creative transition to sound. His early sound musicals were enormously influential in the development of the Hollywood montage style of the 1930s. His early sound comedies are also seminal works in the development of one of Hollywood's best genres, "thirties comedy." In the late 1930s, when political turmoil in Europe was beginning to alter the look of American films, again Lubitsch took a major turn in his career, and by the time of America's entry into the war he had directed two of Hollywood's most successful political satires. The end of his career shortly after the war coincided with the breakup of the Hollywood studio system in which he had been a major force almost from the beginning.

In nine years of making films in Germany Lubitsch directed roughly thirty-seven films. He also appeared as an actor in about twenty of his own films and in around a dozen films directed by others. Almost all the films he made in his early German years (through the summer of 1918) were comedies, ranging in length from one to five reels. Of the roughly nineteen films he directed in this period only three are known to survive. During his later German period Lubitsch directed ten longer comedies (most of them four reels and over) and eight dramatic features. Most of the comedies survive, and they are an uneven lot. Die Austernprinzessin (1919) is a somewhat heavy-handed, occasionally crude satire on the pretensions of rich Americans in Europe, but it is not without redeeming moments (such as the dinner scene when each guest of the American businessman has his own individual waiter for each course). Die Puppe (1919) and Ich möchte kein Mann sein (1920) definitely anticipate Lubitsch's mature comedies in their relatively intricate plots, their sudden flashes of wit, and their skillful managing of sexual anxieties. On the other hand, Romeo und Julia im Schnee (1920), a rustic version of Shakespeare, is a slapstick farce not many grades above an American Keystone comedy. His last German comedy, Die Bergkatze (1921), is one of his most startling works. It is a forgotten classic of surrealism which hovers constantly between the farcical and the grotesque, is filled with bizarre optical effects (especially masks of all shapes and sizes), and has unforgettable futuristic sets by Ernst Stern. Of the eight dramatic features seven are known to survive in some form. Five of these are large-scale costume romances in historical settings --Carmen (nineteenth-century Spain), Madame Dubarry (pre-revolution France), Sumurun (ancient Persia), Anna Boleyn (England during the reign of Henry VIII), and Das Weib des Pharao (ancient Egypt). The sixth, Die Augen der Mumie Mâ, is an Egyptology romance largely set in modern England. Lubitsch's costume spectacles were highly praised at the time they were released for the great advances they made in sets, acting, and general level of intelligence over similar efforts in Italy. Lubitsch's later achievements have tended to eclipse his costume films of these years, and there is something to be said for the argument that they are sometimes as much feats of construction and organization as of art. On the other hand, a film like Madame Dubarry still manages to be impressive even today, especially for its high production values and a surprisingly restrained performance by Emil Jannings as Louis XV. The largest gap in the record for this period involves two small-scale intimate psychological dramas, or Kammerspiele, the genre Lubitsch himself always thought displayed his gifts at their best. Die Flamme (1923), from a play by Danish writer Hans Müller, survives in only a thirty-minute fragment. Rausch (1919), from a play by Strindberg, is apparently lost.

If these two films survived it is possible there would seem less of a jolt between Lubitsch's German films and the small-scale domestic comedies of his first years in America. It is also likely they would greatly increase our appreciation of Lubitsch's first decade in filmmaking. In any case, Lubitsch's total career record in the

German years, 1913 to 1922, rivals any other filmmaker's anywhere for the same period. But, as it turned out, his second decade in film-making was to be even more impressive than his first. In just slightly over ten years in America, Lubitsch directed an astonishing eighteen features plus sections of two multi-director anthology films. Overall, there is a great deal of variety in this output; a silent operetta, an anti-militarist love story involving World War I, several European costume romances, and so on. The heart of the output of these years, however, is in the marital comedies and the musicals. Lubitsch's first film in America, Rosita (1923), was something of a throwback to the German costume romances. But with The Marriage Circle (1924), his second American film, the first outlines of a major pattern emerge.

A man and woman are perfectly suited for one another. They have a potentially ideal relationship, but time has slightly taken the edge off their romance and they have both begun to settle into the routine of taking one another for granted. A third party enters the scene, a sexual rival. One of the partners is lured into a flirtation and possibly a sexual dalliance. The original relationship is threatened. But only temporarily: the interlude of infidelity turns out to be a catalyst to self-awareness and psychological renewal. From this new perspective the faithful partner becomes aware of his or her own faults and vows to mend them, while the unfaithful one gains a new respect for the original mate by coming to recognize the shortcomings of the substitute. Far from endangering a genuine love relationship, the test of infidelity helps to reinvigorate and strengthen it by giving the lovers a better sense of themselves as individuals and a new understanding of their responsibilities to one another. Though the circumstances vary greatly from film to film, this is the predominant conflict and theme of most of Lubitsch's major films from The Marriage Circle (1924) to The Merry Widow (1934). In The Marriage Circle the rival is a woman, an old friend of the wife's, a sexual predator on the prowl for experiences that are lacking in her own loveless marriage. In Kiss Me Again (1925) the rival this time is a man, an "artiste"-type whose Bohemianism is attractive to a woman whose marriage has slightly palled. In The Love Parade (1929), the first of Lubitsch's musicals, the rival is a sexual ideal --the lure of Paris, with its women who know how to please a man-- rather than an actual lover, the wife is the Queen in a mythical European kingdom, and the conflict is whether she can learn to regard her husband as a man and not just as a Prince Consort. Very similar circumstances arise in another "mythical kingdom" musical, The Smiling Lieutenant (1931). One Hour with You (1932) is a musical remake of The Marriage Circle with the original characters and plot conflict retained. In Trouble in Paradise (1932) the couple are a pair of jewel thieves and the rival is one of their rich female victims; though the couple remain steadfastly unmarried, their relationship undergoes the same process of testing and restoration as in the marital films.

Lubitsch's work in sophisticated marital comedy can be seen as part of a broader development. At the time Lubitsch came to America, the Theatre Guild was engaged in a series of revivals of plays by Ferenc Molnár, the master of this genre in modern Europe. Within a few years the genre was thriving on Broadway, in the work of such playwrights as S. N. Behrman, Samson Raphaelson, and Philip Barry. At about the same time a more lithe English strain appeared in the Broadway productions of Noel Coward's plays. Eventually, thanks especially to Lubitsch and the Broadway emigres to Hollywood, the genre flourished on the West Coast, too, and reached its supreme triumph in what Stanley Cavell calls the divorce genre of the late 30s and the 40s--The Awful Truth, His Girl Friday, The Philadelphia Story, The Lady Eve, and Adam's Rib. Lubitsch's own customary starting point in his American comedies was a European source work, most typically a play by one of the nineteenth-century French boulevard dramatists or by one of the now-forgotten Hungarian imitators of Molnár. He once told a newspaper interviewer: "I have a special weakness for the Continental type of thing, works like Molnar's." This impulse, however, is by no means simply a sign of regression to his European past, as it is sometimes made out to be. As a matter of fact, one of the first things Lubitsch did with his source plays was to throw out the translation (if in fact there was one) and start all over again with his screenwriter making a new plot out of the original story idea. Lubitsch's reshaped plots introduced dynamic conflicts not even hinted at in the originals, especially of a sort we might call "conflicts of culture"--an understandable circumstance, certainly, for an artist whose whole mature creative life was torn between past loyalties to Europe and his new life in America. Trouble in Paradise, for instance: despite its Parisian setting and its Continental insouciance, one of the great strengths of this film is the ease and assuredness of its American colloquial dialogue, one of its great pleasures its constant witty turns on familiar American slogans and saws. (A "self-made crook" and "I wouldn't fall for another man if he were the biggest crook on earth!") Or further: in every Lubitsch musical of the thirties the man and woman conflict is also a conflict between a foreign actor with stereotyped European traits and an actress who is as stereotypically American (Maurice Chevalier vs. Jeanette MacDonald four times, Chevalier vs. Miriam Hopkins and MacDonald vs. Jack Buchanan once each). This pattern also carries over into the nonmusical comedies--Trouble in Paradise, for instance, with suave Herbert Marshall facing a choice not only between social respectability and its opposite but also between (despite their role names in this film) two incorrigibly American-girl actresses, Kay Francis and Miriam Hopkins. It even persists into a later phase of Lubitsch's American comedies, though in these the sexual/national roles are usually reversed: Marlene Dietrich vs. Gary Cooper in Desire (1936), Claudette Colbert vs. Cooper in Bluebeard's Eighth Wife (1938), and Garbo vs. Melvyn Douglas in Ninotchka (1939).

The cultural conflict is also at the heart of the way Lubitsch made use of his European source works. Very often little more of the

material in the original story is preserved than the key characters
and the basic plot line--two jewel thieves and a diamond necklace,
two high-society crooks and a missing handbag, and so on. But something else not of the story but of the underlying values of the originals is also carried over. Fundamental to the European comedies is
the assumption that marriage is a relationship that, like any other,
is constantly in need of being tested and renewed. Marriages or love
relationships go sour because of the inconsiderateness or neglect of
the parties involved, and those who are responsible need to be shown
the error of their ways. If sexual dalliance can act as a corrective,
then it is a healthy and even necessary agent in the scheme of things.
This, of course, is comedy operating in its most characteristic fash-
ion--by asking us to reject whatever would tend to make us more mechanical and inflexible and less human, regardless of its social propriety, in favor of whatever brings about the opposite result. But
in this case the values of comedy run directly counter to the more
absolutist moral strictures of the American tradition, which typically hold that marriage is inviolate, sex outside of marriage is sinful,
adultery is reprehensible regardless of the circumstances, and trans-
gressors ought to suffer proper punishment for their misdeeds. This
conflict of values helps to account for the paradox of Lubitsch's
source works, how time after time he was able to breathe life into
pedestrian or inferior material. In the European climate these works
were nothing more or less than sophisticated entertainments for the
affluent classes of European capitals, "well-made plays." But once
transplanted to America, they took on new values and meanings. Their
pallid, dandyish character types suddenly appeared liberated and re-
bellious, their sparkling but basically vacuous wit impudent and ir-
reverent. In short, they became charged with a spirit of subversion,
that sense of being fundamentally in conflict with the narrowness and
repressiveness of American genteel morality that lies behind many of
the great American works of art.

"I thought [Lubitsch] was a very uninspired director," Mary Pickford once told an interviewer. "He was a director of doors." It was
probably inevitable that she and Lubitsch would come to blows <u>what-
ever</u> they worked on together. She was a cherished superstar accustomed to being at the center of her scenes whenever she wanted, while
Lubitsch's typical method was to interrupt the dramatic interchange
of players by focusing on objects or small details that made a witty
or surprising revelation or comment on the main action. As early as
the 1920s that trait was already being referred to as the "Lubitsch
touch." The Lubitsch touch in its purest form ultimately derives
from a standard narrative device of silent film. A good early example of the device can be seen in D. W. Griffith's <u>The Lonedale Opera-
tor</u> (1911). A telegraph operator's daughter takes over for the day
when her father becomes ill. Two shady characters appear at the
train station. The girl signals for help but the robbers manage to
get inside the station before it arrives. She holds them off with
what in medium shot appears to be a gun. After her boy friend arrives and saves the day, a closeup lets the audience in on her little

joke--the "gun" is a wrench with its handle pointed backwards! The most characteristic Lubitsch touches usually involve a wittier or more complex use of this essentially functional narrative device. In The Marriage Circle, for instance, our first intimation that something is amiss in the marriage is a closeup at the beginning of the husband's sock, which has a hole in it. Another good example occurs in Forbidden Paradise. When the Chancellor gets wind of an uprising against the Czarina, he goes to the leader of the uprising and asks him bluntly how much the revolution is worth. The rest is told in three closeups. One shows the general's hand tighten on the hilt of his sword. The next shows the Chancellor's hand going into his pocket for money. The last shows the general's hand relax on the sword. When sound made this kind of narrative closeup less obligatory, Lubitsch continued to use it in new and more complex ways. In Trouble in Paradise, for instance, one whole scene is played almost entirely with closeups of clocks. When Madame Colet, a wealthy widow who owns a perfume factory, is about ready to make a play for her male secretary (who is actually the jewel thief Gaston Monescu in disguise), she calls in his private secretary, Lily (who is really Gaston's partner), and gives her a raise with an order that she clear out every evening at five o'clock. The office clock shows 5:00; on the soundtrack, Lily tells Gaston to behave himself as she leaves for the day. At 5:12 Madame Colet is heard asking Gaston to go out to dinner with her. At 9:05 a phone rings but no one answers. At 10:50 Gaston is heard telling Madame she dances divinely. Closeup of another clock, this one downstairs, a champagne bottle in a bucket nearby, 11:00. Medium shot of a window, looking out into a garden; through the window a tower with a clock on it can be seen; its chimes are striking midnight. Cut to the hall clock outside Madame's door, 2:00 a.m., and finally a pan to Madame saying goodnight to Gaston. The image carries the narrative line, the sound track the action. By itself neither one has its eventual meaning; only by the act of joining together is a new total meaning created. Eisenstein might have called it "sound-image montage," and it is as dynamic a fusion of basic principles of silent and sound filmmaking as can be found in a Hollywood film.

A similar example occurs in a later film, this one involving Lubitsch's celebrated doors. In Ninotchka the three comrades have taken a suite at an elegant hotel. Count Leon arrives and makes them a proposition for the sale of jewels they have brought from Moscow. To soften them up he suggests lunch. Dissolve to waiters carrying food in the hallway outside. They enter and close the ornate twin doors and as we watch the doors from inside a loud "Ahh!" is heard from the comrades. A lovely cigarette girl in a short dress appears and enters; from behind the doors we hear an even louder "Ahh!" from the comrades. One of the waiters comes out and leaves at a normal pace. Then the cigarette girl rushes out, straightens her hair, and takes off down the stairs. Another waiter arrives with champagne and enters. Now three cigarette girls appear, grinning broadly, and enter the suite. From beyond the doors we hear from the comrades the loudest "AHH!" of all.

It may be that a preoccupation with isolated Lubitsch "touches" has tended to obscure his other talents. He was a genuine auteur in the European sense, in full control of every phase of the realization of his films. He was his own producer. He was a masterful director of actors. Several performers who worked with Lubitsch have described his typical working method--how he indicated precisely what he wanted by acting out each role in each scene himself in front of the camera before a foot of film was ever shot. He was at his best with American ingenues such as Jeanette MacDonald and Margaret Sullavan, sophisticated European males such as Maurice Chevalier and Herbert Marshall, and, supremely, Hollywood character actors such as Edward Everett Horton and Charlie Ruggles. (Conversely, he was least successful with wholesome American-boy males such as Gary Cooper and Melvyn Douglas.) He also completely supervised the editing of his films, so that their impeccable sense of timing and pace can be attributed to him. Finally, perhaps most significant of all, he was centrally involved in the writing of his scripts.

Of all Hollywood directors, Lubitsch was probably the one who worked most closely with his writers. His customary method was to begin with a bare outline and work out the story with the writer scene-by-scene from beginning to end. On Trouble in Paradise, for instance, Lubitsch was closeted with Samson Raphaelson, his favorite screenwriter in the sound era, and a secretary, for twelve to fourteen full-time five-day weeks hammering out the script literally detail-by-detail and line-by-line. (Raphaelson says they worked just this way on practically all of their scripts together.) In the Trouble in Paradise script virtually every important detail, including many of the famous visual touches, was spelled out completely in the first draft. Consequently, as was often the case with a Lubitsch film, the "first script" also became the "final script" and plan for shooting. A Lubitsch script is usually as intricately wrought as the best-made play. Lubitsch deserves at least equal writing credit for this, though (as was customary for a director and especially a producer in Hollywood) he almost never took it. He was most dependent on a writer for idiomatic dialogue. This is one reason why so many established writers, especially playwrights, appear in the credits of his sound films--Raphaelson, Ben Hecht, Vincent Lawrence, Edwin Justus Mayer, Samuel Hoffenstein, and so on.

Lubitsch's full talent is displayed at its best in Trouble in Paradise (1932). The film is "based on" an extremely minor Hungarian play which apparently was never even translated into English. It features Herbert Marshall, Miriam Hopkins, and Kay Francis, all in the best roles of their careers, and impeccable performances by a whole stable of Paramount character players. Its elegant modernistic sets by Hans Dreier, which influenced the production design values of a whole decade, are also made to function very skillfully in the story. The musical score by W. Franke Harling, with its standard device of recurring narrative motifs, is used constantly to surprise and amuse rather than just to lead and color the emotions. The film is full of stunning visual and aural effects from beginning to end, such as the playing of a dialogue scene at a garden party from behind glass doors so that no words are heard on the soundtrack; advancing time during an opera by a closeup of riffling pages preceded by a voice singing "I love you" and followed by the same voice singing "I hate you," another classic Lubitsch visual touch borrowed from the techniques of silent film; and a pair of zippy wipe-montages ("Yes, Madame Colet"--"Yes, M. LeVal") with a funny windup ("Maybe, M. LeVal") that tempt one to suggest a comparison with the breakfast table sequence in Citizen Kane. As in many Lubitsch films, a surface of graceful ease in Trouble in Paradise masks an extremely complex plot structure and what Northrop Frye calls an "argument" of comedy. The plot is an unforced fusion of several recognizable plot types. One is the search for a missing object, what Hollywood called the "diamond-necklace" plot: the necklace disappears soon after the beginning, the middle part involves a scramble to recover it, and in the end it is restored to the rightful party. The gimmick (in Trouble in Paradise the missing handbag), what Hitchcock calls the "macguffin," also provides the occasion for disguise and mistaken identity (one of the fundamentals of comic plotting), and constantly serves as a character device (as when the two middle-aged suitors both go to buy substitute handbags). The second plot type is a boy-girl romance--or actually a parody of the type, since the boy and girl have their sexual consummation right away but then have to undergo the customary ordeal anyway and then are re-united at the end. The third plot type is a drawing room version of Robin Hood. The "crooks" in the film are the good people--pragmatic, resourceful, hard-working, realistic --while the respectable people are all shallow and superficial. The crimes of a Gaston and Lily are petty alongside the crimes of those who hide behind wealth and power, the real crooks--Madame Colet, a rich heiress in an elegant world of make-believe who amuses herself by lavishing fortunes on useless baubles "in times like these," and Adolphe J. Giron, a pillar of respectability and propriety in wealthy society, who has made a career out of swindling his closest friends. At the end we cheer when the crooks get away because they are better people than the well-to-do snobs and hypocrites they steal from. As in the opening shot of a garbage gondolier in Venice, Trouble in Paradise works by overturning our customary values and puncturing our romantic notions of "elegance." And at its center is one of Lubitsch's profoundest comic creations, the progenitor of a whole line of stylish crooks in books, movies, and television, Gaston Monescu.

Lubitsch's most prolific decade came to a close with The Merry Widow (1934). After that there was a pause while he served a term as studio production head supervising the work of other directors. He returned to directing early in 1937 with Angel, the last of his great marital comedies and in many ways the most complex. Then, after Bluebeard's Eighth Wife, he left Paramount and went into an independent production venture. This step marks the beginning of a second major phase in his American career that continues until illness forced him onto the sidelines late in 1943. In contrast to the

relative consistency of his themes and subject matter in the earlier
period, the films of these years are characterized by a variety of
comedic subject matters and especially a readiness to experiment with
new and original comedic conceptions and forms. Several background
factors help to explain why Lubitsch's art underwent such a momentous
transformation at the height of his career. For one thing, the Motion
Picture Production Code. The Code contained explicit provisions
against every "European" sexual standard commonly observed in Lubitsch's films. Strict enforcement of the Code, which began in 1934,
put an end to the kind of impudent sexual explicitness that was at
the heart of his films and spelled the death of his special brand of
comedy. The effect can be seen by comparing the endings of the pre-
Code Trouble in Paradise (1932), and the post-Code Desire (1936). In
the earlier film (as William K. Everson points out) "the jewel thieves
escape scot-free (and unmarried) in absolute triumph," while in the
later one a wedding is necessary for jewel thief Dietrich, along with
other satisfactory (and Code-dictated) "moral compensation." But
though American puritanism eventually did have its way with Lubitsch,
by 1934 the lid was off the box. A native strain of sophisticated
comedy was by now one of Hollywood's thriving genres. American directors, of necessity more able to adapt to such things, had learned
the art of beating the Production Code by concealing sexual matters
within ambiguities, as in Bringing Up Baby. Ironically, Lubitsch had
succeeded so well in showing the way, others were able to succeed
even better. In the year the Lubitsch-supervised Desire was released
(1936), so was My Man Godfrey; in 1937, the year of Angel, there were
The Awful Truth, Easy Living, and Nothing Sacred; in 1938, the year
of Bluebeard's Eighth Wife, there were Holiday and Bringing Up Baby.
Alongside these snappy, frenetic domestic efforts set in a recognizable contemporary America, Lubitsch's more restrained Parisian and
Viennese farces must have seemed to many filmgoers of the time to be
quaint and old-fashioned.

Finally, the worsening situation in Europe appears to have had
profound psychological effect on Lubitsch. Already by the beginning
of 1939 the Germans had invaded Austria and were casting ominous
glances toward other neighbors. The Nazi menace in Europe represented not only the destruction of an actual way of life in which Lubitsch had been brought up but also the destruction of an ideal, that
stylized, golden age vision of Europe that had stimulated and nour-
ished his creative imagination throughout his years in America. After 1938 that vision is irrevocably altered in his films. In the
Paris or Vienna or whatever mythical kingdom of the earlier films,
about the only evident signs of the twentieth century we ever saw
were an occasional telephone or radio or automobile. But in Ninotchka (1939), the Paris of old is besieged and threatened by a new and
modern force, the kind of dehumanizing, demystifying bureaucratic-
managerial mentality represented by the Soviet commissariat. And in
That Uncertain Feeling (1941), New York has displaced Paris and Freud
has entered the picture to further complicate the characters' lives.
Lubitsch's vision of the past is also significantly altered in two

27

other major comedies of these years, <u>The Shop around the Corner</u>
(1940) and <u>To Be or Not To Be</u> (1942). There are strongly psychobio-
graphical elements in these two films; in both of them Lubitsch seems
to be using facets of his European past as a means of coming to terms
with his present.

  <u>The Shop around the Corner</u> is set not in an elegant Paris or Vienna but in comparatively provincial Budapest. Its autobiographical
source is equally prelapsarian, Lubitsch's early youth in his father's clothing store in Berlin. Its story is what Northrop Frye
calls "New Comedy," or what Hollywood called "boy meets girl" romance. (This time boy and girl <u>both</u> are American innocents, another
suggestion of how radically the face of Lubitsch's films is altered
after 1938.) According to this plot formula, a young man and a young
woman meet ("boy meets girl"). They are obviously fated to be mates,
but certain obstacles keep them apart--parents (or parent figures), a
rival suitor, social or economic rank, or their own egos ("boy loses
girl"). Eventually all the obstacles are overcome and love triumphs
("boy gets girl"). The triumph over the parents reveals the core
meaning of the plot--the triumph of youth, passion, romance, flexi-
bility, and openness to experience over age, senescence, routine,
and rigidity. At the end the old society is cast off and a new society of right-thinking people forms around the newly united couple.
<u>Shop around the Corner</u> follows the classic prototype exactly, down to
the rival suitor (with an intriguing variation: unknowingly the boy
and girl are romantic pen pals, so that they constantly quarrel with
one another in the flesh but as constantly profess love to one another as phantom identities in their letters) and the ego conflict (appropriately for their bourgeois origins, both are ambitious to succeed in the business and this is what gets in the way).

  There is a sad and haunting quality about <u>Shop around the Corner</u>,
however, that is not to be found in Lubitsch's comedies before <u>Angel</u>.
It is imparted mainly by a subplot, involving the shop's owner, Mr.
Matuschek, the parent-figure (or <u>senex</u>) in the story. At the beginning the old man calls his clerks together to give him an opinion on
a new item he is contemplating stocking in the store. The fawning,
flattering, insidious one tells him what he wants to hear; the good
but slightly cocky one, whom the old man has always treated like a
son, tells him the truth. The old man's pride is wounded, he mistakes truth for ingratitude, the seed of suspicion is planted and begins to grow, and eventually the old man banishes the righteous one
and retains the hypocrite. Almost too late does he learn the truth--
that the false one, not the beloved one, has been having an affair
with Matuschek's wife. If the main plot were not comedy, the subplot
would almost be a retelling of <u>King Lear</u>. But the comic structure
asserts itself just in time to avert a tragic outcome, and the errand boy for the store discovers Matuschek about to commit suicide.
In the end the lovers are united and the old man is reconciled with
his surrogate son. In the meantime, the old man's professional capacity has been put to the test and the young man has beaten him, the

other clerk (also many years his junior) has won out as his sexual
rival, he has lost his wife, and he faces the prospect of a dismal
Christmas dinner alone. But someone has proved worthy to take over
the shop, the errand boy is promoted to clerk, and a new errand boy
is hired in his place. Adversities befall individuals but the cycle
goes on continually renewing itself. Like Shakespeare's late comedies, it is a fable of age learning to come to terms with itself.

There are also strong personal elements in To Be or Not To Be.
From a very early age, Lubitsch had wanted to be an actor. He started his professional career with Max Reinhardt. Though he got out of
the theater once he was on the way to a major career as a film director, it was always in his blood and he maintained close ties with the
stage and stage people throughout his life. As conditions worsened
in Europe in the late 1930s Lubitsch was very concerned about what he
ought to be doing personally and professionally in the face of these
circumstances and also about the appropriateness to the times of the
kinds of films he had always made. Eventually he would become directly involved in the war effort. But in the meantime his response
as an artist was to do what Chaplin had just done in The Great Dicta-
tor (1940), to make a satiric comedy about Hitler himself. Exactly
forty years before, Lubitsch had made his professional debut in Reinhardt's company in Berlin. Now on the eve of the World War he used a
repertory theater company in Warsaw at the time of the invasion of
Poland as his comedic perspective on the Nazi menace.

A Nazi colonel tells a joke that is going the rounds: Napoleon
had a brandy named for him; Hitler will undoubtedly be honored in a
similar fashion--he will go down in history as a piece of cheese.
What a certain actor did to Shakespeare, the same officer says, we
Nazis are now doing to Poland. When an actor playing Hitler is told
he's just a man with a little mustache, another actor quips "But so
is Hitler!" When the Hitler actor makes his entrance in costume and
mustache to a chorus of "Heil Hitler," he heils himself. To a wartime audience it was all grotesque bad taste. But to modern audiences who have seen Dr. Strangelove, M*A*S*H, and Catch-22, it is
authentic black comedy and an early historical landmark in the evolution of a modern genre. To Be or Not To Be is the most daring of Lubitsch's comedies. Not only does it deal with a subject that is
ordinarily antithetical to comedy, but it constantly violates accepted comedic rules and practices. When the Nazis invade Poland the
film explicitly registers the full tragic impact of the event, in
violation of textbook wisdom that a comic work cannot accommodate
heavy tragedy. It allows deep tragic overtones to creep into comic
material, as in the use of the "Hath not a Jew eyes?" soliloquy from
Merchant of Venice as a running gag, a violation of the famous prog-
nosis by Henri Bergson that there must be an absence of feeling in
our laughter. Taboo material is used as a basis for comedy, as when
Jack Benny plays what amounts to a lengthy vaudeville routine with a
dead man as the main prop. The film's plot is also appropriately
complex for its subject matter. It is a curious but highly ingenious

hybrid of three plot types. One is an early version of what came to
be a standard Hollywood espionage story of World War II. A young aviator gets wind of an enemy scheme that endangers the underground
movement in an occupied country. He volunteers to go in behind enemy
lines and do what he can to foil the scheme. After a series of
frighteningly close calls the enemy is finally outsmarted and the
mission is accomplished. A second plot involving a young sexual rival and a threat to a middle-aged marriage is a familiar one for Lubitsch, except that the setting has been changed from the drawing
room to the theater and the husband and wife are actors. The young
aviator is in love with the wife; she is flattered and encourages
him; they arrange an ingenious signal for their trysts: at the point
when the husband is just going into his "To be or not to be" soliloquy onstage the aviator is to come to her in her dressing room. Underneath the zaniness of this lurk two psychological anxieties: when
the aviator walks out, it represents a dual threat, to a husband who
fears losing his wife to a younger sexual rival and to an actor whose
equally mortal dread is to lose his audience. (For the theater plot
Lubitsch undoubtedly owes something to Molnár's play The Guardsman,
which Lunt and Fontanne had a big success with on Broadway and later
did as a film at MGM.) The third plot involves a performance as the
resolution to a political intrigue, as in Hitchcock's The Man Who
Knew Too Much and The 39 Steps. The actors thwart the plot against
the underground by dusting off their costumes and sets for a satiric
play, Gestapo, that never opened, posing as Nazis, and throwing everything into confusion. Finally they manage their escape by staging
an incident with the fake Führer in an opera house while the real
Führer is quietly watching the opera from his box.

   The resolution of To Be or Not To Be is sheer theatrical wish-
fulfillment. As the actors make their escape through the streets of
Warsaw a bomb is heard, a sign that the underground is still at work,
and for a change it is actors, not spies or soldiers-of-fortune, who
have performed the heroic deeds that saved it. But there is a deeper
meaning underlying the thrust of comic affirmation in the film. To
Be or Not To Be raises an issue at the very heart of Lubitsch's (or
any artist's) career and professional identity: of what use are performance and imagination in the face of the reality of disaster? Lubitsch's answer was at once bold and simple: to continue doing what
one does best and therefore to make a comedy out of the disaster. As
a comedy, To Be or Not To Be is a consummate summation of a lifetime's experience on the stage and in films. It is a startlingly
original work motivated by an unshakeable confidence in the power of
comedy to restore our perspective on humanity however great the ad-
versary or the momentary adversity, and it challenges some of our
most fundamental assumptions about the nature of the comic. It was
also to be the final comedic high point of Lubitsch's career. In his
next film, Heaven Can Wait (1943), about an aged playboy telling his
life story to Satan in Hell after his death, the past has ceased to
function as a source of creative conflict with the present and has
become merely a recitation of deeds and events. After that a series

of heart attacks brought Lubitsch down and he finished only one more film as director, Cluny Brown (1946), before his death in 1947.

There is an old adage among actors that however hard something is to do it's not as hard as playing comedy; to which the only safe comeback is, playing comedy isn't as hard as writing or directing it. The gift of comedy involves a number of special talents--subtlety, quick wit, keen intelligence, a way with plots, a mastery of complex emotions, and a profound understanding of human psychology. Above all perhaps it involves a special talent for subterfuge. The comic, according to the psychological theory of it, arises out of a funda- mental paradox, the transformation of the experience of pain in the perceived into the experience of pleasure in the perceiver. The most effective comedic plots are founded on the deepest psychological anx- ieties--the Oedipal conflict, adolescent courtship, fear of a sexual rival, fear of aging and impotency, fear of public exposure, even fear of annihilation. The underlying psychological content of comedy is the same as tragedy; let the misunderstanding over a missing fan or handkerchief not be righted in time and a comic situation is turned into Othello. A comic plot operates, as Northrop Frye tells us, by taking us as near to tragedy as we can possibly come and then suddenly drawing back with a stunning ingenious twist. But though a comic work may be a tragedy averted just in time, the secret of comedy is that the audience should never feel it as such. The mak- ing of comedy involves the ability˜to errect fragile surfaces of unconcern over deep underlying anxieties. One measure of the success of comedy is the grace with which it manages to sustain and manipu- late the pose. Because of this paradox, our comic artists are often our most underrated and least understood. Lubitsch's greatest talent is his ability to deal with matters that are profoundly disturbing in our lives in a fashion that seems positively careless--his gift, in short, for convincing us that the monumental is frivolous. The writer who described Trouble in Paradise as "sparkling froth" was un- wittingly paying Lubitsch the highest tribute as a director of comedy.

31

III. The Films:
Synopsis, Credits and Notes

EARLY GERMAN PERIOD (1913-1918)

*1   MEYER AUF DER ALM   ("MEYER ON THE ALM")
      (1913)

      Cast: Ernst Lubitsch (Meyer), Sophie Pagay.
      Production: Union Film

      Notes:
          Listed in Roberto Chiti's filmography for Paolella (1958)
      and in subsequent filmographies, but not listed in Lamprecht.
      The credit for Sophie Pagay is added in Weinberg (1968).

*2   DIE FIRMA HEIRATET   ("THE FIRM MARRIES")
      (1914)   (The Perfect Thirty-Six)

          A drummer in the employ of a large Berlin clothing store
      discovers the heroine in the clothing store of her aunt in a
      small town. She is a "perfect thirty-six," the ideal size for
      a clothing model, and he persuades the boss back in Berlin to
      give her a job. The drummer isn't there, however, when she
      arrives to report for work and so the boss's nephew takes her
      out to dinner. Eventually the would-be suitors lose out and
      the girl marries the boss. (Adapted from the review of the
      American release in Moving Picture World.)

      Director: Carl Wilhelm
      Scenario: Walter Turszinsky and Jacques Burg
      Photography: Friedrich Weinmann
      Cast: Ernst Lubitsch (Moritz Abramowski),
                                   Resl Orla, Victor Arnold, Albert
                                   Paulig, Franz Schönemann, Anna
                                   Müller-Lincke.
      Production: Projektions-AG "Union," Berlin
      Shot at: Union-Atelier, Berlin-Tempelhof
      Length: 1160m [3806 ft.]
      Opening: January, at Union-Theater
                                   Friedrichstrasse

33

<u>Notes</u>:
Released in the United States as <u>The Perfect Thirty-Six</u>;
intertitles by Montague Glass.

<u>Review</u>:
<u>Moving Picture World</u>, Nov. 7, p. 793.

3   <u>DER STOLZ DER FIRMA</u>   ("THE PRIDE OF THE FIRM")
     (1914)

Rawitsch, a godforsaken place in the outermost corner of
the province of Posen. Siegmund Lachmann, an apprentice in
the Hoffmann Dry Goods Store, is arranging a display window
when his ladder falls through the glass. The display is
ruined, and Siegmund is fired. The lad contemplates suicide,
but decides that he would rather eat first.

After having dinner with his family, Siegmund sends off a
letter of application for a job in Berlin. When Mr. Hoffmann
arrives to relate his "tales" to Mr. and Mrs. Lachmann, Siegmund decides to leave at once for Berlin. He climbs out his
bedroom window and manages to catch a train to Berlin just as
his pursuing ex-boss reaches the station.

Berlin, the fashion salon of J. C. Berg. Preparations for
a fashion show are interrupted by the announcement that Siegmund Lachmann is waiting to see the boss. Mr. Berg finally
recalls Siegmund's letter and wonders why the boy traveled so
far before he had received any answer. Siegmund explains that
he came to get the reply himself and save Mr. Berg the postage.
The boss is won over, and Siegmund gets the job as an apprentice in the salon.

The clumsy Siegmund balks at the physical labors involved
in the job. But in his letters home (written on company time)
he glamorizes his position and says the boss is greatly satisfied with his work. Siegmund's naive and impudent manner helps
him win the hearts of the female employees. One girl in particular, Lilly Maass, attempts to make a gentleman out of the
awkward country boy. When she invites him over for a Sunday
afternoon visit, he asks for an advance on his wages so that
he can buy a new suit.

Siegmund arrives at Lilly's place at the appointed time.
Lilly tries to improve Siegmund's grooming, and she gives him
a manicure, but the visit is abruptly terminated when Lilly's
boyfriend arrives unexpectedly.

Time passes, Siegmund sports a mustache and carries a cane and tophat. He sets his sights higher than Lilly and asks for the hand of the boss's daughter, Isolde. After he is refused, Siegmund places an ad in the paper expressing his desire to marry into a family with a fashion salon. He receives a reply from an interested father, who turns out to be none other than Mr. Berg! Siegmund courts Isolde at a birthday party in her honor, and not long after, the two are wed. They honeymoon to Venice by way of Rawitsch. A son is born, who is "the pride of the firm." The film ends with the former Siegmund, the shabby bumpkin, on the left of the screen confronting the present Siegmund, the immaculate businessman, on the right.

Director:	Carl Wilhelm
Scenario:	Walter Turszinsky and Jacques Burg
Photography:	Friedrich Weinmann
Cast:	Ernst Lubitsch (Siegmund Lachmann), Martha Kriwitz (Lilly Maass), Victor Arnold (J. C. Berg), Albert Paulig (Charly Forst), Alfred Kühne (Herr Hoffmann), Hugo Döblin.
Production:	Projektions-AG "Union," Berlin
Shot at:	Union-Atelier, Berlin-Tempelhof
Length:	1273m [4177 ft.]
Press Showing:	July 30, at Union-Theater Friedrich-strasse
Opening:	January 1915 at Union-Theater Kurfürstendamm

*4   FRÄULEIN PICCOLO   ("MISS PICCOLO")
      (1914)

Lo, daughter of the innkeeper at the "Weißen Schwan," returns home from boarding school. In order to help her father, whose servant girl has run off with Piccolo, she pretends to be a new servant girl and even, when need be, disguises herself as Piccolo. Military maneuvers are taking place nearby. The dashing Lieutenant Clairon falls in love with Lo. A merry game ensues, in which Lo as the servant girl fires up his passions and as Piccolo cools them off. A military ball. Lo, as Piccolo, must look on as the other young ladies admire the Lieutenant and contain her jealousy. But Lo's boarding school friend Röschen arrives unexpectedly, recognizes Lo disguised as Piccolo, sees to it that Clairon (who is Röschen's cousin) finds out who Lo really is, and with this nothing stands in the way of a happy ending. (Translated and adapted from the booklet for the 1967 Berlin Lubitsch Retrospective by Peter B. Schumann; see entry 351.)

Director:	Franz Hofer
Scenario:	Franz Hofer
Photography:	Gotthardt Wolf
Sets:	Fritz Kraencke
Cast:	Dorrit Weixler, Franz Schwaiger, Alice Hechy, Ernst Lubitsch, Max Lehmann, Martin Wolff, Karl Har- bacher, Lene Voss.
Production:	Luna-Film GmbH, Berlin
Shot at:	Luna-Film-Atelier, Friedrichstrasse 224
Length:	1017m [3337 ft.], later cut to 968m [3176 ft.]
Completed:	During the summer of 1914

*5 FRÄULEIN SEIFENSCHAUM   ("MISS SOAPSUDS")
    (1914)

Director:	Ernst Lubitsch
Sets:	Kurt Richter
Cast:	Ernst Lubitsch.
Production:	Projektions-AG "Union," Berlin
Shot at:	Union-Atelier, Berlin-Tempelhof, Summer 1914

Note:
    Direction was once attributed to Franz Hofer.

*6 ARME MARIE   ("POOR MARIE")
    (1914)

    A department store romance.

Director:	Max Mack
Scenario:	Robert Wiene
Photography:	Hermann Böttger
Cast:	Hanni Weisse, Ernst Lubitsch, Felix Basch, Friedrich Zelnik.
Production:	Projektions-AG "Union," Berlin
Shot at:	Union-Atelier, Berlin-Tempelhof
Opening:	April 1915

*7 BEDINGUNG--KEIN ANHANG!   ("CONDITION--NO DEPENDENTS")
    (1914)

Director:	Stellan Rye
Scenario:	Luise Heilborn-Körbitz

Photography:	Guido Seeber
Cast:	Hans Wassmann, Albert Paulig, Ernst
	Lubitsch, Emil Albes, Siddie Sinnen,
	Lene Voss.
Production:	Deutsche Bioscop GmbH, Berlin
Shot at:	Bioscop-Atelier, Neubabelsberg
Length:	748m [2454 ft.]

*8   BLINDEKUH   ("BLIND MAN'S BLUFF")
     (1914)

Director:	Ernst Lubitsch
Sets:	Kurt Richter
Cast:	Ernst Lubitsch, Resl Orla.
Production:	Projektions-AG "Union," Berlin
Shot at:	Union-Atelier, Berlin-Tempelhof

*9   DIE IDEALE GATTIN   ("THE IDEAL WIFE")
     (1914)

Director:	Not Listed
Scenario:	Hanns Heinz Ewers and Marc Henry
Cast:	Lyda Salmonova, Grete Berger, Ernst
	Lubitsch, Paul Biensfeldt.
Production:	Deutsche Bioscop GmbH, Berlin
Shot at:	Bioscop-Atelier, Neubabelsberg

*10   MEYER ALS SOLDAT   ("SOLDIER MEYER")
      (1914)

Cast:	Ernst Lubitsch (Meyer).
Production:	Union Film

Note:
    Listed in Roberto Chiti's filmography for Paolella (1958)
and in subsequent filmographies, but not listed in Lamprecht.

*11   AUFS EIS GEFÜHRT   ("A TRIP ON THE ICE")
      (1915)

Director:	Ernst Lubitsch
Scenario:	Hans Kräly
Cast:	Albert Paulig, Ernst Lubitsch.
Released:	May 28, by Union

Notes:
   Listed by Huff (1947) and in subsequent filmographies, but
not listed in Lamprecht. The scenario credit is added in
Weinberg (1968).

*12   ROBERT UND BERTRAM   ("ROBERT AND BERTRAM")
      (1915)

      Director: Max Mack
      Photography: Max Lutze
      Cast: Eugen Burg, Ferdinand Bonn, Wilhelm
                             Diegelmann, Ernst Lubitsch.
      Production: Projektions-AG "Union," Berlin
      Shot at: Union-Atelier, Berlin-Tempelhof; ex-
                             terior shots at Rothenburg on Tauber
      Length: 843m [2766 ft.]

*13   ZUCKER UND ZIMT   ("SUGAR AND SPICE")
      (1915)

      Directors: Ernst Mátray and Ernst Lubitsch
      Scenario: Ernst Mátray, Ernst Lubitsch, and
                             Greta Schröder-Mátray
      Source: Verse by Ernst Lubitsch and Greta
                             Schröder-Mátray
      Assistant Director: Richard Löwenbein
      Cast: Ernst Mátray, Ernst Lubitsch, Hel-
                             ene Voss, Alice Scheel-Hechy, Paul
                             Ludwig Stein, Victor Colani.
      Production: Mátray-Lubitsch-Film, Berlin
      Released: 1915

*14   WIE ICH ERMORDET WURDE   ("HOW I WAS MURDERED")
      (1915)

      Director: Louis Ralph
      Cast: Ernst Lubitsch.
      Production: Deutsche Bioscop GmbH, Berlin
      Shot at: Bioscop-Atelier, Neubabelsberg

Note:
   Lubitsch wrote to Herman Weinberg in July 1947: "After
having completed [a] series of one-reel comedies, I decided to
switch to feature [that is, two- and three-reel] pictures
again. Like every comedian, I longed to play a straight leading man, a sort of 'bonvivant' role. So together with my collaborators I wrote a screenplay, called ALS ICH TOT WAR ("When
I Was Dead"). This picture was a complete failure as the

audiences were unwilling to accept me as a straight leading
man. I decided to switch back again to the kind of parts
which had brought me my first success in the picture SCHUH-
PALAST PINKUS" (see entry 294). This is the only known reference to Als ich Tot war. Since Lubitsch was writing more
than thirty years later and the titles are so very similar,
it may be that Wie ich ermordet wurde is the film referred to
in his letter.

*15   WO IST MEIN SCHATZ?   ("WHERE IS MY TREASURE?")
       (1916)

       Director: Ernst Lubitsch
       Cast: Ernst Lubitsch.
       Released: February 25, by Union

       Note:
       Listed by Huff (1947) and in subsequent filmographies, but
not listed in Lamprecht.

16   SCHUHPALAST PINKUS   ("SHOE SALON PINKUS")
       (1916)

    Sally Pinkus is awakened for school, but instead of getting
up he goes back to sleep. Finally he gets dressed, and on the
way out he flirts with the housemaid. His father catches him,
animatedly sends the boy on his way, then picks up with the
maid where his son left off. Sally walks a girl to school and
inadvertently loses his books. Late for class, he tries to
sneak in while the teacher's back is turned but is caught. At
gym class Sally is unable to jump over an exercise horse like
the other boys. When the teacher is not looking, he sneaks
under the horse and fakes the jump off to the teacher's approval. After school Sally accompanies five girls home, carrying all their books and buying them all refreshments.

    On exam day, Sally is unprepared and pins a crib note on
the back of the boy seated in front of him. He successfully
answers the instructor's questions, but when the boy with the
note on his back asks to be excused the teacher discovers it
and Sally is expelled.

    Sally is hired as a clerk in a small shoe store. But he is
soon fired when the boss discovers him making romantic advances
to his daughter. Sally is hired by the more fashionable Meyersohn's Shoe Salon. Once again, Sally is attracted to the female employees--and this time to customers as well. While fitting an especially attractive young woman, Sally admires her
foot and playfully tickles it, and is dismissed by the boss.

Melitta Hervé, a well known dancer, comes in to buy shoes. She rejects all the shoes the boss shows her because (she says) their sizes are all too large. Sally comes up with the bright idea of writing the number of a smaller size over the actual size that fits her foot, and when Melitta is satisfied and buys the pair, the boss reinstates him.

The boss is eager to deliver the shoes to Melitta himself. Sally would like this pleasant task for himself, and so he wraps a different sized pair for the boss to deliver. Melitta is disappointed to find the deliveryman is the boss rather than Sally, and she is upset when she finds the wrong shoes. The boss meets Sally outside in the hallway and is about to take the other pair of shoes from him when Sally inquires about how <u>Mrs.</u> Meyersohn is. Melitta is happy when Sally appears with the right pair of shoes.

Melitta suggests that Sally open up his own business, and she volunteers to lend him the needed cash. Shoe Salon Pinkus is an elegant store with a large staff, but there are not many customers. At one of Melitta's dancing recitals, Sally announces to the ecstatic audience that Melitta's shoes were purchased at his shoe salon, and he hands out announcements for a forthcoming show of the latest styles. His business thrives. Sally suggests that rather than divide the money, they marry instead. Melitta consents.

Director:	Ernst Lubitsch
Scenario:	Hans Kräly and Erich Schönfelder
Sets:	Kurt Richter
Cast:	Guido Herzfeld (Meyersohn), Else Kenter (Melitta Hervé), Ernst Lubitsch (Sally Pinkus), Ossi Oswalda, Hans Kräly
Production:	Projektions-AG "Union," Berlin
Shot at:	Union-Atelier, Berlin-Tempelhof
Length:	1080m [3543 ft.]
Opening:	May, at Union-Theater Nollendorfplatz and Union-Theater Kurfürstendamm

*17   DER SCHWARZE MORITZ   ("BLACK MORITZ")
     (1916)

A combination film and stage musical comedy, with Lubitsch in the cast playing in blackface.

Authors:	Louis Taufstein and Eugen Berg
Music:	Martin Knopf

Cast: Ernst Lubitsch, Erna Albert, Margar-
ete Kupfer.

Played: June 2, at Tauentzien Palast

Note:
    Listed by Huff (1947) and in subsequent filmographies but
not listed in Lamprecht.

*18   DOKTOR SATANSOHN   ("DOCTOR SATANSON")
       (1916)

       Director: Edmund Edel
       Scenario: Edmund Edel
       Cast: Ernst Lubitsch (Dr. Satansohn),
                          Erich Schönfelder, Hans Felix, Yo
                          Larte, Marga Köhler.
       Production: Projektions-AG "Union," Berlin
       Shot at: Union-Atelier, Berlin-Tempelhof

*19   DER GEMISCHTE FRAUENCHOR   ("THE MIXED LADIES' CHORUS")
       (1916)

       Director: Ernst Lubitsch
       Sets: Kurt Richter
       Cast: Ernst Lubitsch.
       Production: Projektions-AG "Union," Berlin
       Shot at: Union-Atelier, Berlin-Tempelhof
       Released: 1916

*20   DER G.m.b.H. Tenor   ("THE TENOR, INC.")
       (1916)

       Director: Ernst Lubitsch
       Photography: Theodor Sparkuhl
       Sets: Kurt Richter
       Cast: Ernst Lubitsch, Ossi Oswalda, Victor
                          Janson.
       Production: Projektions-AG "Union," Berlin
       Shot at: Union-Atelier, Berlin-Tempelhof

*21   DER KRAFTMEIER   ("THE BULLY")
       (1916?)

       Director: Ernst Lubitsch
       Sets: Kurt Richter
       Cast: Ernst Lubitsch.
       Production: Projektions-AG "Union," Berlin
       Shot at: Union-Atelier, Berlin-Tempelhof

*22   LEUTNANT AUF BEFEHL   ("LIEUTENANT BY COMMAND")
       (1916)

           Director: Ernst Lubitsch
           Photography: Theodor Sparkuhl
           Sets: Kurt Richter
           Cast: Harry Liedtke, Ernst Lubitsch, Ossi
                                  Oswalda, Erich Schönfelder, Victor
                                  Janson.
           Production: Projektions-AG "Union," Berlin
           Shot at: Union-Atelier, Berlin-Tempelhof

*23   DAS SCHÖNSTE GESCHENK   ("THE MOST BEAUTIFUL GIFT")
       (1916)

           Director: Ernst Lubitsch
           Sets: Kurt Richter
           Cast: Ernst Lubitsch.
           Production: Projektions-AG "Union," Berlin
           Shot at: Union-Atelier, Berlin-Tempelhof
           Length: 233m [764 ft.]

*24   SEINE NEUE NASE   ("HIS NEW NOSE")
       (1917)

           Director: Ernst Lubitsch
           Cast: Ernst Lubitsch.
           Production: Projektions-AG "Union," Berlin
           Shot: Late 1916 and early 1917

       Notes:
          The film played in Dresden in 1917. Whether it is the same
       film that played later in the year in Berlin as Die Schiefe
       Nase ("The Crooked Nose") is not known. (Lamprecht)

*25   HANS TRUTZ IM SCHLARAF-   ("HANS TRUTZ IN NEVER-NEVER LAND")
          FENLAND
       (1917)

           Director: Paul Wegener
           Scenario: Paul Wegener
           Photography: Frederik Fuglsang
           Sets: Rochus Gliese
           Cast: Paul Wegener, Lyda Salmonova, Ernst
                                  Lubitsch (Devil), Wilhelm Diegel-
                                  mann, Rochus Gliese, Gertrud Welck-
                                  er, Fritz Rasp.

```
          Production:        Projektions-AG "Union," Berlin
          Shot at:           Union-Atelier, Berlin-Tempelhof
          Length:            1225m [4019 ft.]
          Opening:           November, at Union-Theater
                             Kurfürstendamm
```

*26   WENN VIER DASSELBE TUN   ("WHEN FOUR DO THE SAME")
       (1917)

```
          Director:          Ernst Lubitsch
          Scenario:          Ernst Lubitsch and Erich Schönfelder
          Sets:              Kurt Richter
          Cast:              Ossi Oswalda, Emil Jannings, Margar-
                             ete Kupfer, Fritz Schulz, Ernst Lu-
                             bitsch.
          Production:        Projektions-AG "Union," Berlin
          Shot at:           Union-Atelier, Berlin-Tempelhof
          Length:            1076m [3530 ft.]
          Released:          November
```

Note:
    See Jannings (1951) for an account of his role in this
film.

*27   DER BLUSENKÖNIG   ("THE BLOUSE KING")
       (1917)

```
          Director:          Ernst Lubitsch
          Scenario:          Hans Kräly
          Sets:              Kurt Richter
          Cast:              Ernst Lubitsch, Käthe Dorsch, Guido
                             Herzfeld, Max Zilzer.
          Production:        Projektions-AG "Union," Berlin
          Shot at:           Union-Atelier, Berlin-Tempelhof
```

Also see:
    *Der Film, no. 8, p. 30.

*28   OSSIS TAGEBUCH   ("OSSI'S DIARY")
       (1917)

```
          Director:          Ernst Lubitsch
          Sets:              Kurt Richter
          Cast:              Ossi Oswalda, Hermann Thimig.
          Production:        Projektions-AG "Union," Berlin
          Shot at:           Union-Atelier, Berlin-Tempelhof
          Length:            972m [3189 ft.]
```

*29   <u>PRINZ SAMI</u>   ("PRINCE SAMI")
      (1918)

      Director: Ernst Lubitsch
      Sets: Kurt Richter
      Cast: Ernst Lubitsch, Ossi Oswalda, Wil-
                           helm Diegelmann, Margarete Kupfer,
                           Victor Janson, Erich Schönfelder.
      Production: Projektions-AG "Union," Berlin
      Shot at: Union-Atelier, Berlin-Tempelhof,
                           1917
      Released: January

      <u>Also see:</u>
        *<u>Der Film</u>, no. 8 (1917), p. 30.

*30   <u>EIN FIDELES GEFÄNGNIS</u>   ("THE MERRY JAIL")
      (1918)

      Director: Ernst Lubitsch
      Source: The operetta, <u>Die Fledermaus</u> (1874),
                           by Johann Strauss
      Sets: Kurt Richter
      Cast: Harry Liedtke, Emil Jannings (Frosch
                           the Jailer), Ossi Oswalda, Paul
                           Biensfeldt, Erich Schönfelder.
      Production: Projektions-AG "Union," Berlin
      Shot at: Union-Atelier, Berlin-Tempelhof
      Length: 1170m [3839 ft.]
      Released: Early in 1918
      Alternate Title: <u>Das fidele Gefängnis</u>

      <u>Note:</u>
        <u>See</u> Emil Jannings (1951) for an account of his involvement
      in this film.

*31   <u>DER FALL ROSENTOPF</u>   ("THE ROSENTOPF CASE")
      (1918)

      Director: Ernst Lubitsch
      Sets: Kurt Richter
      Cast: Ernst Lubitsch, Trude Hesterberg.
      Production: Projektions-AG "Union," Berlin
      Shot at: Ufa-Union-Atelier, Berlin-Tempelhof
      Length: 1083m [3553 ft.]
      Opening: September 20, at the Union-Theater
                           Friedrichstrasse

*32   DER RODELKAVALIER   ("THE TOBOGGAN CAVALIER")
       (1918)

   "Sportlustspiel," featuring tobogganing and winter scenes.
A spoiled daughter is to marry a man she doesn't love. She
runs away to find the romantic hero of her dreams (Horak,
1975, p. 66).

       Director: Ernst Lubitsch
       Scenario: Ernst Lubitsch and Erich Schönfelder
       Sets: Kurt Richter
       Cast: Ossi Oswalda (Spoiled Daughter),
                          Harry Liedtke (Romantic Hero), Ernst
                          Lubitsch (Ossi's Suitor), Ferry
                          Sikla.
       Production: Projektions-AG "Union," Berlin
       Shot at: Union-Atelier, Berlin-Tempelhof
       Length: 995m [3264 ft.]
       Released: 1918

   Review:
       *Der Kinematograph, no. 582 (1918), p. 22.

GERMAN FEATURE PERIOD (1918-1923)

33   DIE AUGEN DER MUMIE MÂ   (THE EYES OF THE MUMMY)
      (1918)

   Egypt, the present. Albert Wendland, a young English
painter, is fascinated by the stories he hears about the tomb
of Queen Mâ, and inquires at his hotel about the possibility
of going to see it. The guide warns him that the tomb is said
to be haunted and a fatal curse falls on all who visit it. A
dazed tourist warns him that the eyes of the mummy are alive.

   After his efforts to recruit a guide prove unsuccessful,
Wendland goes to the tomb alone. Radu, guardian of the tomb,
shows him to the mummy, whose glowing eyes move and blink.
After a struggle with Radu, Wendland breaks into an adjoining
room and there discovers Mâ, a beautiful young girl, who tells
him Radu has kept her captive and forced her to look through
the mummy's eyes to frighten away intruders. Wendland promises his eternal fidelity to her.

   The two escape together on horseback. Radu chases after
them on foot for a time but finally collapses in the desert.
He is rescued by Prince Hohenfels, an English explorer returning from an expedition. After Radu recovers, he pledges his

45

faithful service to Hohenfels back in Europe. Radu privately vows that he will not rest until he finds Mâ and seeks his revenge.

Back in England, Wendland gives a party for Mâ. When an Oriental song is played on the piano, she begins to dance as if in a trance. One of the guests, a theatrical agent, insists that Mâ's talents belong in a variety show, and he instantly produces a contract for her to sign.

Mâ is a big success as a dancer at the Alhambra Theatre. One day Hohenfels and his servant Radu take in the show. In the middle of a dance Mâ sees her former captor in the audience, faints, and has to be carried off the stage.

Some time later, Wendland and Mâ meet Hohenfels at the opening of an art exhibition in which Wendland's portrait of Mâ is on display. Later, the couple visit Hohenfels to view his art collection. Mâ sees Radu's reflection in a mirror and falls ill. While Mâ is recuperating, Wendland receives a message from Hohenfels, via Radu, that he has bought the portrait of Mâ. Mâ implores Wendland to get the painting back from Hohenfels.

Meanwhile, Radu has seen the portrait and he stabs it, leaving his dagger implanted in the canvas. He returns to seek revenge on Mâ as Wendland arrives at Hohenfel's home. While Wendland and Hohenfels talk business, Radu breaks into Wendland's house in search of Mâ. Hohenfels and Wendland discover Radu's dagger in the painting. Back at Wendland's Radu finds Mâ and as he lifts a knife to her throat, she goes unconscious and falls down the stairs. When Radu sees she is dead, he stabs himself. Wendland returns home to find the two bodies lying dead on the floor.

Director:	Ernst Lubitsch
Scenario:	Hans Kräly and Emil Rameau
Photography:	Alfred Hansen
Sets:	Kurt Richter
Cast:	Pola Negri (Mâ), Emil Jannings (Radu), Harry Liedtke (Wendland, a Painter), Max Laurence (Prince Hohenfels), Margarete Kupfer.
Production:	Projektions-AG "Union," Berlin
Shot at:	Ufa-Union-Atelier, Berlin-Tempelhof
Length:	1193m [3914 ft.] (Lamprecht); 3805 ft. [1160m] (Moving Picture World); 4112 ft. [1253m] (Publicity Sheet)
Opening:	October 3, at Union-Theater Nollendorfplatz and Union-Theater Kurfürstendamm, Berlin

46

Notes:
   Die Augen der Mumi Ma was retitled The Eyes of the Mummy
for U.S. release. It was distributed by Paramount. The New
York opening was August 2, 1922.

Reviews:
   *Der Film, no. 41, p. 82; Variety, Aug. 18, 1922, p. 42;
Moving Picture World, Aug. 19, 1922, p. 613.

Also see:
   Moving Picture World, July 1, 1922, p. 28, Dec. 23, 1922,
p. 772.

*34   DAS MÄDEL VOM BALLETT   ("THE BALLET GIRL")
      (1918)

      Director: Ernst Lubitsch
      Scenario: Hans Kräly
      Photography: Theodor Sparkuhl
      Sets: Kurt Richter
      Cast: Ossi Oswalda, Margarete Kupfer,
                             Harry Liedtke, Victor Janson, Rein-
                             hold Schünzel, Ferry Sikla, Juliette
                             Brandt, Joe Konradi.
      Production: Projektions-AG "Union," Berlin
      Shot at: Ufa-Union-Atelier, Berlin-Tempelhof
      Opening: December 6, at Union-Theater
                             Nollendorfplatz, Union-Theater
                             Friedrichstrasse, and Union-Theater
                             Alexanderplatz
      Length: 693m [2274 ft.]

35   CARMEN   (GYPSY BLOOD)
      (1918)

      Frame: around a campfire a gypsy tells a
                             tale of long ago....

   Spain, around 1820. Don José Navarro, Spanish dragoon, is
spending a furlough at home in the Baztan Valley with his
mother and his fiancée when word comes that he has been promoted to sergeant and is to return at once to Seville to take
charge of his men.

   One of the girls at a cigarette factory across from where
Don José is quartered, La Carmencita, a gypsy, flirts with Don
José. One day the hot-tempered Carmen stabs a fellow worker
who is taunting her and Don José assumes responsibility for
taking her to jail. Carmen persuaded him to let her escape and
for this Don José himself is thrown in jail. Carmen arranges

for him to escape while she keeps the elderly jailkeeper distracted, but Don José can't bring himself to do it. Later he is stripped of his rank and sent back to jail.

Sometime after, Carmen is called to dance at a party Colonel Rodriguez gives for his friends. When she arrives in the Colonel's carriage Don José is standing guard duty like a raw recruit. Later he watches through the window as the Colonel makes advances to Carmen. As she leaves she tells Don José to come to her later at the tavern of Lillas Pastia, a hangout for her and her band of gypsy smugglers. When they meet, Don José makes the mistake of telling her where he will be standing guard that evening; she goes to him there at midnight and forces him to pay attention to her while the smugglers slip past his post.

Next day Carmen and Don José are together at her place when the Colonel pays her a visit. He and Don José quarrel and in the ensuing fight the Colonel is killed. Don José has no choice but to flee to the gypsy smugglers and join their band.

The band operates out of a mountain camp. One day Carmen leaves the camp for Gibraltar. Sometime later she returns as the companion of an unsuspecting dragoon, whom she leads into an ambush. The gypsies are about to kill him when Don José intercedes and permits his escape. The soldier alerts the garrison in Seville and leads the troops back to the gypsy camp. Don José is wounded in their attack but he and Carmen manage to escape.

When she was in Gibraltar Carmen became involved with Escamillo, the famous matador, who promised to take her to the great bullfight in Seville as his lady a month hence. On the day of the bullfight Don José, still recuperating from his wound, hears of it and rushes to the arena in time to see the matador triumph in the ring and then present himself before Carmen in front of the crowd. Don José is waiting for Carmen as she leaves the arena to meet her lover. He pulls a dagger and stabs her and collapses in grief on her lifeless body. (Synopsis prepared from the American release version.)

Director:	Ernst Lubitsch
Scenario:	Hans Kräly
Source:	The story, <u>Carmen</u> (1846), by Prosper Mérimée
Photography:	Alfred Hansen
Sets:	Kurt Richter
Associate:	Karl Machus
Costumes:	Ali Hubert
Music:	Artur Vieregg
Cast:	Pola Negri (Carmen), Harry Liedtke (Don José Novarro), Leopold von Ledebur (Garcia, Smuggler), Grete Diercks (Dolores), Wilhelm Diegelmann (Guard Housekeeper), Heinrich

	Peer (English Officer), Margarete Kupfer (Old Lady at Carmen's), Sophie Pagay (Don José's Mother), Paul Conradi (Don Cairo, Smuggler), Max Kronert (Rementale, Smuggler), Magnus Stifter (Escamillo, Toreador), Paul Biensfeldt, Victor Janson, Albert Venohr.
Production:	Projektions-AG "Union," Berlin
Shot at:	Ufa-Union-Atelier, Berlin-Tempelhof, and at the chalkpits in Berlin-Rudersdorf
Length:	1784m [5853 ft.] (Lamprecht); 6040 ft. [1841m] (Wid's Daily)
Opening:	December 17, at the Union-Theater Kurfürstendamm, Berlin

Notes:
   Carmen was retitled Gipsy [or Gypsy] Blood for U.S. release. It was distributed by First National. Titles for the American version were by Myron Stearns. The New York opening was May 8, 1921.

Reviews:
   *Der Film, no. 52, p. 52; New York Times, May 9, 1921, p. 16; Variety, May 13, 1921, p. 42; Wid's Daily, May 15, 1921, p. 5; Moving Picture World, May 21, 1921, p. 321; Exceptional Photoplays, May 1921, p. 7; London Times, Mar. 1, 1927, p. 12.

Also see:
   Moving Picture World, May 28, 1921, p. 387, Sept. 24, 1921, p. 430; Motion Picture, June 1921, pp. 49-53, 86, 99-100.

*36 MEINE FRAU, DIE FILM-   ("MY WIFE, THE MOVIE STAR")
     SCHAUSPIELERIN
     (1919)

   "A temperamental film diva manages to transform a studio into a madcap circus, while her director tears his hair out" (Horak, 1975, p. 81).

Director:	Ernst Lubitsch
Scenario:	Hans Kräly and Ernst Lubitsch
Photography:	Theodor Sparkuhl
Sets:	Kurt Richter
Cast:	Ossi Oswalda (Ossi, the Movie Star), Victor Janson (The Director), Hans Kräly, Paul Biensfeldt (Writers), Julius Dewald (Erik Frank), Max Kronert (Hans, a Porter).
Production:	Projektions-AG "Union," Berlin

Shot at:	Ufa-Union-Atelier, Berlin-Tempelhof, 1918
Length:	1084m [3556 ft.]
Opening:	January 24, at the Union-Theater Kurfürstendamm

*37   <u>MEYER AUS BERLIN</u>   ("MEYER FROM BERLIN")
          (1919)

Director:	Ernst Lubitsch
Cast:	Ossi Oswalda (Teenager), Ernst Lubitsch (Apprentice), Erich Schönfelder (Her Father).
Production:	Projektions-AG "Union," Berlin
Shot at:	Ufa-Union-Atelier, Berlin-Tempelhof
Length:	1019m [3343 ft.]
Opening:	February, at the Union-Theater Nollendorfplatz

<u>Also See</u>:
   *<u>Licht-Bild-Bühne</u>, no. 4, p. 79.

*38   <u>DAS SCHWABEMÄDLE</u>   ("THE GIRL FROM SWABIA")
          (1919)

Director:	Ernst Lubitsch
Cast:	Ossi Oswalda, Carl Auen.
Production:	Projektions-AG "Union," Berlin
Shot at:	Ufa-Union-Atelier, Berlin-Tempelhof
Length:	956m [3136 ft.]

<u>Note</u>:
   According to Horak (1975, p. 80n), *<u>Der Kinematograph</u> (January) gives Ernst Jacoby as director of this film.

39   <u>DIE AUSTERNPRINZESSIN</u>   ("THE OYSTER PRINCESS")
      (1919)

     In the European villa of Mr. Quaker, an American businessman, the "oyster king." The oyster king smokes his fat cigars as his many servants and secretaries see to his needs and carry out his work. A message is brought to him about his daughter. She has just read an item in the paper that the daughter of the shoepolish king has married a count, and she is throwing a tantrum and smashing up the furniture and won't stop until her father agrees to buy her a prince.

Assistance is sought from a marriage broker. He recommends
Prince Nuki. The prince is penniless (he is washing his own
clothes when the matchmaker arrives) and he jumps at the opportunity to make a wealthy match. However, he sends his
manservant, Josef, to impersonate him to the Quakers and to
find out for sure that the prospective spouse is wealthy.

Miss Quaker grows impatient waiting for her prince and
throws another tantrum. She yanks the newspaper out of her
father's hands. She does it again and again but each time he
takes another paper from his pocket and continues reading.
Josef arrives and presents himself as the prince. He is kept
waiting while Miss Quaker is bathed and massaged and dressed.
(Meanwhile, Papa Quaker relaxes and sleeps.) Finally she appears and Josef is whisked away at once to be married.

An elaborate dinner is given by Papa Quaker in honor of the
the newly wedded couple. Each of the many guests has a different waiter for each course of the meal. Josef is called
upon to deliver a toast. Not knowing what to say and beginning to feel his many drinks, he announces he is glad to be
eating so well after such a long time. A fox trot follows
dinner, but Josef continues to eat and drink during the dancing.

The real prince arrives. The Women's Society to Prevent
Drunkenness, of which the oyster princess is a member, argue
over who shall have the opportunity to minister to such a
handsome but inebriated client. A boxing match is held among
the women to decide. The oyster princess wins. She and the
real prince get on well. Josef looks through the keyhole of
her door and sees another man on her bed. When he discovers
it's Prince Nuki, he informs the happy couple that since he
married the princess in the prince's name, they are legally
married.

Mr. Quaker and his daughter and the real son-in-law dine
together. Nuki and the princess play footsie under the table.
They leave the table without Quaker noticing. When Quaker
discovers he is alone, he follows them to his daughter's room
and looks through the keyhole. The married couple are in bed.
Nuki turns out the light. The oyster king is happy.

Director:	Ernst Lubitsch
Scenario:	Hans Kräly
Photography:	Theodor Sparkuhl
Sets:	Kurt Richter
Cast:	Ossi Oswalda (The Princess, Daughter of The Oyster King), Victor Janson (Quaker, The Oyster King), Julius Falkenstein (Josef, Servant of Nuki),

Harry Liedtke (Prince Nuki), Max
Kronert (Seligson, of the Matrimo-
nial Agency), Curt Bois (Orchestra
Director), Albert Paulig, Gerhard
Ritterband. Kosmorama (1976) adds
Hans Junkermann.

Production:	Projektions-AG "Union," Berlin
Shot at:	Ufa-Union-Atelier, Berlin-Tempelhof
Length:	1144m [3753 ft.]
Opening:	June 25, at the Union-Theater Kurfür-stendamm

*40   RAUSCH   ("INTOXICATION")
      (1919)

   Paris, around the turn of the century. Maurice, a selfish,
egotistical playwright, neglects his faithful mistress, Jeanne,
and their five-year-old daughter, Marion. On opening night of
his new play, Maurice skips a gathering put on for him by his
friends and goes off with Henriette, a sculptress and mistress
of his best friend, Adolphe. The play is a smash hit. Intox-
icated with his success, Maurice begins to feel his child by
Jeanne stands in the way of his happiness with Henriette and
wishes her out of the way. The child dies from unexplained
causes. Maurice is suspected. His fortunes turn--the police
harass him, the neighbors turn against him, his friends desert
him, and the play is closed. Driven by uncontrollable feelings of guilt, he and Henriette begin to psychologically lac-
erate one another. Eventually it comes out that the child
died from natural causes, but not before the suffering and remorseful Maurice has learned his lessons--that outward success
is hollow and that each man must learn to come to terms with
the dark side of his nature. (Synopsis based on Strindberg's
play.)

Director:	Ernst Lubitsch
Scenario:	Hans Kräly
Source:	The play, Brott och Brott (There Are Crimes and Crimes) (1900), by August Strindberg
Photography:	Karl Freund
Sets:	Rochus Gliese
Cast:	Asta Nielsen (Henriette), Alfred Abel (Maurice), Carl Meinhard (Adolphe), Grete Diercks (Jeanne), Marga Köhler (Henriette's Mother), Frieda Richard (Housekeeper), Sophie Pagay (Mme. Catherine), Rudolf Klein-Rohden (Investigator), Heinz Stieda (The Abbé).

Production:	Argus-Film GmbH, Berlin
Shot at:	Filmatelier Chausseestrasse 123
	(formerly Bioscop Atelier)
Length:	1796m [5892 ft.]
Opening:	August, at the Union-Theater Kurfür-
	stendamm

Also see:

Asta Nielsen, Den tiende Muse, vol. II (Kфbenhaven: Gyldendal, 1946), pp. 149-51. (German translation, *Die schweigende Muse, Rostock: Hinstorff, 1961).

41 MADAME DUBARRY   (PASSION)
    (1919)

France, the late eighteenth century. On her way to deliver a hat to an important customer, Jeanne Marie Vaubernier, a milliner's apprentice, stops off to see her lover, a student, Armand de Foix. After a time she leaves, promising to see him again on Sunday. Resuming her errand, she comes upon a procession for Don Diego, Spanish envoy to the court. Don Diego's horse runs over the millinery box. Jeanne's employer, Madame Labille, is very angry and slaps the girl but about that time Don Diego appears and insists on taking full responsibility for the accident. He comforts the pretty apprentice, tells her she could be better placed, and invites her to dinner with him on Sunday.

Jeanne has to decide which engagement to keep. She settles on rank and tells Armand her employer is sending her on an errand to fit a robe for the wife of the Spanish envoy. Armand insists on accompanying her to Don Diego's door and waits outside. During dinner Don Diego makes advances to Jeanne. When the Comte Dubarry is admitted on urgent business, she hides behind a screen. As he discusses business with Don Diego, Dubarry sees Jeanne in a mirror and is attracted to her. Meanwhile, the waiting Armand is informed by a guard that Don Diego is unmarried.

Two days later Armand receives a letter from Jeanne begging his forgiveness and entreating him to meet her at the Opera Ball. At the Ball Armand and Don Diego argue and fight a duel and the Spaniard is killed. Armand is led away under guard. Dubarry leaves with Jeanne.

Dubarry becomes Jeanne's protector. He sends her to Choiseul, Louis XV's minister, to arrange it so that he will be reimbursed for a military expedition he financed. Choiseul turns down the request and has her escorted out. As she sits dejectedly on a bench outside, the King notices her and sends for her. But Choiseul, whose overpowering ambition is to have his sister, the Duchess de Grammont, become Queen of France, informs her she is trespassing and orders her to leave. The King sends an emissary, Lebel, to search for her.

Lebel finds Jeanne at Dubarry's and invites her to dine with the King. The King is enthralled with her. At dinner he removes Dubarry's petition from her bosom and signs it and kisses her. When Choiseul brings papers condemning Armand to death for having killed Don Diego, Jeanne tells the King Armand is her cousin and the King declares that he shall go free.

Choiseul and his sister scheme to cause the King embarrassment over his new mistress. They pay street singers to chant unflattering things about her. When the King hears of the songs, he reacts by issuing an order that Jeanne will be received at court. Lebel informs Dubarry it will be necessary for Jeanne to be married to a nobleman in order for her to be received at court and asks who a likely matrimonial candidate might be. Dubarry suggests his brother Guillaume, who will do anything for a price. Jeanne marries him.

Armand is unaware of what has happened to Jeanne or of her intervention for his pardon. He decides to devote his life to the man who spared it and becomes a soldier of the King's guard. When Jeanne sees him in that station, she has him made an officer.

Choiseul's sister schemes to have unpleasant things happen during Jeanne's formal presentation at Versailles. At an appointed signal, the mob outside yells "Down with Dubarry." Jeanne's spirits are lifted when she sees it is Armand who attempts to control the unruly crowd. Jeanne has him brought to her and he learns the truth about her. She admits to him she was responsible for his pardon.

Paillet, a cobbler, is about to be arrested for failing to pay his taxes. He is forced to give the small amount of money he has for bread for his family to the King. Armand tells Paillet what has become of Jeanne and assures Paillet's family they will get bread. Armand becomes a leader among the rioters. When he is arrested, Choiseul tells him that Jeanne is ruining France as she ruined him. Armand convinces Choiseul he could stop Jeanne if he were free. Choiseul lets him go in order to save France.

Disguised as a man, Jeanne goes to Gourdan's where Armand and his comrades are plotting. After the others leave, Jeanne reveals herself to Armand. He agrees to give her one more chance but tells her to beware if she doesn't mend her ways.

The King faints while he and Jeanne play blindman's bluff. His ailment is diagnosed as smallpox. The dying King calls out for Jeanne. Choiseul sees to it that Jeanne is not permitted to get to him, and the King is already dead when she is finally admitted. Choiseul issues a proclamation that bans Jeanne from Paris and will force her to live in seclusion.

Meanwhile, Jeanne has had Paillet, who was among the rioters, arrested. Armand is incensed over this final treachery of Jeanne's. He helps to stir up the populace to storm the Bastille and the palace, setting off a revolution. Jeanne is taken captive and is sentenced to death by Citizen Armand de Foix. But Armand realizes he cannot let Jeanne die. In disguise he goes to her in her cell in order to save her but is recognized and shot as a traitor. Jeanne is led to the guillotine.

Director:	Ernst Lubitsch
Scenario:	Fred Orbing [pseud. Norbert Falk] and Hans Kräly
Photography:	Theodor Sparkuhl
Sets:	Kurt Richter
Associate:	Karl Machus
Costumes:	Ali Hubert
Technical Advisor:	Kurt Waschneck
Production Manager:	Carl Moos
Cast:	Pola Negri (Jeanne Vaubernier, later Mme. Dubarry), Emil Jannings (Louis XV), Reinhold Schünzel (Duke of Choiseul, Minister of State), Harry Liedtke (Armand de Foix), Eduard von Winterstein (Count Jean Dubarry), Karl Platen (Guillaume Dubarry), Paul Biensfeldt (Lebel, the King's Chamberlain), Magnus Stifter (Don Diego, Spanish Envoy), Willi Kaiser-Heyl (Commandant of the Guards), Else Berna (Duchess of Gramont), Fred Immler (Duke of Richelieu), Gustav Czimeg (Duke of Aiguillon), Alexander Ekert (Paillet), Marga Köhler (Madame Labille), Bernhard Goetzke, Robert Sortsch-Plá.
Production:	Projektions-AG "Union," Berlin
Shot at:	Ufa-Union-Atelier, Berlin-Tempelhof; Sans Souci Park scenes in Potsdam
Length:	2280m [7480 ft.]
Opening:	September 18, at the Ufa-Palast am Zoo, Berlin

Notes:
 Madame Dubarry was retitled Passion for U.S. release. It
was the first German film shown in this country after World
War I. It premiered in New York on December 12, 1920, and set
new attendance records. It had been purchased for American
distribution by Associated First National when no other distributor would touch it even at its lowest price. "At the
time that the production was finished in Berlin, the latter
part of last year, the German producers would have been glad
to take $10,000 for the American rights, which finally were
sold for $40,000.... Conservative estimates place the value
of the American rights today in excess of $500,000" New York
Times, Dec. 23, 1920, p. 28). Titles for the American version
were by Katherine Hilliker; title effects were by S. L. Rotha-
fel and were photographed in color by Prizma. Credits were
unlisted for the premiere; Variety referred to the director
"Emil Subitch." Concerning a benefit showing of Passion at
Carnegie Hall January 21, 1921: "At the previous presentation,
for two weeks at the Capitol Theatre, a six reel version was
used. The Passion shown at Carnegie Hall extended to nine
parts. The difference in length was hardly noticeable, so
great is the power of holding the onlookers' interest in the
historical and beautifully presented story" (Moving Picture
World, Feb. 5, 1921, p. 678). Passion had an unprecedented
return run at the Capitol Theatre beginning June 24, 1923.

Reviews:
 New York Times, Dec. 13, 1920, p. 19 and Jan. 30, 1921,
VI.2; [revival] June 26, 1923, p. 14 and July 1, 1923, VI.2;
Variety, Dec. 17, 1920, p. 40; Wid's Daily, Oct. 10, 1920,
p. 4; Moving Picture World, Nov. 27, 1920, pp. 469, 513; Chi-
cago Daily News, May 10, 1921, p. 22; Exceptional Photoplays,
Nov. 1920, p. 3; London Times, Nov. 28, 1922, p. 10.

Also see:
 Bibliography entry 84 on "German Invasion." Variety,
Dec. 3, 1920, p. 34, Dec. 17, 1920, pp. 1, 45, p. 41, Jan. 14,
1921, p. 46, Feb. 25, 1921, p. 41; Moving Picture World, Dec.
4, 1920, p. 599, Dec. 11, 1920, p. 714, p. 750, Dec. 18, 1920,
p. 907, Dec. 25, 1920, p. 992, p. 1050, p. 1055, Jan. 1, 1921,
p. 47, Mar. 5, 1921, p. 70, May 28, 1921, p. 411, July 16,
1921, p. 328, July 9, 1927, p. 77, July 16, 1927, p. 147,
Aug. 20, 1927, p. 531 (a recut version released by Tiffany);
New York Times, Dec. 12, 1920, VI.2.

*42 DER LUSTIGE EHEMANN   ("THE MERRY HUSBAND")
     (1919)

     Director: Leo Lasko
     Scenario: Ernst Lubitsch, after an idea of
                               Richard Wilde

Photography: Theodor Sparkuhl
Sets: Kurt Richter
Cast: Victor Janson (in a dual role), Irm-
                     gard Bern, Marga Köhler, Heddy Jen-
                     dry, Wally Koch.
Production: Projektions-AG "Union," Berlin
Shot at: Ufa-Union-Atelier, Berlin-Tempelhof
Length: 757m [2484 ft.]
First Shown: October

43   DIE PUPPE   (THE DOLL)
     (1919)

     Prologue: Lubitsch assembles a miniature set,
                         containing a cottage and grounds and
                         a little pond....

     The set comes to life: the young man who lives in the cot-
tage, Lancelot, is plagued by bad fortune, but the sun comes
out and shines on him, auguring well for his future. Lancelot's uncle, the Baron von Chanterelle, insists that the young
man get married. Lancelot flees to a monastery to escape the
horde of girls who have heard the news of his availability and
are in hot pursuit of him. The fat, greedy monks take him in.
When they see the Baron's notice in the paper begging Lancelot
to come back and promising 300,000 francs as a wedding gift,
the monks come up with a solution--let Lancelot marry a doll
and give them the money.

     At the shop of Hilarius, a maker of lifesize mechanical
dolls, Hilarius' daughter is posing as a model for the dollmaker's latest creation. While the dollmaker is out of the
room, his apprentice dances with the doll and accidentally
breaks off her arm. The daughter poses as the doll to spare
the boy a licking. Lancelot appears and purchases the daughter.

     Lancelot presents the "doll" to his uncle as his new wife.
When they are alone later he starts to change her clothes,
but she slaps him and indicates with a mechanical-looking gesture that she can do it herself. Meanwhile, Hilarius discovers the truth and there is a wild spree through his shop as
the dollmaker tries to catch his apprentice to punish him.

     At the wedding party the girl manages to eat and dance yet
comically conceal all her actions from her new husband.
Lancelot gets his money and returns with it and his doll to
the delighted Brothers. As Lancelot gets ready for bed, he
looks at his doll, sighs because she isn't real, and hangs
his clothes on her. In his dreams the doll comes to life.

In reality she does too, but Lancelot can't believe it's true. Suddenly she is frightened by a mouse, and Lancelot sees she is indeed a real-life woman. (At this point there is a cutout insert of a cock that raises its head and crows.) Lancelot and his bride leave the monastery. They meet the dollmaker and show him with their marriage license that all is well, and the happy couple go off together.

Director:	Ernst Lubitsch
Scenario:	Hans Kräly and Ernst Lubitsch
Source:	Inspired by themes of E. T. A. Hoffmann and their operatic adaptations by A. M. Willner
Photography:	Theodor Sparkuhl
Sets:	Kurt Richter
Costumes:	Kurt Richter
Technical Advisor:	Kurt Waschneck
Cast:	Ossi Oswalda (The "Doll," Daughter of Hilarius), Hermann Thimig (Lancelot, Nephew of the Baron), Victor Janson (Hilarius, Dollmaker), Jacob Tiedtke (Prior of the Abbey), Gerhard Ritterband (Apprentice to Hilarius), Marga Köhler (Wife of Hilarius), Max Kronert (Baron von Chanterelle), Josefine Dora (Lancelot's Nurse), Paul Morgan, Arthur Weinschenk, Herr Lapitski.
Production:	Projektions-AG "Union," Berlin
Shot at:	Ufa-Union-Atelier, Berlin-Tempelhof
Length:	1375m [4511 ft.]
Opening:	December 5, Ufa-Palast am Zoo, Berlin

Notes:
   Die Puppe was shown as The Doll at a few selected locations in the U.S. in 1928. Film Daily Yearbook lists "55th St. Playhouse Group" as the distributor. There were said to be censorship problems over the clerical scenes. Between two Boston showings on separate days, the reviewer for the Boston Evening Transcript wrote: "The Doll reminds one hardly at all of Lubitsch's later work. Except for its delightful inconsequence and its undercurrent of satire it would be a pleasing enough but harmless fairy story" (Nov. 2 [?], 1928). For a plot summary of the operetta La Poupée, by Maurice Ordonneau and Edmond Audran, which A. M. Willner translated into German, see Mark Lubbock, The Complete Book of Light Opera (London: Putnam, 1962), pp. 121-23.

44   ICH MÖCHTE KEIN MANN   ("I WOULDN'T WANT TO BE A MAN!")
      SEIN!
      (1920)

     Ossi plays poker, smokes, drinks, and does other things her uncle and governess say don't become a respectable young lady. When the uncle is called away to New York on business, he leaves Ossi in the care of the governess and a new male guardian, Dr. Kersten, who assures her he'll "cut her down to size" and make her behave like a lady. Ossi chafes under his strict regimen and decides to try living as a man. She has herself fitted out in a gentleman's wardrobe. But very soon she begins to discover living a man's life won't be as easy as she thought. She has to stand for women on the streetcar; in crowds the men all jostle one another very roughly; women pursue her relentlessly. Out for an evening on the town, Ossi sees her guardian at a ball with a female companion. Ossi consoles him after his girl jilts him and the two drink and smoke cigars together. The smoking makes Ossi sick; she is sure she "wouldn't want to be a man." The two companions get drunk and have to be taken home in a carriage. On the way, in their drunkenness they kiss. Meanwhile, the driver gets the addresses mixed up and next morning Ossi wakes up in a strange bed. When she arrives home still dressed as the night before, her guardian has slept in her bed. She announces she has come to see her cousin Ossi; the guardian begs his acquaintance of the night before not to mention their little escapade. When he goes to Ossi's room to wake her up, he finds her still in her gentleman's clothing letting down her long hair. "I'll cut you down to size," Ossi promises him, and they embrace passionately. A final title reads "I wouldn't want to be a man!"

Director:	Ernst Lubitsch
Scenario:	Ernst Lubitsch and Hans Kräly
Photography:	Theodor Sparkuhl
Sets:	Kurt Richter
Cast:	Ferry Sikla (The Uncle), Ossi Oswalda (Ossi, His Niece), Margarete Kupfer (Governess), Kurt Götz (Dr. Kersten), Victor Janson.
Production:	Projektions-AG "Union," Berlin
Shot at:	Ufa-Union-Atelier, Berlin-Tempelhof
Length:	907m [2976 ft.]
First Shown:	1920

*45   KOHLHIESELS TÖCHTER   ("KOHLHIESEL'S DAUGHTERS")
      (1920)

     Innkeeper Kohlhiesel has two marriageable daughters, Gretel and Liesel. Gretel is a saucy, strapping wench who is being

courted by two young huntsmen, Xaver and Seppl. According to
peasant tradition, however, she may not marry until her older
sister has found a husband. But Liesel is uncouth, shrewish,
and overbearing, and men are not interested in her. Xaver,
the heftier of the two fellows, makes his intentions known to
old Kohlhiesel, who can only tell him: "Get a man for Liesel
first." Seppl therefore suggests that Xaver first marry Liesel, then get a divorce and marry Gretel. This seems like a
good idea. But Xaver turns out to be a disgusting oaf of a
husband and this makes Liesel very sad. Liesel changes her
ways and with Gretel's help becomes a devoted wife. Xaver and
Liesel are reconciled and so nothing stands in the way of
Gretel's marriage to Seppl. (Translated and adapted from the
synopsis in the booklet for the 1967 Berlin Lubitsch Retrospective by Peter B. Schumann; see entry 351.)

Director:	Ernst Lubitsch
Scenario:	Hans Kräly and Ernst Lubitsch
Photography:	Theodor Sparkuhl
Sets:	Jack Winter
Cast:	Henny Porten (in dual roles, Gretel and Liesel, The Daughters), Emil Jannings (Peter Xaver), Gustav von Wangenheim (Paul Seppl), Jacob Tiedtke (Mathias Kohlhiesel).
Production:	Messter-Film GmbH, Berlin
Shot at:	Ufa-Messter-Atelier, Berlin-Tempel-hof, 1919/1920
Length:	1129m [3704 ft.]
Opening:	March 9, at the Ufa-Palast am Zoo, Berlin

Notes:
   Verdone (1964) credits costumes to Jan Baluschek; Kosmorama
(1976) gives source as a story by Friedrich Raff and Julius
Urgiss.

46   ROMEO UND JULIA IM SCHNEE ("ROMEO AND JULIET IN THE SNOW")
     (1920)

   A tale inspired by Shakespeare. A mountainous region of
Swabia. Court day. Feuding families, the Capulethofers and
the Montekugerls, seek resolution of a dispute. Seated on
facing benches while waiting for their case to be called, the
parents of both families turn to the wall rather than look at
one another. As they go in they break down the door to the
courtroom quibbling over who shall go first. The judge places
sausages each side has given him on the scale of justice and
pronounces both sides in the right. Therefore, both sides are
also in the wrong, and both sides must pay a fine.

Outside a boy sticks out his tongue at children of the opposing family and a fight ensues. It spreads into a huge
brawl as gangs from all over rush to the scene. A policeman
arrives and puts a stop to it.

A son of friends of the Capulethofers, a great lummox, is
presented as a marriage prospect for Julia. Julia's father
leaves them alone in a hayloft and the prospective fiancé begins to make advances toward her. She moves away. He pursues
her and falls down a flight of steps into a haystack.

Romeo sees Julia outside and throws a snowball at her.
Later, as the two stare out their windows at one another, Romeo blows her a kiss. Julia's father discovers her infatua-
tion with a member of the opposing family and chases her outside in a rage. Romeo throws another snowball and this time
hits the father.

At a masquerade, the fiancé, dressed as an angel, is seated
with a bored Julia and her parents. Romeo changes costumes
with him and goes to join Julia and she and Romeo dance. Her
parents are pleased when they see her kissing who they think
is the son of their friends. But the ruse is discovered when
the fiancé returns to their table, and Romeo flees.

Romeo climbs a ladder to Julia's bedroom and declares his
love for her. But the parents remain adamantly opposed to the
romance. Romeo and Julia visit a chemist and ask for a poison.
They go to a hayloft and both drink some of the potion. They
weep, kiss, and collapse backwards into the hay. Nothing happens, so they repeat the process.

Meanwhile, Julia's father discovers a suicide note his
daughter left behind. Everyone joins him in a search for the
couple except the fiancé, who continues to eat. When they
hear the approaching voices, the lovers pretend to be dead.
Both sets of parents are overcome with grief. The fathers are
remorseful, each one trying to take the blame on himself for
the tragedy. The mothers embrace one another. Suddenly the
lovers open their eyes, raise up and kiss. (The chemist
actually only gave them sugared water.) The feuding families
have learned their lesson; all accept the union and embrace.
The fiancé continues to eat heartily.

Director:	Ernst Lubitsch
Scenario:	Hans Kräly and Ernst Lubitsch
Photography:	Theodor Sparkuhl
Sets:	Kurt Richter
Cast:	Lotte Neumann (Julia), Gustav von Wangenheim (Romeo), Jacob Tiedtke (Kapulethofer), Marga Köhler (His Wife), Ernst Rückert (Montekugerl),

61

	Julius Falkenstein (The Fiancé), Paul Biensfeldt (Magistrate), Hermann Picha (Clerk), Josefine Dora, Paul Passarge.
Production:	Maxim-Film-Ges. Ebner and Co., Berlin
Shot at:	Maxim-Film-Atelier, Blücherstrasse 32; exterior scenes in Garmisch
Length:	947m [3107 ft.]
First Shown:	March 28

Also see:
   Robert Hamilton Ball, Shakespere on Silent Film (New York: Theatre Arts Books, 1968), p. 372.

47   SUMURUN   (ONE ARABIAN NIGHT)
      (1920)

   Bagdad, the ninth century. In the noonday heat a tiny caravan crawls lazily across the sands toward the city. In the main wagon is a small troupe of performers--a juggler, a dancer, a hunchback, and an old hag. The hunchback is in love with the wild, dark-haired dancer. She loves no man but has been loved by many, and enjoys playing the tease with other men in the hunchback's presence in order to arouse his jealousy. A slave dealer, Achmet, passes by and is struck with the dancer's beauty. Months before he was sent out by Zuleika, favorite wife of the Sheik of Bagdad, to find a woman more beautiful than she is to replace her in his harem. (She is in love with a handsome young merchant, Nour-ed-din, and longs to be free of the old Sheik.) Meanwhile, in the city, the jealous old Sheik has stumbled upon what appears to be a tryst or flirtation of Zuleika's and is threatening to kill her when his eunuch brings news of Achmet and the beautiful dancer.

   The old Sheik's son happens to ride past during the troupe's first performance in the city, is much attracted to the dancer, and directs Nour-ed-din to take expensive gifts to her. She is more taken with the handsome merchant than with the gifts and throws herself at him. When he resists, the hunchback, much relieved, tells Nour-ed-din he has earned his eternal gratitude.

   The old Sheik condemns Zuleika to death for her presumed unfaithfulness and her continued obstinacy. She is spared at the last minute when the young Sheik hears of her plight and rushes to his father to explain it was he who made the advances, but Zuleika showed no interest in him.

   That night the old Sheik and the young Sheik both come to see the dancer perform. Afterwards the old Sheik indicates to Achmet she is to be brought to him. In despair at losing her, the hunchback takes pills which induce a deathlike trance. The old woman finds him and stuffs his body into a sack.

Nour-ed-din's servants steal the sack, thinking it contains valuables, and take it to their master's shop. Zuleika and Haidee, her friend in the harem, order a selection of goods from Nour-ed-din for the harem and hide the merchant inside one of the chests containing the shipment. (The sack containing the hunchback is also inside.) Zuleika and Nour-ed-din are united inside the palace.

Achmet dresses and perfumes the new beauty and sends her to the palace. The old Sheik takes a string of pearls from around Zuleika's neck and bestows them on the dancer, signifying that she now occupies Zuleika's former position in the harem. At dawn, after the old Sheik has fallen asleep, the young Sheik arrives and the dancer begins to receive his attentions. Meanwhile, the old hag has succeeded in rousing the hunchback, who climbs a wall just in time to see the old Sheik wake up in a rage and kill both the lovers. Shortly after, the old Sheik discovers Nour-ed-din and Zuleika and is about to kill this unfaithful pair too when the distraught hunchback rushes in and stabs the old Sheik in the back. The doors are flung open, the girls of the harem have their freedom, and Zuleika and Nour-ed-din walk slowly away from the palace together. (Synopsis prepared from the American release version.)

Director:	Ernst Lubitsch
Scenario:	Hans Kräly and Ernst Lubitsch
Source:	The hunchback episode of <u>The Arabian Nights</u> and its adaptation as a stage pantomime, <u>Sumurûn</u> (first performed 1910), by Friedrich Freksa, music by Victor Holländer, produced by Max Reinhardt
Photography:	Theodor Sparkuhl
Technical Advisor:	Kurt Waschneck
Sets:	Kurt Richter
Associate:	Ernö Metzner
Costumes:	Ali Hubert
Cast:	Pola Negri (Dancer), Jenny Hasselqvist (Zuleika, "Sumurun," the Sheik's Favorite), Aud Egede Nissen (Haidee), Paul Wegener (Sheik), Harry Liedtke (Nur-al-Din, a Merchant; Nour-ed-din in the American version), Carl Clewing (Sheik's Son), Ernst Lubitsch (Hunchback Clown), Margarete Kupfer (Old Woman), Jacob Tiedtke (Chief Eunuch), Paul Graetz, Max Kronert (Servants of Nur-al-Din), Paul Biensfeldt (Slave Dealer).

Production:	Projektions-AG "Union" (Union-Film der Ufa), 1920
Shot at:	Ufa-Union-Atelier, Berlin-Tempelhof
Length:	2400m [7874 ft.] cut to 2379m [7805 ft.] by censors. "The original German version...was in 12 reels. This was cut to about 6500 feet before the general idea of the American version was arrived at. Then it was discovered that the entire picture would have to be re-edited for the American market.... When the picture is finally shown here it will contain about 7,800 feet with titles" (Variety, Sept. 2, 1921, p. 62). American trade reviews listed the film at both 7650 ft. [2332m] and 7850 ft. [2393m].
Opening:	September 1, at the Ufa-Palast am Zoo, Berlin

Notes:
   Sumurun was retitled One Arabian Night for U.S. release. It was distributed by First National. The American version was titled and edited by Lesley Mason. The New York opening was October 2, 1921.

Reviews:
   New York Times, Oct. 3, 1921, p. 16; Variety, Oct. 7, 1921, p. 43; Wid's Daily, Sept. 25, 1921, p. 3; Moving Picture World, Oct. 1, 1921, p. 574, Oct. 8, 1921, p. 629; Chicago Daily News, Nov. 1, 1921, p. 30; Nation, Oct. 5, 1921, pp. 375-76; Exceptional Photoplays, Oct. 1921, pp. 3-4; London Times, Apr. 9, 1923, p. 10.

Also see:
   *Licht-Bild-Bühne, no. 34 (1922), p. 56; Variety, July 1, 1921, p. 31, Aug. 12, 1921, p. 38, Sept. 2, 1921, p. 62, Oct. 7, 1921, p. 46, Jan. 13, 1922, p. 47; Moving Picture World, Sept. 4, 1921, p. 428, Oct. 1, 1921, p. 557, Oct. 15, 1921, p. 759, Oct. 22, 1921, p. 880, Jan. 7, 1922, p. 28, Mar. 4, 1922, p. 44; Motion Picture, Dec. 1921, pp. 51-55, 86 [fictionalization]; Richard Riess, Sumurun: ein Roman aus dem Morgenlande [novelization] (Berlin: Erich Reiss Verlag, 1920).

48   ANNA BOLEYN   (DECEPTION)
     (1920)

   England, 1532. Anne Boleyn, daughter of Sir Thomas Boleyn and niece of the Duke of Norfolk, returns from France to become a lady-in-waiting to Queen Catherine. She is in love with Henry Norris, a knight, but soon after her arrival King Henry the Eighth becomes interested in her and, with the aid of the Duke of Norfolk, seeks to make her his mistress. At a tennis match he openly displays his passion for her before the whole court. The King's increasing attentions to Anne cause a rift between her and Henry Norris. The King continues to pursue her vigorously and eventually she gives in to him.

When the Pope refuses to grant the King a divorce, the King, who has already secretly married Anne, breaks with the Church of Rome, declares his marriage to Queen Catherine annulled and his present marriage valid, and, despite the opposition of his angry subjects, has Anne crowned Queen in Westminster Abbey.

The royal couple are happy for a time, but before long the fickle King's eyes begin to wander. At a Spring festival he takes up with a dancing girl and they go off into the woods together. Meanwhile, as the Queen walks in the woods, she meets Mark Smeaton, a court singer, who professes his love for her. When she spurns him, he makes a sarcastic remark about her "fidelity" to Henry Norris. The Queen faints and the King carries her home.

Anne Boleyn gives birth to a daughter. The King is enraged it isn't a boy and orders the crowd gathered to hail the royal birth driven away. The King begins to pay attention to Jane Seymour, another lady-in-waiting. He takes her on a hunt. The Queen follows and pleads with the King to give this new interest up, but to no avail.

At a banquet Smeaton sings a song suggesting there is a special relationship between the Queen and a certain knight. The angry King sends Smeaton to the Tower; then he takes the baby Elizabeth away from her sleeping mother and asks Jane Seymour if she thinks the child resembles him. The once imperious Queen goes to the lady-in-waiting and begs her on her knees to break with the King. The King enters and he and his lady scorn and humiliate the Queen and go off together.

At a tournament the Queen appears unexpectedly in the royal box. When she sees that a knight wounded in the lists is Henry Norris, she is overcome with emotion. The King sees her behavior as confirmation of the rumors and has her banished to the Tower. Her case is put in the hands of her uncle, who turns against her. Henry Norris appears to testify to her innocence but dies before he can reach the witness stand. The uncle has Smeaton tortured and obtains from him a confession that he has been the Queen's lover. The Queen is sentenced to be beheaded and is led to the place of execution.

```
Director:          Ernst Lubitsch
Scenario:          Fred Orbing [pseud. Norbert Falk]
                   and Hans Kräly
Photography:       Theodor Sparkuhl
Sets:              Kurt Richter
Costumes:          Ali Hubert
Cast:              Henny Porten (Anne Boleyn), Emil
                   Jannings (King Henry the Eighth),
                   Paul Hartmann (Sir Henry Norris),
                   Ludwig Hartau (Duke of Norfolk), Aud
                   Egede Nissen (Jane Seymour), Hedwig
                   Pauly (Queen Catherine), Hilde Mül-
                   ler (Princess Marie), Maria Reisen-
                   hofer (Lady Rochford), Ferdinand
                   von Alten (Mark Smeaton), Adolf
                   Klein (Cardinal Wolsey), Paul Biens-
                   feldt (Jester), Wilhelm Diegelmann
                   (Cardinal Campeggio), Friedrich
                   Kühne (Archbishop Cranmer), Karl
                   Platen (Physician), Erling Hanson
                   (Count Percy), Sophie Pagay (Nurse),
                   Josef Klein (Sir William Kingston).
Production:        Messter-Film GmbH, Berlin, and Pro-
                   jektions-AG "Union," Berlin
Shot at:           Ufa (Messter and Union)-Ateliers,
                   Berlin-Tempelhof
Length:            2793m [9163 ft.] (Lamprecht);
                   9297 ft. [2834m] (Wid's Daily)
Opening:           December 14 (?), at the Ufa-Palast
                   am Zoo, Berlin
```

Notes:
   Anna Boleyn was retitled Deception for U.S. release. Deception was distributed by Paramount; the New York opening
was April 17, 1921.

Reviews:
   New York Times, Apr. 18, 1921, p. 8 and Apr. 24, 1921,
VI.2; Variety, Jan. 21, 1921, p. 45 (Berlin opening) and
Apr. 22, 1921, p. 40; Wid's Daily, Apr. 24, 1921, p. 3; Moving
Picture World, Apr. 30, 1921, p. 989; Chicago Daily News,
Aug. 11, 1921, p. 25; Exceptional Photoplays, Apr. 1921,
pp. 3-4, 7, May 1921, p. 3; London Times, Jan. 21, 1924, p. 8.

Also see:
   Variety, Jan. 14, 1921, p. 46, Mar. 25, 1921, p. 46, May 13,
1921, p. 46, May 20, 1921, p. 45; Moving Picture World,
Jan. 22, 1921, p. 398, Apr. 9, 1921, p. 583, Apr. 30, 1921,
p. 946, May 7, 1921, p. 47, May 14, 1921, p. 190, p. 203,
May 21, 1921, p. 307.

49   <u>DIE BERGKATZE</u>   ("THE MOUNTAIN CAT" or "THE WILD CAT")
     (1921)

A surrealistic military satire. Fort Tossenstein, near
Piffkaneiro, early in the twentieth century. Reveille: The
Fort Commander supervises the men as they prepare for the day.
Once he leaves, they all go back to bed.

When a letter comes from Lieutenant Alexis, the Commander
and (especially) his wife see a lively marriage prospect for
their daughter, Lilli.

All the women are in love with the handsome Lieutenant
Alexis. They gather along the roads as he leaves for the day
and block his passage; his men have to let loose a sackful of
mice to disperse them so that he can get through. As he
passes, a crowd of children wave flags and cry "Papa!"

At a mountain camp a brigand chief inspects the loot his
men have taken. One of their victims was the Lieutenant, who
is now seen wandering in the snow in his shirtsleeves.

News of the robbers' foragings reaches the Fort. The Commander sends at once for Alexis, who will lead an expedition
against them. When he arrives Alexis is also coaxingly introduced to the Commander's daughter.

Rischka, the brigand chief's daughter, a wild mountain
girl, gets articles taken from Alexis and falls in love with a
photograph of him she finds in one of the pockets. Later,
when she pelts the occupant of a passing sleigh with a snowball, it turns out to be Alexis, and Rischka gets to see her
lover in the flesh.

The soldiers set out with grand pomp to attack the robber
camp. Alexis encounters Rischka in battle and finds her bra-
vado very exciting. Though the campaign is an utter rout, the
Commander pronounces it a great victory and rewards Alexis
with the hand of his daughter.

During the ensuing celebration the brigands arrive and begin to loot the fort. Rischka lags behind and begins trying
on Lilli's clothing. Her companions come back for her and end
up putting on uniforms, passing for soldiers, and joining in
the revelry. Alexis recognizes Rischka and pursues her
through the fort. He gets her in a room and kisses her.
Lilli observes through the keyhole and when Alexis goes away
for a time, orders her out. Rischka gathers together the
drunken brigands and leaves.

Rischka dreams of Alexis. (In the dream sequence he takes
out his heart and gives it to her and she begins to eat it.
Later they dance to the accompaniment of an orchestra of snow-
men.) Rischka's father senses she is lovesick and declaires
she must marry. Pepo, one of the band, steps forward and volunteers. On Rischka's wedding day news comes of Alexis' betrothal to Lilli. Saddened by their plight, Rischka and
Alexis both go wandering and run into one another in the snow.
Alexis takes Rischka to the fort and she is perfuming and
dressing to receive him when Lilli shows up, crying because
Alexis loves Rischka more than he loves her. Rischka feels
sorry for her and when Alexis returns she deliberately scares
him off with her "wildness," leaving the field open to Lilli.
Rischka returns to the mountain camp and her sorrowing husband.

Director:	Ernst Lubitsch
Scenario:	Hans Kräly and Ernst Lubitsch
Photography:	Theodor Sparkuhl
Sets:	Ernst Stern and Max Gronert
Costumes:	Ernst Stern
Assistant Director:	Walter F. Fichelscher
Cast:	Pola Negri (Rischka, The "Wildcat"), Paul Heidemann (Lieutenant Alexis), Victor Janson (Commander of Fort Tossenstein), Hermann Thimig (Pepo), Edith Meller (Lilli, Daughter of Commander), Marga Köhler (Wife of Commander), Wilhelm Diegelmann (Claudius, Rischka's Father, Brigand Chief), Paul Biensfeldt (Dafko), Paul Grätz (Zofano), Max Kronert (Masilio), Erwin Kopp (Tripo).
Production:	Projektions-AG "Union," Berlin
Shot at:	Ufa-Union-Atelier, Berlin-Tempelhof; exterior scenes in the Bavarian Alps, near Garmisch
Length:	1818m [5965 ft.]
Opening:	April 14, at the Ufa-Palast am Zoo, Berlin

Note:
  Kosmorama (1976) adds co-costume credit, Emil Hassler.

Review:
  Variety, June 3, 1921, p. 4.

*50   DAS WEIB DES PHARAO   (THE LOVES OF PHARAOH)
      (1922)

To Amenes, Pharaoh of the Egyptians, comes Samlak of Ethio-
pia, bringing his daughter Makeda to become Pharaoh's wife and
thus effect an alliance between the two nations.

Outside the city, while the final beautifying touches are
being applied to Makeda, her beautiful Greek serving girl,
Theonis, incurs her wrath and is dismissed and beaten. She is
rescued by Ramphis, son of Sothis, an architect, and the two
instantly fall in love.

Homage is paid by the Ethiopians to Amenes and vast trea-
sures are laid before him for storing in the Treasure House.
Ramphis and Theonis are happy in their love, but one night the
girl hides from him and goes to view the Treasure House, which it
is forbidden, under pain of death, to approach. Ramphis vain-
ly tries to warn her. The two are captured and brought before
Amenes. The King immediately falls in love with the girl and
offers to save her own life if she agrees to marry him. She
refuses angrily. He decrees that Ramphis must die, but that
he will save the latter's life if she consents to become Queen
of Egypt. Her love for Ramphis causes her to consent, but unknown to her Ramphis is condemned to the slave quarries for
life.

Samlak is furious when he sees what has occurred and leaves,
vowing vengeance on the Egyptians. From his own country he
brings his armies and declares war on Egypt. Theonis is made
Queen of Egypt.

Then the Egyptians march away to war, but before they go,
Amenes places his wife in the Treasure House, the entrance to
which is known to Sothis alone. He orders the eyes of Sothis
to be put out. The people are incensed at the thought of war,
but they have to fight or suffer annihilation.

On the desert outside the city the two armies meet and the
Egyptians are thrown into flight. They retire in confusion to
the city and there a hasty consultation is held. Ramphis, who
is now a soldier, advances a daring plan to lure the Ethiopians into the city, as into a baited trap, and destroy them.
He is put in command of the army. The plan is a success, and
the Egyptians win the day.

But in the battle on the desert Amenes has been seen to
fall, and is believed dead. The city rejoices with the victory, and the death of Amenes, for he had been a tyrant, and
now the populace wants a new Pharaoh. Sothis guides Ramphis,
by his sense of direction to the secret entrance to the

Treasure House, and Theonis is released. When she has to choose a new husband who will become the Pharaoh, she takes Ramphis, and he is crowned ruler.

In the midst of the ceremonies, Amenes, who has only been wounded, crawls to the Palace and tries to make himself known. But the populace howls that Amenes is dead, and when the ex-ruler sees the fierce opposition to him, he falls dead on the steps of the throne. Then Ramphis and Theonis are free to enjoy the happiness that is rightfully theirs. (Synopsis from the pressbook for the American release version deposited for copyright in the Library of Congress.)

Director:	Ernst Lubitsch
Scenario:	Norbert Falk and Hans Kräly
Photography:	Theodor Sparkuhl and Alfred Hansen (and numerous others for the mass scenes)
Sets:	Ernst Stern and Kurt Richter
Costumes:	Ernst Stern, Ali Hubert, and Ernö Metzner
Music:	Eduard Künneke
Technical-Architectural Management:	Max Gronau
Cast:	Emil Jannings (Pharaoh Amenes), Harry Liedtke (Ramphis), Dagny Servaes (Theonis), Paul Wegener (Samlak, Ethiopian King), Lyda Salmonova (Makeda, His Daughter), Albert Bassermann (Sotis, Architect), Friedrich Kühne (High Priest), Paul Biensfeldt (Menon), Elsa Wagner, Mady Christians.
Production:	Ernst Lubitsch-Film GmbH, Berlin, in association with Europäischen Film-Allianz GmbH (Efa); Paul Davidson, Executive Producer
Shot at:	Efa-Ateliers am Zoo; exterior shots on the lot in "Rauhen Bergen," Berlin-Steglitz
Length:	2976m [9764 ft.] (Lamprecht); 7476 ft. [2279m] (Film Daily)
Opening:	March 14, at the Ufa-Palast am Zoo, Berlin

Notes:
  Das Weib des Pharao was retitled The Loves of Pharaoh for U.S. release. It was distributed by Paramount. Titles for the American version were by Julian Johnson and Randolph Bartlett. The New York opening was February 21. Variety reported that the film "has been given a happy ending by the simple expedient of leaving off the epilog" (Feb. 3, p. 46).

Reviews:
New York Times, Feb. 22, p. 13 and Mar. 5, VI.3; Variety,
Mar. 3, p. 41; Film Daily, Feb. 26, p. 2; Moving Picture World,
Mar. 4, p. 40, p. 79; Chicago Daily News, June 7, p. 32; Ex-
ceptional Photoplays, Jan./Feb., pp. 2-3.

Also see:
*Film und Presse, no. 25/26 (1921), p. 227; Variety, Aug.
5, 1921, p. 27, Nov. 18, 1921, p. 43; New York Times, Dec. 18,
1921, VI.3, Dec. 25, 1921, p. 13, Feb. 12, VI.3, Feb. 19, VI.2;
Moving Picture World, Oct. 1, 1921, p. 512, Dec. 31, 1921,
p. 1075, Apr. 1, p. 544, Apr. 22, p. 839, May 20, p. 276,
Sept. 2, p. 35; Scott O'Dell, Representative Photoplays Analyzed (Hollywood: Palmer Institute of Authorship, 1924),
pp. 429-33.

*51   DIE FLAMME   (MONTMARTRE)
       (1923)

     Yvette, a milliner, spends most of her time dancing and
flirting in the Cafe Flora. She attracts Raoul who makes a
scene when she dances for Papa Lemonier and is about to take
from him a 100 franc note much needed for her board. By accident, Yvette meets Andre, a musician and falls in love with
him and resolves to reform. Andre calls on her and brings
Raoul who is his cousin. Andre learns of Yvette's past but
marries her anyway. He is ashamed of her and keeps her away
from his concert so she returns to the cafe. Repentant she
returns home but Raoul always seeking to make trouble for her
finds money in her pocket and Andre leaves her. Andre's mother goes to get her to go away but discovers she is expecting
to become a mother and goes to send Andre to her. Andre comes
in time to save her from suicide. (Synopsis of the American
version from Moving Picture World, Oct. 11, 1924, p. 523.
According to Weinberg [1968], in the European version Yvette
loses Andre "because she cannot, despite all her efforts and
suffering, become a meaningful part of his life," and she
"throws herself from the window of their home in despair"
[p. 43].)

Director: Ernst Lubitsch
Scenario: Hans Kräly
Source: The play, Die Flamme (1920), by
                   Hans Müller [pseud. Hans Lothar]
Photography: Theodor Sparkuhl and Alfred Hansen
Sets: Ernst Stern and Kurt Richter
Cast: Pola Negri (Yvette), Hermann Thimig
                   (Andre, Her Husband, a Composer),
                   Alfred Abel (Raoul, His Cousin, a
                   Musician), Hilde Wörner (Louise),

71

	Frieda Richard (Madame Vasal), Jacob Tiedtke (Petit Bourgeois), Max Adalbert (Journalist), Ferdinand von Alten (Man of the World), Jenny Marba (Andre's Mother).
Production:	Ernst Lubitsch-Film GmbH, Berlin, for Efa
Shot at:	Efa-Atelier am Zoo
Length:	2540m [8333 ft.] and 2555m [8383 ft.] (Lamprecht); 6715 ft. [2047m] (Film Daily)
Opening:	September 11 (?), at the Ufa-Palast am Zoo, Berlin

Notes:

Some filmographies list co-writer credit: Rudolph Kurtz. Die Flamme was released in the U.S., with an alternate "happy" ending, as Montmartre. It was distributed by Paramount. Titles and editing for the American version were by Hector Turnbull. The New York opening was July 1, 1924, "at Loew's New York, one day...as half bill...Montmartre got off to a bad start with poor notices, and Paramount has done little for it since" (Variety, July 9, 1924, p. 25).

Reviews:

Variety, July 9, 1924, p. 25; Film Daily, July 6, 1924, p. 11; Moving Picture World, Oct. 11, 1924, p. 523; Exceptional Photoplays, Feb./Mar. 1924, p. 5.

AMERICAN SILENT PERIOD (1923-1929)

52 ROSITA
(1923)

Spain, the seventeenth century. At the Royal Palace, the King is engaged in one of his favorite pastimes, dawdling with the ladies of the court. The Prime Minister enters with orders of execution for the King's signature, but the royal business is postponed when the King is distracted by some other ladies playing a game in the garden.

Carnival time in old Seville, with dancing and merrymaking in the streets. A pretty street singer attracts a crowd with her song. In the crowd is Count Don Diego of Alcala; his eyes meet the singer's and she takes a rose from her hair and tosses it to him. A cry goes up that the King is passing nearby, and the crowd deserts the singer to follow the royal coach. Rosita sings to support her family, and this disturbance deprives her of her collections. In anger, she composes a song about the King and his weakness for the ladies and later sings it to the great delight of the crowd.

News of Rosita's song reaches the King. He mingles with the crowd incognito and instead of being angered by the song, determines to make its pretty singer one of his conquests. But meanwhile the Prime Minister orders her arrest, and when Don Diego interferes and kills one of the soldiers in the scuffle, he is also taken to prison.

Rosita is brought to the Royal Palace and offered fine clothes and jewels. She resists the King's advances, but later, at her mother's urging, accepts his offer of a royal villa and moves into it with her family. To elevate Rosita's rank and station the King orders that she be married to Don Diego, who has been sentenced to be executed for treason. They are blindfolded during the ceremony but afterwards Rosita sees she has been married to the man she really loves. She goes to the King and pleads that he be spared. The King writes out an order for a fake execution. After Rosita leaves, however, he remands it and orders that the real execution be carried out as planned. But the Queen is onto the King's chicanery, and she now directs that the guns be loaded with blanks.

Rosita is permitted to be with Don Diego in his cell. She tells him he is to fall when the soldiers fire and to pretend to be dead. After he goes to face the firing squad she learns of the King's counter-order, hears the shots, and presumes Don Diego is dead. She orders his body placed in the chapel in the villa.

The King comes to visit the newly widowed Countess. She receives him and they dine together. Suddenly she opens the door to the chapel, reveals the body, and is just about to stab the King with a dagger when Don Diego rises from his bier.

Crestfallen and shamed, the King leaves to find the triumphant Queen waiting for him outside in his carriage.

Director:	Ernst Lubitsch
Scenario:	Edward Knoblock
Story:	Norbert Falk and Hans Kräly
Source:	The play, <u>Don César de Bazan</u> (1844), by Philippe François Pinel Dumanoir and Adolphe Philippe Dennery
Photography:	Charles Rosher
Set Design:	Svend Gade
Costumes:	Mitchell Leisen
Musical Score:	Louis F. Gottschalk
Assistant Director:	James Townsend

Cast: Mary Pickford (Rosita), Holbrook
                               Blinn (King), Irene Rich (Queen),
                               George Walsh (Don Diego), Charles
                               Belcher (Prime Minister), Frank
                               Leigh (Prison Commandant), Mathilde
                               Comont (Rosita's Mother), George
                               Periolat (Rosita's Father), Bert
                               Sprotte (Big Jailer), Snitz Edwards
                               (Little Jailer), Mme. de Bodamere
                               (Serving Maid), Phillipe de Lacey,
                               Donald McAlpin (Rosita's Brothers),
                               Doreen Turner (Rosita's Sister),
                               Mario Carillo (Majordomo), Marian
                               Nixon, Charles Farrell.
Production: Ernst Lubitsch for Mary Pickford;
                               released through United Artists
Shooting: Begun March 5 at the Pickford-Fair-
                               banks Studio and completed May 31
Length: 8800 ft. [2682m]
Released: September 3
Temporary Production
Title: The Street Singer

Notes:
    Article in International Film Guide 1968 (p. 38) lists
William Cameron Menzies as art director. Rosita has been out
of circulation for many years; see Mary Pickford (1955) in the
bibliography for details.

Reviews:
    New York Times, Sept. 4, p. 14 and Sept. 9, VII.4; Variety,
Sept. 6, pp. 22-23; Film Daily, Sept. 9, p. 3; Moving Picture
World, Sept. 15, pp. 262, 265; Chicago Daily News, Nov. 10,
p. 15; Life, Sept. 27, p. 22; Exceptional Photoplays, Oct./
Nov., p. 5; Photoplay, Nov., p. 74; London Times, Jan. 16,
1924, p. 10; Bioscope, Jan. 24, 1924, p. 53.

Also see:
    New York Times, Mar. 4, VII.3, Mar. 11, VIII.3; Moving Pic-
ture World, Mar. 17, p. 358, Mar. 24, p. 458, May 19, p. 247,
June 2, p. 417, June 30, p. 770, Sept. 15, p. 277 (excerpts
reviews from New York papers), Nov. 17, p. 320 (excerpts reviews from Chicago papers), May 3, 1924, p. 40; Scott O'Dell,
Representative Photoplays Analyzed (Hollywood: Palmer Institute of Authorship, 1924), pp. 481-87; David Chierichetti,
Hollywood Director: The Career of Mitchell Leisen (New York:
Curtis, 1973), p. 32.

53 THE MARRIAGE CIRCLE
    (1924)

Vienna, early in the twentieth century. A close-up of a toe
peeping out through a hole in a sock suggests all is not well
in Professor Stock's marriage. His wife Mizzie reads a letter
from her best friend, Charlotte Braun, saying she is hurt because the Stocks, who have recently moved to Vienna, haven't
visited yet.

On her way to the Brauns Mizzie gets into a taxi. By coincidence it is engaged and waiting for its rider, Dr. Franz
Braun, Charlotte's husband, to return from an errand. The two
strangers agree to share the cab. The Professor looks out of
his window, sees the two drive off together, smiles, and continues shaving.

In the taxi Mizzie tries to get Franz to pay attention to
her. There is a sudden turn and she practically falls into
his lap. She bends over him to look into the mirror on his
side of the cab. He refuses to submit to Mizzie's alluring
gestures and stops the cab and gets out. Mizzie arrives at
Charlotte's. The two old friends are getting reacquainted
when Franz arrives and the startled taxi companions recognize
one another.

Back at home, Mizzie feigns an illness so that Doctor Franz
will be forced to pay her a visit. Franz is reluctant to go
but Charlotte persuades him. Mizzie prepares for his arrival
by powdering her face and putting on perfume and moving a
chair away so he will be forced to sit next to her on the di-
van. As Franz takes Missie's pulse, she holds his wrist. They
are in this situation when the Professor enters, and a closeup shows the quick change from holding the wrist to taking the
pulse.

Breakfast at the two households: Charlotte and Franz embrace while the camera focuses on their coffee and eggs. Mizzie and the Professor sit at opposite ends of a long table.

Mizzie goes to Franz's office and begins trying to seduce
him again. Franz's partner, Dr. Mueller, who is in love with
Charlotte, enters. He only sees Franz's back with the woman's
arms around his neck, assumes it's Charlotte, and then is
startled to see Charlotte sitting in the waiting room.

The Brauns give a dinner party. Franz switches the place
cards so he won't be seated next to Mizzie. Charlotte thinks
he does it in order to sit next to another woman, Miss Hoffer,
and switches them back again. Charlotte confides her suspicions to Mizzie and asks her to help keep Franz away from the

75

other woman. Mizzie switches the place cards again. At the
dinner table Charlotte is very upset when she sees the final
seating arrangement. She leers at her husband and pretends to
flirt with her dinner companion, Dr. Mueller.

A title reads: "There is more danger in dancing than in
dinner." Mizzie dances with Franz. Charlotte dances with Dr.
Mueller. Mizzie brings Franz close to her as they dance and
persuades him to go out on the terrace. She schemes to get
him into the garden. On a garden bench she puts her arm
around his leg and puckers her lips. She tosses away her
scarf. Dr. Mueller and Charlotte come into the garden looking
for Franz and Dr. Mueller's foot drags the scarf. Charlotte
notices it's Mizzie's and finds her soon after, but without
Franz, who by now is on the terrace again, talking with Miss
Hoffer.

Mizzie slips a note to Franz saying she will be waiting for
him in a cab around the corner after the party. He rips it up
and shakes his head but goes after all when Charlotte scolds
him and kicks him out. After he leaves, Charlotte mistakes
Dr. Mueller for Franz and opens her eyes in horror to see
she's been kissing another man. She orders him to leave.
Meanwhile, Mizzie is unsuccessful in her attempts to seduce
Franz.

The Professor receives evidence of his wife's promiscuous
activity and sends her packing. He pays a visit to Franz, who
denies his accusations. Charlotte senses something is wrong
between the Professor and Mizzie and goes to console Mizzie at
her hotel. Mizzie has sent Franz a letter instructing Franz
to come to her hotel and she leaves Charlotte in her room
while she goes to meet him in the lobby. She rides down in
one elevator as Franz rides up in another. Charlotte realizes her husband is the alleged other man. He protests his
innocence and shows her Mizzie's letter, which reads, "Why did
you come over if you wanted to say that you do not love me."

To get even with her husband, Charlotte admits her rendezvous with Dr. Mueller. Franz doesn't believe her but signals
Mueller to admit it and pretends to. The Brauns are reconciled. As Dr. Mueller leaves the Brauns' and walks slowly
down the road Mizzie passes him in a cab and waves to him.
He sets out after the cab.

Director:	Ernst Lubitsch
Scenario:	Paul Bern
Source:	The play, <u>Nur ein Traum</u> (<u>Only a Dream</u>) (1909), by Lothar Schmidt [Goldschmidt]
Photography:	Charles J. Van Enger

Assistant Directors: James Flood and Henry Blanke
Cast: Adolphe Menjou (Prof. Joseph Stock),
         Marie Prevost (Mizzie Stock), Monte
         Blue (Dr. Franz Braun), Florence
         Vidor (Charlotte Braun), Harry Myers
         (Detective), Creighton Hale (Dr.
         Gustav Mueller), Dale Fuller (Nerv-
         ous Patient), Esther Ralston.
Production: Ernst Lubitsch for Warner Brothers
Shooting: September and October 1923 at the
             Warner Brothers West Coast studios
Length: Listed at 8200 ft. [2499m] and
           8300 ft. [2530m]
World Premiere: Los Angeles (Grauman's Rialto)
New York Opening: February 3
Released: February 16

Notes:
    Studio records list co-photography credit: Henry Sharp.
There is an English-language typescript of the source play in
the Theatre Collection of the Library of the Performing Arts
at Lincoln Center. Remade by Lubitsch in 1932 as One Hour
with You.

Reviews:
    New York Times, Feb. 4, p. 23 and Feb. 10, VII.5; Variety,
Feb. 7, p. 22; Film Daily, Feb. 10, p. 5; Moving Picture
World, Feb. 16, p. 581; Chicago Daily News, Mar. 20, p. 31;
Exceptional Photoplays, Dec./Jan., pp. 1-2; Life, Feb. 21,
p. 24; London Times, May 21, p. 12; Spectator, May 17, p. 788.

Also see:
    Moving Picture World, July 28, 1923, p. 323, Sept. 1, 1923,
p. 58, Sept. 22, 1923, p. 356, Oct. 6, 1923, p. 512, Nov. 10,
1923, p. 243, Jan. 19, p. 186, Jan. 26, p. 282, Feb. 2, p. 374,
Feb. 9, p. 454 (excerpts reviews in Los Angeles papers),
Feb. 16, p. 544 (excerpts reviews in New York papers), Feb. 23,
p. 631, Aug. 2, p. 384; Motion Picture Classic, Feb., pp. 38-
39, 80 (interview with Lubitsch on the set of Marriage Circle);
Picture-Play, Mar., pp. 26-27, 109-110 (interview with Lubitsch); New York Times, Mar. 30, VIII.4; London Times, Jan.
18, 1926, p. 12; Eileen Bowser, Film Notes (New York: Museum
of Modern Art, 1969), pp. 50-51; The [London] Film Society
Programmes 1925-1939 (New York: Arno Press, 1972), p. 15.

54   THREE WOMEN
      (1924)

    It has been said there are two types of women--the mistress
and the mother. This story concerns itself with Mabel Wilton,
the mistress type, a charming widow no longer young, who is

not happy unless she has a man dangling about somewhere, and who keeps her only daughter away at school in California so she won't interfere with her affair with Lamont, a man about town, who in truth is more infatuated with her fortune than with her.

Mrs. Wilton's eyes have looked so long upon the pleasures of the world that they have grown a little weary. She has fought against time with all the weapons at a pretty woman's disposal, but even she has been forced to admit that in spite of electrical treatments and long hours with the beauty specialists, time at last is beginning to show its ravaging effects. Accordingly, she decides that she wants to marry Lamont, so that when she ceases to be alluring to all men, there will be one bound to her lawfully that she can depend on. Everything is going beautifully when Jeanne, her daughter, unexpectedly returns from California. The mother is torn between joy at seeing her daughter and fear that this fresh young girl might interfere with her plans.

Lamont is instantly attracted to Jeanne, as the mother feared. In a frenzy at the thought of losing him, the mother treats her daughter very coolly and scolds her for showing up and being a nuisance. The girl, not understanding the situation and thinking Lamont only has business dealings with her mother, is grateful for his solicitousness to her and begins to entertain his advances. The mother, feeling a coolness in Lamont's attentions, seeks the cause and finds out that her daughter has been making clandestine visits to his apartment. Distraught at what her own selfishness may have brought her, she goes to his apartment, finds her daughter there, and demands an explanation. Lamont admits to having compromised Jeanne and cynically offers reparation by marrying the girl. Mrs. Wilton is forced to give her consent.

Jeanne's boyfriend at school, Fred Armstrong, wants to marry her but has refrained from proposing to her until he has finished his medical training. Now when he arrives to ask for her hand, she is already married.

Jeanne's happiness in her marriage does not last very long. Supplied with plentiful funds, Lamont returns to his old haunts and to Harriet, a well known gold digger. One evening, Lamont escorts Harriet to a popular cabaret and, having had too much to drink, attacks a man who has tried to flirt with her. A brawl breaks out and Lamont is hit over the head with a bottle. Fred is a guest at the cabaret and he offers his services as physician. When he takes Lamont home in his car he is amazed to find out he is Jeanne's husband. For Jeanne's sake Fred does not go into the details of the accident, but she guesses the truth. By subterfuge, Jeanne learns all about Harriet and angrily goes home to mother.

Jeanne secures Harriet's address and goes to see her. She is taken aback when Harriet taunts her by saying it was not worse for her to steal Lamont from Jeanne than for Jeanne to steal him from her mother. Realizing for the first time what the real situation was and sensing what her mother must have suffered, Jeanne rushes to her mother's, but Mrs. Wilton has just gone to see Lamont.

Mrs. Wilton demands that Lamont give her daughter her freedom. He threatens to create a public scandal by exposing the mother's love affair with him if she insists upon the divorce. Jeanne arrives in time to hear Lamont suggesting insidiously that her mother is still in love with him and to see her mother, angered beyond control, shoot Lamont dead.

In the trial that follows, Mrs. Wilton makes full confession of her affair with Lamont. She has no regrets for her crime; she only regrets her negligence as a mother. The jury acquits her. Fred joins mother and daughter in the courtroom, and the true lovers, Fred and Jeanne, are united at last. (Synopsis from a Warner Brothers publicity sheet deposited for copyright in the Library of Congress, edited to correspond to what appears on the screen.)

Director:	Ernst Lubitsch
Scenario:	Hans Kraly
Story:	Ernst Lubitsch and Hans Kraly
Source:	The novel, <u>Lillis Ehe</u> (<u>Lilli's Marriage</u>), by Iolanthe Marees
Photography:	Charles J. Van Enger
Art Director:	Svend Gade
Assistant Directors:	James Flood and Henry Blanke
Cast:	May McAvoy (Jeanne Wilton), Pauline Frederick (Mabel Wilton), Marie Prevost (Harriet), Lew Cody (Edmund Lamont), Willard Louis (Harvey Craig), Pierre Gendron (Fred Armstrong), Mary Carr (Mrs. Armstrong), Raymond McKee (Fred's Friend).
Production:	Ernst Lubitsch for Warner Brothers
Shooting:	Begun in April at the Warner Brothers West Coast studios and completed in June, with brief location shooting at San Bernadino
Length:	Contemporary reviews vary from 7900 ft. [2408m] to 8200 ft. [2499m] (A running time of about 95 minutes can be reconstructed from a Music Cue Sheet.)
New York Opening:	October 5

Notes:
    Studio records list co-photography credit: John Mescall.
Studio records and the United Artists Contracts file identify
the source story; the United Artists file (at Wisconsin Center
for Film and Theatre Research) contains an English translation
of this work.

Reviews:
    New York Times, Oct. 6, p. 25 and Oct. 12, VIII.5; Variety,
Oct. 8, p. 27; Film Daily, Oct. 19, p. 4; Moving Picture
World, Sept. 27, p. 334; Chicago Daily News, Aug. 28, p. 16;
Life, Oct. 30, p. 26; London Times, Sept. 15, p. 10; Bioscope,
Sept. 11, p. 40.

Also see:
    Moving Picture World, Mar. 22, p. 283, May 10, p. 198,
May 17, p. 282, p. 306, May 24, p. 360, July 12, p. 125,
p. 129, Oct. 4, p. 384, Nov. 8, p. 163.

55   FORBIDDEN PARADISE
      (1924)

    The Czarina rules over a small European kingdom. She has
an iron will, meeting all the intrigues of the court with
masterful assurance. Underneath it all, however, she is a
woman, tempestuous, elemental.

    The Chancellor is her faithful ally. Alexei is a young
officer in the army at the front. He discovers a plot to
overthrow the Czarina and rides three horses to death to warn
her. The conspirators are quickly sent to prison. As for
Alexei, his youth, his strength and good looks appeal to the
queen, and she rewards him with her favor and advancement.

    Weeks pass. Alexei's star is in its zenith. He has cast
aside his betrothed, Anna, first lady-in-waiting to the Czarina, and is basking in the sunshine of his queen's love. Nevertheless, Alexei suffers. He is ambitious to become a figure
in governmental affairs, but the Czarina laughs at his aspira-
tions. She wants him to amuse her, help her forget the cares
of her position. Alexei resents this--he realizes she is the
complete master, and he but a plaything, a servant.

    Rumors reach him that the Czarina has been untrue to him,
and maddened by the thought he joins in a conspiracy against
her.

    Later, when the Chancellor informs the queen that he has
discovered a plot against her in which Alexei is implicated,
she refuses to believe him. Furthermore, she thinks that the

Chancellor is trying to take advantage of her jealousy to get Alexei out of the way.

The Chancellor leaves--and the Czarina sends for Alexei. She is all woman--pleading, sobbing that she loves only him. Suddenly from the courtyard below there comes an ominous sound. The conspiracy is in full swing. Thoroughly scared, Alexei admits the plot but assures the queen that no harm will come to her. Both are surprised when the Chancellor comes marching in at the head of the Czarina's private guards and announces that he has crushed the revolt and arrested the chief conspirators. The Czarina orders him to arrest Alexei also.

During the days that follow the Czarina is irritable, unhappy, restless. Alexei is still very dear to her and she cannot find it in her heart to sign his death warrant. The crafty Chancellor, understanding her mood, introduces to her the young and charming French ambassador who is eager to have the queen sign a treaty that will cement a friendship with France.

The ambassador's cleverness, his ease of manner, his subtle compliments find instant favor with the Czarina. She has discovered a new lover and is happy. Her new-found happiness prompts her to pardon Alexei. She sends him back to the army, settles an estate on him, and gives him Anna for a wife. (Synopsis from the pressbook deposited for copyright in the Library of Congress. The print the authors saw was incomplete.)

Director:	Ernst Lubitsch
Scenario:	Hans Kraly and Agnes Christine Johnston
Source:	The play, <u>The Czarina</u> (1913), by Lajos Biró and Melchior Lengyel
Photography:	Charles J. Van Enger
Set Design:	Hans Dreier
Cast:	Pola Negri (The Czarina), Rod La Rocque (Alexei), Adolphe Menjou (Chancellor), Pauline Starke (Anna), Fred Malatesta (French Ambassador), Nick De Ruiz (General), Carrie Daumery (Lady-in-Waiting), Clark Gable (Extra--Grenadier).
Production:	Ernst Lubitsch for Famous Players-Lasky; released through Paramount
Shooting:	Begun at the Lasky Studio mid-July and completed in September
Length:	7543 ft. [2299m]
Released:	October 27
New York Opening:	November 16

Notes:
   The Czarina, "adapted by Edward Sheldon from the Hungarian," and starring Doris Keane, opened on Broadway January 31, 1922; for cast list and plot synopsis see Best Plays of 1921-22, pp. 502-03. Remade in 1945 as A Royal Scandal, directed by Otto Preminger and produced by Lubitsch.

Reviews:
   New York Times, Nov. 17, p. 16 and Nov. 23, VIII.5; Variety, Nov. 19, p. 31; Film Daily, Nov. 30, p. 13; Moving Picture World, Nov. 29, p. 448; Chicago Daily News, Nov. 7, p. 32; Life, Dec. 11, p. 24; Motion Picture Classic, Feb. 1925, pp. 47, 94; Bioscope, Feb. 12, 1925, p. 53; Spectator, Feb. 21, 1925, p. 281.

Also see:
   Moving Picture World, Mar. 8, p. 113, May 31, p. 449, July 12, p. 99, Aug. 16, p. 555, Sept. 6, p. 33, Oct. 4, p. 384, Oct. 11, p. 495, Oct. 18, p. 576, Oct. 25, p. 670, Nov. 22, p. 356.

*56   KISS ME AGAIN
      (1925)

   Paris, the 1920s. The music room at the house of Gaston Fleury, a well-to-do businessman. Maurice Ferrière, a long-haired "artiste"-type, is playing the piano vigorously as Gaston's wife, Loulou, sits beside him, enraptured. In his study Gaston is reading the financial page of his newspaper. Just as Maurice is about to reach a crashing climax Gaston slams the door to his study and shatters Maurice's concentration. Maurice resumes playing but is distracted by Loulou. He stops and kisses her. She is afraid her husband will be suspicious if the piano stops. Maurice takes out a player-roll, puts it in the piano, and continues to press his attention on Loulou as it plays. When she rejects him, he leaves the room and she follows. Gaston enters and sees the piano playing by itself. He leaves to answer the telephone. Loulou and Maurice return and Maurice resumes his playing. Maurice starts to leave and Loulou sees him to the door. Just when she is about to let him kiss her, they hear the tune start again on the player piano. Maurice rushes out. Gaston remarks how much better Maurice's playing is; Loulou thinks he's serious, breathes a sigh of relief, and begins to giggle. Gaston flings a cushion at her. She thinks he's flirting; she throws it back, gives him a sweet and tempting smile, and runs out of the room.

   Gaston asks lawyer Dubois' advice. Dubois says he's been neglecting Loulou, being too much a husband and too little a lover. Dubois' secretary Grisette gets an orchid every day

from her fiancé--does Gaston get the idea? Gaston leaves a
basket of orchids beside Loulou's place at the dinner table.
When she finally notices them she says, "Isn't that sweet of
Maurice?" Gaston flies into a murderous rage. Maurice arrives and enters at one door. Gaston storms out another door,
jerking on Maurice's hat and coat without noticing. Loulou
sees him from the window, feels sorry for him, and begins to
cry. Maurice kisses and consoles her.

Gaston goes to Maurice's to wait for him but a suspicious
housekeeper won't admit him. As he paces in front of the
house he reaches in his pocket for a cigarette and brings out
an elegant gold cigarette case inscribed "To the great master
Maurice Ferrière from Loulou." Suddenly it dawns on him where
Maurice is.

Gaston finds Maurice passionately kissing Loulou. While
Loulou distracts Gaston, Maurice tries to sneak out. He gets
as far as the study; Gaston follows him in and locks the door.
A motorcycle backfires outside and Loulou fears the worst.
Shortly after, Gaston emerges to say he is giving Loulou what
she apparently wants--half his fortune and Maurice. After
Gaston leaves, Maurice surveys his new domain proudly and
lights a big cigar, but Loulou is despondent.

Dubois is drawing up the divorce papers. When he asks who
the guilty party is, Gaston nobly volunteers to serve in place
of his wife. They arrange to stage a quarrel in front of a
witness, the secretary. At the height of it, Gaston is to
strike Loulou. After several tries, he can't bring himself to
do it. The lawyer says there's only one alternative--adultery
--and he winks at Gaston to fall in with the act. Loulou is
enraged when Gaston pretends there is already someone else,
but she tries to affect indifference. Meanwhile, the secretary, Grisette, begins to flirt outrageously with Gaston.

Gaston is installed in a suite at the Hotel Claridge. Loulou and Maurice are finishing their dinner when a large basket
of flowers arrives. Loulou thinks Maurice ordered them and is
pleased. A card in the basket from Gaston wishes them con-
gratulations on their betrothal. Loulou is pleased until it
occurs to her perhaps Gaston is glad to be rid of her; angrily
she throws the basket down in the study. Maurice answers the
telephone and tells Gaston rudely they do not wish to be disturbed. When Loulou hears it was Gaston, she is elated. She
tries to hide it in front of Maurice, but shortly after we see
her hand reach in and right the overturned basket of flowers.

Late that evening, at Loulou's prompting, Maurice is about
to leave her house when Gaston walks in without a word, goes
into the bedroom, and begins to undress. Maurice is flabbergasted, but shortly Gaston reappears in formal dress saying he

had to have these clothes to go to a dance. He hints it's getting late; he waits for Maurice, then offers to walk him home. We see them much later in front of Gaston's hotel, both exhausted from walking one another home. After Maurice leaves in a taxi Gaston takes another taxi back to his house. He finds Loulou safe in bed alone. As he is about to leave the phone rings, and he answers it out of habit. A flabbergasted Maurice is at the other end.

Early next morning Loulou is awakened by Maurice loudly playing the piano. He searches the house and demands to know where Gaston is. Loulou shrugs, "How should I know?" He vents his rage in playing the piano. Loulou is very annoyed at this and, during a break, she locks the piano. Maurice leaves in a rage, ranting jealously just like Gaston. Loulou says to herself, "They're all alike."

Maurice rushes to Gaston's hotel. Gaston tries to mollify him by inviting him to play the piano. When Grisette arrives with a letter from Dubois, Gaston pretends he went dancing with her last night and convinces Maurice he made a mistake. After Maurice leaves, Grisette says "Now we must really go out together."

Maurice and Loulou are bored--he because she has closed the piano down and she because they aren't doing anything to have fun. She prods him into going dancing. At a cabaret he orders the cheapest champagne and confesses he can't dance. Loulou begins to see him through new eyes. Suddenly they see Gaston and Grisette dancing. Loulou is furious. Gaston senses it and flirts outrageously with Grisette.

Gaston drops Grisette off at her home and thanks her for her help in making Loulou jealous. (She is enraged.) Gaston discovers she left her handbag in the car but decides to return it later. When Loulou shows up at Gaston's hotel, he decides to use the situation to teach her a lesson. He makes sure she sees the handbag and pretends Grisette is in the bedroom. He leads Loulou on and obviously enjoys the humiliation he's putting her through. While he is in the bedroom Grisette bursts in in search of the bag. Loulou sees what's going on but plays along, letting Gaston think he has scored a full victory over her.

Gaston and Loulou are in an amorous mood in their own bedroom again. Suddenly they hear the piano playing. Gaston goes out in his pajamas, taps Maurice on the shoulder, says with a friendly nod, "not so loud, please," and goes back into the bedroom. Shortly after, Maurice, deeply mortified, takes his picture out of the frame on the piano and leaves. Gaston comes out and locks the front door, takes a deep breath and a

stiff drink, and heads back to the bedroom. (Derived from the
release script of the film deposited for copyright in the Library of Congress.)

Director:	Ernst Lubitsch
Scenario:	Hans Kraly
Source:	The play, Divorçons (Let's Get a Divorce) (1880), by Victorien Sardou and Émile de Najac
Photography:	Charles J. Van Enger
Cast:	Marie Prevost (Loulou Fleury), Monte Blue (Gaston Fleury), John Roche (Maurice Ferrière), Clara Bow (Grisette), Willard Louis (Dubois).
Production:	Ernst Lubitsch for Warner Brothers
Shooting:	Early in January to late March at the Warner Brothers West Coast studios
Length:	6722 ft. [2049m]
Released:	August 1

Notes:
    Studio records give the following credits: "From the story...Hans Kraly, And from the play...Lawrence Schwab, Adaptation...Hans Kraly." Remade by Lubitsch as That Uncertain Feeling (1941).

Reviews:
    New York Times, Aug. 3, p. 10 and Aug. 16, VII.3; Variety, Aug. 5, p. 31; Film Daily, Aug. 9, p. 7; Moving Picture World, Aug. 15, p. 736; New Yorker, Aug. 1; Life, Aug. 20, p. 26; Theatre Magazine, Oct., p. 32; Bioscope, June 4, p. 36.

Also see:
    Moving Picture World, Oct. 25, 1924, p. 686, Jan. 17, p. 280, Jan. 24, p. 386, p. 387, Jan. 31, p. 494, Feb. 7, p. 595, Feb. 14, p. 725, Mar. 28, p. 380, Apr. 18, p. 715, May 16, p. 357 (excerpts reviews in Los Angeles papers for Hollywood preview), June 20, p. 896, Aug. 15, p. 699, Aug. 22, p. 843 (excerpts reviews in New York papers); New York Times, Feb. 22, VII.5 (press interview with Lubitsch); Eric Bentley, ed., 'Let's Get a Divorce!' and Other Plays (New York: Hill and Wang, 1958), p. 347.

57   LADY WINDERMERE'S FAN
      (1925)

    London, early in the twentieth century. Lord Darlington pays a visit to Lady Windermere as she is preparing the seating arrangements for a dinner party. She is obviously attracted to

this suave and handsome young man, who is even more obviously
interested in her, but to avoid temptation she introduces him
to her husband as if he had come to see him.

Lord Windermere has received a letter from a Mrs. Erlynne
saying she wishes to see him on a matter of extreme urgency.
After a life of adventure abroad, Mrs. Erlynne has drifted
back to London, her means and social standing a thing of the
past. She reveals to Lord Windermere she is his wife's mother
and shows him proof of her identity. Since Lady Windermere
worships the memory of the mother she thinks long since dead,
Lord Windermere wishes to spare and protect her and begins
giving money to Mrs. Erlynne in exchange for her silence.

At the racetrack three Duchesses are gossiping about Mrs.
Erlynne, who is seated nearby. Lord Windermere defends her
and one of them wonders aloud, Why? Lady Windermere is curious too but lets it pass. Lord Augustus, an aging friend of
the Windermeres, develops an interest in Mrs. Erlynne and begins calling on her.

Lady Windermere receives a magnificent fan as a birthday
gift. She is suspicious when she sees from the window her
husband dismisses his own car and takes a taxi. Lord Darlington, who arrived shortly before, drops suggestive hints and
finally mentions Mrs. Erlynne's name. (He says he does it because he loves Lady Windermere.)

Mrs. Erlynne pleads with Lord Windermere for an invitation
to his wife's birthday party that evening. She says the social recognition might help to clear the way for her to marry
Lord Augustus and threatens to go to his wife if he fails.
Meanwhile, Lady Windermere has found a check made out to Mrs.
Erlynne in her husband's desk. Lord Windermere assures her it
isn't what she thinks and says she'll find out for herself
that very evening at her party what a fine person Mrs. Erlynne
is. Lady Windermere says if the woman dares to show up she'll
strike her in the face with her fan.

Mrs. Erlynne assumes a letter of refusal from Lord Windermere is an invitation and rushes off to the party without opening it. As she is about to be turned away at the door, Lord
Augustus arrives, and in the confusion Mrs. Erlynne is announced. Lady Windermere is grudgingly polite to her but extremely disturbed. When she sees Mrs. Erlynne in an intimate
conversation on the terrace with who she thinks is her husband
(it is actually Lord Augustus, at that very moment asking her
to marry him), she decides to retaliate by going off to Lord
Darlington. Mrs. Erlynne follows her to Lord Darlington's
apartment. She swears there has never been anything between
her and Lord Windermere and begs Lady Windermere to return

home before she ruins herself. Through the window they see
Lord Darlington and several of his friends arriving and they
hide in the library. Lady Windermere has left her fan on the
sofa. When it is discovered Mrs. Erlynne comes out in order
to save her daughter's reputation and pretends she took Lady
Windermere's fan by mistake.

Next morning Mrs. Erlynne comes to say goodbye as she is
leaving for France. Lord Windermere retires without a word
but Lady Windermere greets her visitor warmly. Afterwards
Mrs. Erlynne meets Lord Augustus on the street and tells him
his behavior last evening was outrageous and she won't marry
him after all. He looks perplexed but follows her to her car
and they drive off together.

Director:	Ernst Lubitsch
Scenario:	Julien Josephson
Source:	The play, <u>Lady Windermere's Fan</u> (1892), by Oscar Wilde
Photography:	Charles J. Van Enger
Assistant:	Willard Van Enger
Art Director:	Harold Grieve
Assistant Director:	George Hippard
Cast:	Ronald Colman (Lord Darlington), Irene Rich (Mrs. Erlynne), May McAvoy (Lady Windermere), Bert Lytell (Lord Windermere), Edward Martindel (Lord Augustus), Carrie Daumery (Duchess of Berwick), Helen Dunbar, Billie Bennett (Duchesses).
Production:	Ernst Lubitsch for Warner Brothers
Shooting:	September and October at the Warner Brothers West Coast studios, with location shooting in Toronto for the race track scenes
Length:	7816 ft. [2382m]
World Premiere:	Casa Lopez, New York City, December 1
Released:	December 26

Notes:
  Harold Grieve submitted a brief memoir of his work with Lubitsch at Warner Brothers to the authors; it includes an account of his art work on <u>Lady Windermere's Fan</u>. Edgar G. Ulmer
claimed in an interview with Peter Bogdanovich (<u>Film Culture</u>,
no. 58-59-60, 1974, p. 199) that he was art director on this
film.

Reviews:
  <u>New York Times</u>, Dec. 28, p. 19 and Jan. 3, 1926, VII.5; <u>Va-
riety</u>, Jan. 13, 1926, p. 42; <u>Film Daily</u>, Dec. 6, p. 4; <u>Moving</u>

Picture World, Dec. 12, p. 575; *Chicago Daily News*, Jan. 4, 1926, p. 26; *New Yorker*, Dec. 12; *Life*, Dec. 31, p. 24; *New Republic*, Mar. 24, 1926, p. 144; *New Movies*, Mar./Apr. 1926, pp. 11-12; *Bioscope*, Feb. 4, 1926, p. 42; *London Mercury*, July 1926, p. 305.

Also see:
Moving Picture World, June 27, p. 992, July 25, p. 441, Aug. 15, p. 761, Sept. 26, p. 340, Oct. 3, p. 416, Oct. 24, p. 634, Nov. 21, p. 226, Nov. 28, p. 333, Dec. 5, p. 443, Dec. 12, p. 551, p. 554, Jan. 2, 1926, p. 79, Jan. 9, 1926, p. 161 (excerpts reviews in New York papers); *New York Times*, Oct. 25, VIII.5, Dec. 27, VII.5; *Play Pictorial*, Jan.-June 1926, Supplement pp. xiv-xvi; Edmund Wilson, *The American Earthquake* (Garden City, N.Y.: Doubleday Anchor, 1958), pp. 78-79; Dewitt Bodeen, "May McAvoy," *Films In Review*, Oct. 1968, pp. 490-91.

58 SO THIS IS PARIS
    (1926)

Paris, the 1920s. On camera a sheik stabs a harem girl and she expires. A pan across the room to an accompanist reveals that it is the Lallés, Maurice and Georgette, rehearsing their act. When Maurice has trouble trying to lift her, Georgette intimates that his sexual performances are also weak. Meanwhile, across the way, Mme. Suzanne Giraud, in an aroused state from reading one of her "hot Arabian romances," catches a glimpse of Lallé at his window in his sheik's costume. He appears to be nude, and Suzanne's husband, Paul, a physician, takes his cane to go over and give the fellow a thrashing.

Mme. Lallé, it turns out, is an old paramour of Dr. Giraud. They become so involved in recalling old times that Paul forgets his cane when he leaves. He tells Suzanne he smashed it to bits giving Lallé a beating. Shortly after, as Paul is taking a nap, Maurice returns the cane, tells Suzanne how nice her husband is, and begins to flirt with her. She is obviously interested, but since her husband is in the next room she sends him away. However, she gives Maurice back the cane.

To arrange a rendezvous, Georgette leaves a phony message with Suzanne that her husband, M. Moreau, is gravely ill, and she gives the address of a café. Racing to what he thinks is a sick man's bedside, Paul is stopped for speeding, but is let go when he explains. Shortly afterwards, when the policeman sees him going into the café with Georgette, they get into an argument, which results in Paul's receiving a three-day jail sentence for insulting an officer. (Meanwhile, while the doctor was out on his errand of mercy, Maurice paid a visit to Suzanne.)

Making light of his sentence, Paul arranges to attend an artist's ball with Georgette. When he is served a summons at home to appear and serve his sentence, he is delighted because it gives him an excuse to go off with Georgette. Maurice pretends to his wife he's too ill to go out and again, while Paul is out, Maurice calls on Suzanne. A detective who has come to arrest Paul finds them together and Maurice pretends to be Paul to avoid compromising Suzanne. After taking several parting kisses, Maurice goes off to serve Paul's sentence.

Suzanne hears on the radio that Paul and Georgette have won the Charleston contest at the ball. She goes to the ball wearing a mask. Not recognizing her, Paul begins to flirt and she takes him home with her. Once home, Suzanne takes off her mask, bawls Paul out, says she pleaded to get him pardoned, and tells him from now on she's going to be boss. Georgette arrives home from the ball to find a wire from Maurice saying the doctor has sent him to a sanitarium for three days for a cure. She immediately telephones a man who flirted with her at the ball.

Paul and Suzanne coo like lovebirds at breakfast the next morning. When they see in the paper that Giraud was taken to jail after a tender farewell scene with his wife, Paul fails to catch on and says it "shows how much you can believe in the newspapers." An insert shows Maurice marching in line in jail, and we fade out on the happy couple at their breakfast table.

Director:	Ernst Lubitsch
Scenario:	Hans Kraly
Source:	The play, Réveillon (1872), by Henri Meilhac and Ludovic Halévy
Photography:	John Mescall
Assistant:	Bert Shipman
Art Director:	Harold Grieve
Titles:	Robert Wagner and Robert Hopkins
Electrical Effects:	F. N. Murphy
Art Titles:	Victor Vance
Assistant Directors:	George Hippard and Ernst Laemmle
Cast:	Monte Blue (Dr. Paul Giraud), Patsy Ruth Miller (Suzanne Giraud), André Beranger (Maurice Lallé), Lilyan Tashman (Georgette Lallé), Max Barwin (Detective), Myrna Loy (Maid), Sidney d'Allbrook (Cop), George Bowe (Charleston Dancer).
Production:	Ernst Lubitsch for Warner Brothers
Shooting:	Begun at the Warners Brothers West Coast studios March 25 and completed in May

Released:	July 31
Length:	6135 ft. [1870m]
Temporary Production	
Title:	Réveillon

Notes:
    So This Is Paris was one of the "American Film Classics"
selected for the 1976 American Film Institute National Tour.
George Bowe, a featured dancer in the Charleston sequence,
doubled for the dancing feet of Monte Blue (see his Feb. 26,
1965 letter in the files of the Museum of Modern Art).

Reviews:
    New York Times, Aug. 16, p. 10 and Aug. 22, VII.2; Variety,
Aug. 18, p. 58; Film Daily, Aug. 15, p. 7; Moving Picture
World, Sept. 4, p. 41; Chicago Daily News, July 19, p. 20;
New Yorker, Aug. 21; Life, Sept. 9, p. 26; Bioscope, Oct. 7,
p. 46; Play Pictorial, Jan.-June 1927, Supplement pp. xviii-
xix.

Also see:
    Moving Picture World, Apr. 10, p. 427, May 22, p. 310.

59 THE STUDENT PRINCE IN OLD HEIDELBERG
    (1927)

    Karlsburg, Germany, ancestral home of the Princes of Karls-
burg, around 1890. The inhabitants have turned out for their
first look at their Prince and heir-apparent, Karl, age 7,
nephew of the present King. The King is formal and stiff and
forbidding. The Prince is a frightened little boy. A loud
salute begins firing in welcome as he arrives, and he retreats
back into his governess' arms. Later at the palace we see the
kind of cold regimentation the Prince is subjected to. A
group of boys about the Prince's age play ball in the street,
but the Prince must toss a ball with three aging footmen. The
Prince's governess is sent away quietly because the King dis-
approves of sentimental farewells ("a Prince never cries").
Her replacement is a tutor, Doctor Juttner, who fortunately
is a kind and compassionate man. Doctor Juttner quickly becomes the Prince's comrade and understanding friend as well as
his teacher.

    When the Prince is eighteen, King Karl decides to send him
to Heidelberg. His tutor goes along. The Prince is joyfully
happy there. He is immediately accepted as one of them by
the members of the Saxonia corps, and he falls in love with
Kathi, a girl at the inn where he and Juttner have taken
rooms. He vows that one day Kathi will be his Princess. (In
the meantime Juttner suppresses the information that the King
has decided the Prince will marry Princess Ilse.)

90

News comes that the King is dying and the Prince must return to Karlsburg. The King's last request is that the marriage to Princess Ilse take place, and the Prince has to re-
lent. When he goes back to Heidelberg everything is changed.
Doctor Juttner is dead, and his former companions in the corps
greet him stiffly and formally. After a final impassioned
meeting with Kathi, he resigns himself to his fate.

As the royal newlyweds ride through the streets of Karlsburg a few days later, an ironic title with one of the film's
leitmotifs flashes on--"It must be wonderful to be a King."

Director:	Ernst Lubitsch
Scenario:	Hans Kraly
Sources:	The story, <u>Karl Heinrich</u> (1900), by Wilhelm Meyer-Förster, and its play version, <u>Alt-Heidelberg</u> (1901), and the operetta, <u>The Student Prince</u> (1924), by Dorothy Donnelly and Sigmund Romberg
Photography:	John Mescall
Art Directors:	Cedric Gibbons and Richard Day
Titles:	Marian Ainslee and Ruth Cummings
Musical Arrangements:	David Mendoza and William Axt
Editor:	Andrew Marton
Wardrobe:	Ali Hubert
Assistant:	Eric Locke
Assistant Director:	George Hippard
Technical Advisor:	Capt. John S. Peters
Cast:	Ramon Novarro (Prince Karl Heinrich), Norma Shearer (Kathi), Jean Hersholt (Dr. Juttner), Gustav von Seyffertitz (King Karl VII), Phillipe de Lacey (Heir Apparent), Edgar Norton (Lutz), Bobby Mack (Kellerman), Edward Connelly (Court Marshal), Otis Harlan (Old Ruder), John S. Peters, George K. Arthur (Students), Edythe Chapman, Lionel Belmore, Lincoln Steadman.
Production:	Ernst Lubitsch for Metro-Goldwyn-Mayer; Executive Producer, Irving Thalberg
Shooting:	Begun at MGM Studios in Culver City December 1926; location footage in Germany shot by Lubitsch in May 1927 (days of shooting: 108)

Length: 9435 ft. [2876m] (Film Daily);
                              9541 ft. [2908m] (Moving Picture
                              World)
New York Opening: September 21
Released: January 30, 1928
Temporary Production
Title: Old Heidelberg

Notes:
"M-G-M, recent purchase[r] of the rights to the operetta
The Student Prince, founded on the play, Old Heidelberg, which
Ernst Lubitsch has been months in making, has changed the title of the picture to The Student Prince. A subtitle will add
In Old Heidelberg. This latest purchase of The Student Prince
makes available the oper[e]tta effects and the music of Sigmund Romberg" (Moving Picture World, June 25, p. 563). For a
partial account of the complicated source history of The Student Prince, see Motion Picture Classic, November 1927, pp. 28-
29, 68. In this same source Hans Dreier is said to have been
involved in the art direction. Edgar G. Ulmer told Peter Bogdanovich in an interview (Film Culture, no. 58-59-60, 1974,
p. 199) that he was involved in the art direction on this film
("I created Heidelberg"). In Mayer and Thalberg: The Make-
Believe Saints (New York: Random House, 1975, p. 255) Samuel
Marx reports that The Student Prince cost $1,205,000 and
showed a loss of $307,000 on world-wide returns after five
years from date of release.

Reviews:
New York Times, Sept. 22, p. 33 and Sept. 25, VIII.7; Variety, Sept. 28, p. 24; Film Daily, Oct. 2, p. 6; Moving Picture World, Sept. 24, p. 250; Time, Oct. 3, p. 27; Life,
Oct. 13, p. 26; National Board of Review Magazine, Oct.,
pp. 8-9, 14; Motion Picture, Dec., p. 55; London Times, Feb.
10, 1928, p. 12; Bioscope, Feb. 16, 1928, p. 55; Illustrated
London News, Feb. 18, 1928, pp. 254, 280; Close Up, May 1928,
pp. 52-54; La Revue du Cinéma, July 1930, no. 12, p. 68.

Also see:
Moving Picture World, Nov. 29, 1926, p. 278, Dec. 25, 1926,
p. 579, p. 581, Jan. 15, p. 194, Jan. 29, p. 354, Feb. 12,
p. 497, Feb. 19, p. 567, May 2, p. 787, p. 829, June 25,
p. 567, Sept. 17, p. 151; New York Times, June 1, p. 25,
Sept. 18, VII.5 (press interview with Lubitsch), Sept. 28,
p. 29; Films in Review, Mar. 1962, p. 167.

*60   THE PATRIOT
       (1928)

       Emperor of All the Russias, Paul the First, is a strange
combination of tyrant, coward, weakling and mad man. He is

feared and hated by his subjects whose resentment and bitterness are inward and without visible protest. But even as Paul
creates terror and woe in the hearts of his subjects, so does
Paul himself live in constant dread and fear of these subjects. He is harrassed by suspicion and doubt, afraid even to
eat, drink or sleep. He fears he will meet the end that had
been the fate of some of his ancestors.

There is only one living soul in whom Paul places any
trust, and that only at intervals. He is the Prime Minister,
Count Pahlen, who has won a powerful influence in the Empire
by virtue of this trust. He can handle the Czar like a child.
His position is unapproachable save only by the Czar himself.

Count Pahlen is in love with the Countess Ostermann, wife
of an army officer. They are surprised by the husband. He
picks up one of Pahlen's boots to throw out a window but is
the victim of a Cossack bullet. One of the Czar's edicts is
that no one shall present himself at a window when he rides
by. The Czar and his Cossack guard had just passed.

The Conspiracy

Pahlen--"The Patriot,"--pitying the Czar, is at the same
time bleeding for his suffering country. He determines to use
his love, the Countess, as a pawn to lure the Czar into a game
of death.

At St. Michael, built as a murder-proof castle by Paul, the
Czar is more concerned with the number of buttons on the gait-
ers of Stephan, than with matters of international importance.
He whips Stephan for not having enough buttons. Stephan suffers in silence.

Pahlen arrives, and after an audience with the Czar sees
Stephan. He presses the soldier into service as his personal
bodyguard promising Stephan revenge. He also outlines plans
of the dethroning of the Monarch to court attaches.

Alexander, the Crown Prince, is an idealist with a yearning
towards his father, and Pahlen's proposition shocks and horri-
fies him. When Pahlen realizes that his plea to the young man
has been in vain, he determines to take drastic steps and warn
the Czar against Alexander. The Czar has no love for his son,
for he knows the attitude of his subjects towards the crown
prince. They love him. Paul therefore immediately places his
son under arrest.

The Plans Are Outlined

Pahlen's next step is to surround himself with his faithful
followers and outline his plan minutely whereby the Czar will

be pressed for his abdication, and failing in this, he is to be assassinated, thus clearing the way for Alexander's being placed on the throne.

On the day of the night the plan is to materialize, Paul suddenly decides to leave the city with Lapoukhine his mistress. This will upset the plans and in desperation Pahlen manages to put the Czar in contact with a snuff box which he, Pahlen, owns. In this snuff box, hidden by a secret lid, there is an alluring likeness of Countess Ostermann, Pahlen's love.

The Czar becomes excited and calls off the trip. He must meet the Countess. Pahlen arranges this, and ingeniously manages to leave the Countess alone with the Czar. He clumsily makes love to her. The Countess, outraged with her betrayal by Pahlen, discloses the minister's plans to the Czar.

The Czar is Satisfied

The Count is summoned and he explains that he has been in the service of the conspirators to learn of their plans. He pledges his life for the Czar's life. Paul is satisfied and retires to his quarters.

Later that night while the Czar sleeps fitfully, his officers appear. They gain entrance to his bedroom. He shrieks in fear and calls for Pahlen. The Count waits outside weeping. The officers are subdued for the moment by the Czar's dramatic plea: "I am the Czar by Divine Right!" Then from behind appears Stephan. He rushes up to the Czar and presently the Czar is dead.

While the bells toll ominously outside, and the peasants hail their new Czar, Pahlen and Stephan face each other in Pahlen's home. Stephan holds a pistol. As the clock strikes the hour a shot rings out. Pahlen is mortally wounded.

At this moment the Countess appears. She embraces Pahlen. He turns to her and says: "I have been a bad friend and lover --but I have been a 'Patriot.'"

With these words, "The Patriot" falls dead. (Synopsis from the Paramount Pressbook deposited for copyright in the Library of Congress.)

Director:	Ernst Lubitsch
Scenario:	Hans Kraly (Academy Award)
Source:	The play, <u>Der Patriot</u> (1927), by Alfred Neumann
Photography:	Bert Glennon

Set Design: Hans Dreier
Titles: Julian Johnson
Musical Direction: Nathaniel Finston
Original Music: Domenico Savino and Gerard Carbonaro
Costumes: Ali Hubert
Technical Advisor: Nicholas Kobliansky
Cast: Emil Jannings (Czar Paul the First),
                           Lewis Stone (Count Pahlen), Florence
                           Vidor (Countess Ostermann), Neil
                           Hamilton (Crown Prince Alexander),
                           Harry Cording (Stephan), Vera Voro-
                           nina (Mlle. Lapoukhine).
Production: Ernst Lubitsch for Paramount Famous
                           Lasky Corp.; released through Para-
                           mount
Exhibited: In a silent version and in a sound
                           version with talking sequences,
                           sound effects, and music score
Shooting: January 3 to early March
Length: 10,172 ft. [3100m]; silent version
                           9819 ft. [2993m] (AFI Catalog)
New York Opening: August 17
Released: September 1
Temporary Production
Title: High Treason

Notes:
    According to Harold Dunham, The Patriot had "music and
sound effects--raps on doors, sleighbells, the yapping of a
dog--and one or two badly synchronized spoken lines" (Films
in Review, Jan. 1970, p. 32). Variety reported on April 24,
1929 (p. 6) that Emil Jannings obtained cancellation of his
Paramount contract because of dissatisfaction over a double
speaking his lines in The Patriot. Studio records contain
the following undated length notations: 9738' American,
9969' Foreign. The Patriot, a "drama in eight scenes, adapted
from the German of Alfred Neumann by Ashley Dukes" opened on
Broadway January 19, 1928; for cast list and plot synopsis see
Best Plays of 1927-28, pp. 494-95.

Reviews:
    New York Times, Aug. 18, p. 7 and Aug. 26, VII.5; Variety,
Aug. 22, p. 14; Film Daily, Aug. 26, p. 4; Life, Sept. 14,
p. 24; New Yorker, Sept. 15; National Board of Review Maga-
zine, Sept., pp. 6-8; New Republic, Oct. 3, p. 177; London
Times, Jan. 1, 1929, p. 10; Bioscope, Jan. 2, 1929, p. 48;
Spectator, Jan. 5, 1929, p. 12; Les Annales Politiques et
Littéraires, Mar. 15, 1929, p. 278; La Revue du Cinéma (Paris),
1930, no. 7, p. 63.

Also see:
New York Times, July 29, VII.4, Sept. 2, VII.4, Sept. 9,
IX.3, Oct. 28, IX.5; Variety, Oct. 26, 1927, p. 9, Dec. 21,
1927, p. 4, Jan. 11, p. 4, Feb. 15, p. 11, Mar. 14, p. 16,
Mar. 28, p. 11, Sept. 26, p. 6, p. 48; Gary Carey, Lost Films
(New York: Museum of Modern Art, 1970), pp. 72-75.

*61   ETERNAL LOVE
       (1929)

       Commanded by an invading army to give up their firearms un-
der the threat of bringing punishment to the whole community,
the liberty-loving mountaineers of Switzerland grumble. Without weapons their hunters cannot procure meat. The revered
pastor of Pontresina successfully restrains his flock from any
violent action. But Marcus Paltram, daredevil hunter, defies
the law. Fearless, foolhardy, he is an incorrigible to all--
save Ciglia, his sweetheart.

       Marcus has a rival for the hand of Ciglia in Lorenz Gruber,
wealthy and violently jealous. And Ciglia also has a rival
for the affections of Marcus. She is Pia, a wild mountain
girl, whose passionate quest of the hunter has become an ob-
session. She hates Ciglia, and awaits an opportunity to blast
the romance between Marcus and his betrothed.

       This opportunity comes after a masquerade party given in
the village inn. Giddy with the wine he has drunk, Marcus
makes love to Ciglia. Frightened, she persuades him to take
her home. To escape her sweetheart's drunk-mad attentions,
Ciglia invites a masked girl walking along the dark roadway,
to ride with them. She does not dream that this girl is Pia.

       Arrived at Ciglia's house, Pia vanishes, while Marcus sees
his loved one to her door. Then at his own house, Marcus is
confronted by Pia, who throws herself at him. He drives her
off. Afraid of himself Marcus seeks to strengthen his powers
of resistance with more wine. But the continued advances of
Pia prove too much, and Marcus falls a victim to her wiles.

       The next morning Marcus comes to the full realization of
what has happened. A note from Ciglia forgiving him for his
conduct adds to his misery. Worried because he has not come
to her, Ciglia visits him at his home. Her assurance that
she loves him only tortures Marcus. While they are talking a
knocking is heard at the door.

       To protect her reputation, Marcus persuades Ciglia to hide
in another room until the visitor leaves. Pia's mother has
come to demand that justice be done her daughter.

Bowing to the stern code of the village, Marcus disconso-
lately marries Pia, while Ciglia with a heavy heart allows
Lorenz Gruber to resume his attentions to her. She finally
consents to his proposals, and they are wed. Lorenz is a devoted husband, and for a time the couple live quite happily.

Recklessly Marcus continues to hunt in all kinds of weather.
One day, while he is far up in the mountains, the worst storm
in years suddenly breaks. In vain Pia tries to urge the vil-
lagers upon a rescue expedition. Desperately she rushes to
Gruber's house, crying out Marcus' peril. Ciglia's screams
shock Gruber into a realization that he can never have his
wife's love.

The crash of an avalanche resounds through the valley as
Ciglia pleads with Lorenz unavailingly to save Marcus. She
hurries to her uncle for help, and on the way meets Marcus,
safely returned from the wilds.

The next day Gruber offers Marcus a bag of gold if he will
leave the village. The hunter spurns the proposition. There-
upon Gruber trails his wife's sweetheart into the mountains
and attempts to assassinate him. The hunter, in self-defense,
kills his enemy.

Accused of murder, Marcus flees into the mountains with
Ciglia, a mob at their heels. Resolved to brave any perils
together sooner than be again separated, they walk into the
path of an avalanche and perish in each other's arms. (Synopsis from the press sheet deposited for copyright in the Library of Congress.)

Director:	Ernst Lubitsch
Scenario:	Hans Kraly
Source:	The novel, Der König der Bernina (1928), by Jacob Christoph Heer
Photography:	Oliver Marsh
Sets and Costumes:	Walter Reimann
Musical Arrangement:	Dr. Hugo Riesenfeld
Editor:	Andrew Marton
Titles:	Katherine Hilliker and H. H. Caldwell
Assistant Director:	George Hippard
Cast:	John Barrymore (Marcus Paltram), Camilla Horn (Ciglia), Victor Var- coni (Lorenz Gruber), Hobart Bosworth (Rev. Tass), Bodil Rosing (House- keeper), Mona Rico (Pia), Evelyn Selbie (Pia's Mother).
Production:	Ernst Lubitsch for United Artists (Joseph M. Schenck, Executive Pro- ducer; John W. Considine Jr., Asso- ciate Producer).

Exhibited: In a silent version and in a sound
version with synchronized music score
and sound effects

Shooting: Location shooting in the Canadian
Rockies late August and early Septem-
ber, and studio shooting at Universal
Studios in Universal City into November

Length: 6515 ft. [1986m] Sound; 6498 ft.
[1981m] Silent

Released: May 11

Temporary Production
Titles: Avalanche, King of the Mountains

Notes:
Eternal Love has long been out of circulation. Copyright
to the film is owned by Mary Pickford Corporation. (The authors attempted unsuccessfully to arrange a screening.) A
print also survives in an East European archive.

Reviews:
New York Times, May 13, p. 27 and May 19, IX.7; Variety,
May 15, pp. 23, 27; Film Daily, May 19, p. 9; Life, May 31,
p. 31; Outlook and Independent, June 5, p. 235; Bioscope,
Mar. 13, p. 45.

Also see:
Variety, Sept. 5, 1928, p. 11, Nov. 7, 1928, p. 16; Gene
Fowler, Good Night, Sweet Prince: The Life and Times of John
Barrymore (Philadelphia: Blakiston, 1945), pp. 304-306.

AMERICAN SOUND PERIOD (1929-1948)

62   THE LOVE PARADE
       (1929)

       Paris, about 1920. Count Alfred Renard, military attaché
from Sylvania, is entertaining a lady friend, Paulette, in his
bedroom. Paulette is furious because she thinks Alfred is de-
ceiving her with other women. She pulls a tiny jewelled pistol, but Alfred gently dissuades her from using it and lays it
aside on a table. Paulette's husband forces his way in,
seizes the gun, and fires at Paulette, who falls at his feet.
The husband then fires at Alfred, who shows no reaction. (The
gun is loaded with blanks.) Alfred takes the gun and puts it
in a drawer alongside several others like it. The husband is
satisfied just to have his wife alive, but she is angered because she has lost her Alfred. Shortly after Alfred is informed that he is being recalled by the Queen of Sylvania because of his amorous escapades.

Sylvania. The aged cabinet ministers of the country are
worried over the fact that Queen Louise is unmarried. The
Queen explodes that all she ever hears is marriage. (Outside,
the Royal Band strikes up "The Wedding March.") Count Alfred
arrives for an audience. The Queen, after reading a report of
his scandalous doings in Paris, commands him to dine with her
that evening. The Court is pleased at their growing romantic
interest in one another. So are Jacques, Alfred's valet, and
Lulu, the Queen's maid, who engage in a flirtation of their
own.

Louise and Alfred are soon married, though he hesitates at
the vow that calls for <u>him</u> to obey. Prince Consort Alfred is
soon bored with having nothing to do. Complications arise in
the marriage because he is expected to treat his wife as he
would be expected to treat his Queen. But Sylvania is in a
bad way financially, and Alfred manages to keep up appearances
in order not to hurt the chances of an impending foreign loan.
Quietly Alfred works out a plan for allocation of natural resources that will make the foreign loan unnecessary, but the
Prime Minister refuses to receive it and Alfred is told to
leave the room.

Alfred has been ordered to attend the opera that evening
with the Queen and to be on his best behavior because the foreign ambassador will be present. He tells the Queen he will
not go and that he intends to go back to Paris. She goes to
the opera alone, to the audience's astonishment, but suddenly
Alfred appears after all. When the Queen is peevish, Alfred
starts to go and forces her to beg him to stay. He explains
he came not to humiliate her personally but to save her publicly, but he's still going to Paris tomorrow and as soon as
the foreign loan is signed will file for a divorce.

Later, in their quarters, as he is packing, the Queen says
she will follow him to Paris or wherever he goes, and that he
will always be "her king." He relents, they reach an understanding about their public and personal "duties" to one another, and they live happily ever after.

Director:	Ernst Lubitsch
Screenplay:	Ernest Vajda
Libretto:	Guy Bolton
Source:	The play, <u>Le prince consort</u> (ca. 1919), by Léon Xanrof [pseud. Léon Fourneau] and Jules Chancel
Photography:	Victor Milner
Art Director:	Hans Dreier
Music:	Victor Schertzinger
Lyrics:	Clifford Grey
Editor:	Merrill White

Dialogue Director:	Perry Ivins
Costumes:	Travis Banton
Sound Engineer:	Franklin Hansen
Cast:	Maurice Chevalier (Count Alfred), Jeanette MacDonald (Queen Louise), Lupino Lane (Jacques), Lillian Roth (Lulu), Eugene Pallette (War Minister), E. H. Calvert (Ambassador), Edgar Norton (Master of Ceremonies), Lionel Belmore (Prime Minister), Albert Roccardi (Foreign Minister), Carl Stockdale (Admiral), Russell Powell (Afghan Ambassador), Andre Cheron (Le Mari), Yola d'Avril (Paulette), Winter Hall (Priest), Ben Turpin (Crosseyed Lackey), Anton Vaverka, Albert de Winton, William von Hardenburg (Cabinet Ministers), Margaret Fealy (First Lady in Waiting), Virginia Bruce, Josephine Hall, Rosalind Charles, Helene Friend (Ladies in Waiting), Jean Harlow (Extra in Theater Box).
Songs:	"Champagne" ("Ooh, La La"), "Paris Stay the Same," "Dream Lover," "Anything to Please the Queen," "Let's Be Common," "My Love Parade," "Nobody's Using It Now," "The Queen Is Always Right," "Gossip," "March of the Grenadiers"
Production:	Ernst Lubitsch for Paramount
Shooting:	June and July (and possibly into August) at the Paramount Studios in Hollywood
Length:	Published running times vary from 106 to 115 minutes. Some recorded footage counts are: 10,022 ft. [3055m] (AFI Catalog); 10,131 ft. [3088m] (cutting continuity); 10,264 ft. [3128m] (Museum of Modern Art print).
New York Premiere:	November 19
Released:	January 18, 1930

Notes:
A French-language version, <u>Parade d'amour</u>, was also shot. Also released in a silent version, 7094 ft. [2162m] (AFI Catalog).

Reviews:
  New York Times, Nov. 20, p. 32 and Nov. 24, X.6; Variety,
Nov. 27, p. 21; Film Daily, Nov. 24, p. 8; Time, Dec. 2,
pp. 39-40; Outlook and Independent, Dec. 4, p. 551; Life,
Dec. 13, pp. 22, 28; National Board of Review Magazine, Jan.
1930, pp. 6-7; Cinema (New York), Jan. 1930, p. 38; London
Times, Feb. 13, 1930, p. 10; Bioscope, Feb. 19, 1930, p. 27;
Illustrated London News, Mar. 1, 1930, p. 334.

Also see:
  Variety, Feb. 6, p. 7, Apr. 17, p. 7, May 1, p. 5; New York
Times, April 21, IX.4; July 28, VIII.3; Aug. 4, VIII.4; Aug.
18, VIII.4; Russell Holman, The Love Parade [novelization]
(New York: Grosset and Dunlap, 1930), 275 pp.; Jerome Beatty,
"The Girl Who Sang in the Bathtub," American Magazine, July
1937, pp. 32-33, 138-41; Lillian Roth, I'll Cry Tomorrow (New
York: Frederick Fell, 1954), pp. 60-67; James Dillon White,
Born to Star: The Lupino Lane Story (London: William Heine-
mann, 1957), pp. 182-87; Eileen Bowser, Film Notes (New York:
Museum of Modern Art, 1969), pp. 75-76; Souvenir Programs of
Twelve Classic Movies 1927-1941, ed. Miles Kreuger (New York:
Dover, 1977), pp. 41-60.

63   PARAMOUNT ON PARADE
     (1930)

     A variety revue. The episodes numbered 5, 11, and 19 were
directed by Lubitsch. Episodes marked (C) were originally
filmed in Technicolor.

	Episode	Songs	Performers
1.	Showgirls on Parade (C)	"Paramount on Parade" by Jack King and El-sie Janis	Virginia Bruce, Paramount Publix Ushers; danced by Mitzi Mayfair
2.	Introduction	"We're the Masters of Ceremony" by Dave Dreyer and Ballard MacDonald	Jack Oakie, Skeets Gallagher, Leon Errol
3.	Love Time	"Any Time's the Time to Fall in Love" by Jack King and Elsie Janis	Charles "Buddy" Rogers, Lillian Roth
4.	Murder Will Out		William Powell (Philo Vance), Clive Brook (Sher-lock Holmes),

Eugene Pallette
(Sergeant Heath),
Warner Oland (Dr.
Fu Manchu), Jack
Oakie (Victim)

Lubitsch Sequence

5. Origin of the Apache. Maurice Chevalier introduces his
sequence--something a little bit naughty and typically French:
he will explain the origin of the Apache dance, which, con-
trary to rumor, did not derive from gangsters in the Paris
underworld.

A man (Chevalier) and a woman (Evelyn Brent) return home
from a show. To musical accompaniment, she accuses him of
flirting with the girl on his right. He denies it. She
changes her strategy and weeps while repeating her accusation.
Soothingly, he denies it. Now she rebukes him gently and flir-
tatiously, but he, caressingly, still remains adamant in his
denial. Their argument becomes more and more violent as they
shove and slap one another to the beat of Apache music. As
they come to rhythmical blows, he removes his jacket and she
takes off her dress. Articles of clothing are seen flying
across the screen. Finally a cut reveals the couple in full
dress attire, about to embark on an evening on the town.

6.	Song of the Gondolier (C)	"Come Back to Sorrento" by Ernesto de Curtis and Leo Robin	Nino Martini
7.	In a Hospital		Leon Errol, Helen Kane, Phillips Holmes, David Newell, Jean Arthur
8.	In a Girls' Gym	"I'm in Training for You" by L. Wolfe Gilbert and Abel Baer	Jack Oakie (Trainer), Zelma O'Neal (Jealous Sweetheart); danced by Mitzi Mayfair
9.	The Toreador	"I'm Isadore the Toreador," lyrics by David Franklin to music from Bizet's Carmen	Harry Green, Kay Francis; Marion Morgan Dancers
10.	The Montmartre Girl	"My Marine" by Richard A. Whiting and Ray Egan	Ruth Chatterton sings to Fredric March, Stuart Erwin, Jack Pennick, Stanley Smith

The Films: Synopsis, Credits and Notes

Lubitsch Sequence
11. A Park in Paris. Song: "All I Want Is Just One Girl" by
Richard A. Whiting and Leo Robin, sung by Maurice Chevalier.
Gendarme Chevalier patrols in a Paris park; lovers of all nations are embracing according to their national customs. He
gives one couple a citation in order to get the woman's address. He scolds a man reading a paper alone for wasting
benches and sends him on his way. A woman calls him over and
points out her husband on a bench embracing another woman.
When he sees the man is enjoying himself, he knocks out the
wife with his club. The husband tips his hat appreciatively.
With Tyler Brooke (?), Jack Pennick, Rolfe Sedan.

12.	Mitzi Herself	"All I Want Is Just One Girl" (repeated)	Mitzi Green sings imitating Charles E. Mack of the Two Black Crows and then Chevalier
13.	The Schoolroom	"What Did Cleopatra Say?" by Jack King and Elsie Janis	Helen Kane (Teacher), Mitzi Green, Jackie Searle
14.	The Gallows Song (C)	"Nichavo!" by Mme. Mana-Zucca and Helen Jerome	Dennis King, Skeets Gallagher
15.	Dance Mad	"Dancing to Save Your Sole" by L. Wolfe Gilbert and Abel Baer	Nancy Carroll, Abe Lyman and His Band, danced by Al Norman
16.	Dream Girl (C)	"Let Us Drink to the Girl of My Dreams" by L. Wolfe Gilbert and Abel Baer	Richard Arlen, Jean Arthur, Virginia Bruce, Mary Brian, Gary Cooper, James Hall, Phillips Holmes, David Newell, Joan Peers, Fay Wray, Eugene Pallette
17.	The Redhead	"I'm True to the Navy Now" by Jack King and Elsie Janis	Clara Bow, Jack Oakie, Skeets Gallagher, Chorus
18.	Impulses		George Bancroft, Cecil Cunningham, Kay Francis, William Austin, Henry Fink, Mischa Auer, Jack Pennick, Jack Luden

103

Lubitsch Sequence
19. The Rainbow Revels. (C) Song: "Sweeping the Clouds Away"
by Sam Coslow. Chevalier and a bevy of girls appear as Paris
chimney sweeps. For the finale, Chevalier climbs a ladder to
the clouds and the girls form a giant rainbow. (Sequence outline and credits based on Miles Kreuger's program notes for a
July 17, 1971 showing in the Museum of Modern Art's retrospective "Roots of the American Musical Film," and on Per Calum's
filmography in Kosmorama, 1976.)

Directors:	Dorothy Arzner, Otto Brower, Edmund Goulding, Victor Heerman, Edwin H. Knopf, Rowland V. Lee, Ernst Lubitsch, Lothar Mendes, Victor Schertzinger, A. Edward Sutherland, Frank Tuttle
Photography:	Harry Fishbeck and Victor Milner
Color Sequences:	Technicolor
Set Design:	John Wenger
Choreography:	David Bennett
Editor:	Merrill White
Sound Engineer:	Harry M. Lindgren
Production Supervisor:	Elsie Janis
Production:	Albert S. Kaufman for Paramount
Shooting:	The Lubitsch-Chevalier sequences were shot late in October 1929.
Running Time:	128 minutes, cut to 102 minutes
New York Opening:	April 19
Released:	April 26

Notes:
    Also shot in a French-language version, Paramount en parade,
directed by Charles de Rochefort; reviewed in Variety, Dec. 24,
pp. 21, 29. Also made in various European versions.

Reviews:
    New York Times, Apr. 21, p. 20 and Apr. 27, IX.5; Variety,
Apr. 23, pp. 24, 36; Film Daily, Apr. 20, p. 10; New Yorker,
Apr. 26; Life, May 16, p. 18; Time, May 5, p. 32; Cinema (New
York), June, p. 41; London Times, June 17, p. 12; Bioscope,
June 18, p. 23.

Also see:
    New York Times, Aug. 3, VIII.3; Liberty, Nov. 21, 1936,
pp. 55-57.

64   MONTE CARLO
      (1930)

    Europe, the present. The outdoor procession for the wed-
ding of Countess Helene Mara and the wealthy Duke Otto is

interrupted by a sudden rainshower. Matters worsen when the
Duke discovers his bride-to-be has fled. The thrice-jilted
Duke appears to explain the situation to the impatient guests,
who demand the return of their gifts.

On a train bound for Monte Carlo, the Countess, clad only
in a negligee, tells her maid her dress didn't fit properly
and therefore it was fated that she would not go through with
the wedding. As the train rhythmically accelerates toward its
destination, the Countess sings "Beyond the Blue Horizon."
Workers in the passing fields join in her song.

At a casino in Monte Carlo Count Rudolph Farrière watches
the Countess at the gambling table. His presence proves extremely lucky for her, but after he leaves the table she loses
everything back again. The Count sends flowers to her in her
hotel room and telephones and sings a love song to her over
the phone. After she hangs up the infatuated Countess continues singing the song as she retires for the night.

The following day the Count runs into the Countess' new
hairdresser and arranges to go to the Countess' posing as him.
The Countess' maid, Bertha, warns him never to flirt with the
chambermaids, but adds that <u>she</u> is not a chambermaid. It soon
becomes apparent that the new hairdresser knows very little
about hairdressing. The Countess fires him but relents and
asks him to stay after he begins giving her a soothing, ca-
ressing massage.

After losing repeatedly at the gambling table, the Countess
is flat broke. She tells the Count, who is now her chauffeur,
that she must dismiss him in order to save money. Meanwhile,
Duke Otto has followed his fiancée to Monte Carlo, and he offers to give her the money to pay her debts. She confesses
she cares for the Duke only for his money, but the thickwitted
Duke is not displeased. In an effort to prevent the Countess
from marrying for money, the Count tells her of his never-fail
method for winning at the tables: If he is next to a brunette,
he bets on red; if next to a redhead, on black. The Countess
asks what if he is next to a blonde; he says in that case he
never loses. The Countess gives him her last 1,000 francs and
they set out for the casino. When she sees her fiancé is at
the gambling table, the Countess leaves. Later the Count
takes a large sum of his own money to her and pretends he won
it. The position of the hairdresser/chauffeur is secure.

The Countess has her hair done for an evening at the opera.
The opera turns out to be "Monsieur Beaucaire," a romantic
tale of a lady and a prince who poses as her hairdresser. The
Countess recognizes the similarity between the situation in
the opera and her own. The Count admits to his masquerade,
and he and the Countess are united at last.

Director:	Ernst Lubitsch
Screenplay:	Ernest Vajda
Additional Dialogue:	Vincent Lawrence
Source:	The play, Die blaue Küste (The Blue Coast or The Love Coast) (1914), by Hans Müller [pseud. Hans Lothar], and episodes from the operetta Monsieur Beaucaire (1901), by Booth Tarkington and Evelyn Greenleaf Sutherland, based on Tarkington's novel Monsieur Beaucaire (1900)
Photography:	Victor Milner
Art Director:	Hans Dreier
Music:	Richard A. Whiting and W. Franke Harling
Lyrics:	Leo Robin
Sound Engineer:	Harry D. Mills
Cast:	Jack Buchanan (Count Rudolph Farrière), Jeanette MacDonald (Countess Helene Mara), Claud Allister (Duke Otto von Liebenheim), ZaSu Pitts (Bertha, Maid to the Countess), Tyler Brooke (Armand), John Roche (Paul, a Ladies' Hairdresser), Lionel Belmore (Prince Gustav von Liebenheim), Albert Conti (Master of Ceremonies), Helen Garden ("Lady Mary"), Donald Novis ("Monsieur Beaucaire"), Erik Bey (Lord Winterset), David Percy (Herald), Billy Bevan (Train Conductor), Sidney Bracey (Hunchback at Casino), Geraldine Dvorak (Extra at Casino; Garbo look-alike). Knowles (1975) adds: Frances Dee (Receptionist), Rolfe Sedan (Hairdresser), John Carroll (Wedding Guest Officer).
Songs:	"Day of Days," "I'm a Simple-Hearted Soul," "She'll Love Me and Like It," "Beyond the Blue Horizon," "Give Me a Moment, Please," "Trimmin' the Women," "Whatever It Is, It's Grand" ("This Is Something New to Me"), "Always in All Ways"
Production:	Ernst Lubitsch for Paramount
Shooting:	Begun at the Paramount Studios in Hollywood April 21
Running Time:	90 minutes
New York Premiere:	August 27
Released:	September 4
Temporary Production Title:	The Blue Coast

106

Notes:
AFI Catalog also lists silent version. Publicity sheets
and most filmographies have listed Edgar Norton in the cast;
he was replaced by Lionel Belmore.

Reviews:
New York Times, Aug. 28, p. 22 and Sept. 7, IX.5; Variety,
Sept. 3, pp. 19, 41; Film Daily, Aug. 31, p. 10; Exhibitors
Herald-World, Aug. 2, pp. 26-27 and Sept. 6, p. 38; New Yorker,
Sept. 6; Time, Sept. 8, p. 25; Outlook and Independent, Sept.
17, p. 112; Life, Sept. 19, p. 18; Nation, Oct. 1, pp. 356-57;
Theatre, Nov., p. 48; Cinema (New York), Dec., p. 38; London
Times, Jan. 13, 1931, p. 10; Bioscope, Jan. 14, 1931, p. 45;
Illustrated London News, Jan. 31, 1931, p. 160.

Also see:
New York Times, June 8, IX.6; Variety, Mar. 26, p. 8, Sept.
10, p. 2, Jan. 14, 1931, p. 7.

65   THE SMILING LIEUTENANT
(1931)

Vienna and, later, the mythical kingdom of Flausenthurm,
the late nineteenth century. Lieutenant Niki's latest sweetheart has departed and he is preparing to retire for the night
when his friend, Max, comes to him with a problem. Max (who
is happily married) has become interested in Franzi, the beautiful leader of a girls' band appearing at a nearby beer garden, but is afraid to try to meet her alone. Niki agrees to
accompany his friend.

Franzi rebuffs Max's attempt to get acquainted with her but
is impressed with Niki and his knowledge of music. The two
stroll through a park while Max, carrying Franzi's violin
case, follows after them. Niki brings Franzi to his apartment
to play chamber music and invites her to have breakfast next
morning with him. Franzi objects: "First tea. Then dinner.
Then--maybe--breakfast." Next the couple are seen having
breakfast together.

Meanwhile, on a train headed for Vienna, King Adolf XV of
Flausenthurm and his staid daughter, Princess Anna, receive a
telegram of welcome from the King's cousin, the Emperor of
Austria. The King is insulted when he sees the name of his
kingdom spelled without an 'h' but is soon pacified when he
reads of the Emperor's good will toward him and his daughter.

In Vienna, the royal guard is called out for an elaborate
welcome for the visiting King. While Niki stands at attention, Franzi waves to him from across the street and blows him

a kiss. He smiles and winks back at her. Just at this moment the royal carriage passes by and Princess Anna thinks the Lieutenant is smiling at her. Outraged newspaper headlines announce that a blatant insult has been directed at the Princess.

Matters look grim for Niki when he is summoned to appear before the King. His arrival is greeted by six doleful ladies-in-waiting and a sobbing Anna. The King orders him to spell Flausenthurm. When he correctly includes the 'h,' the ladies are relieved and murmur agreement that "he certainly knows his alphabet." The King is equally ecstatic, but Anna is quick to remind him of the seriousness of the Lieutenant's affront. The King demands that Niki explain his behavior. Niki dissembles and says the crime came about because he suddenly found himself staring at the most beautiful girl he had ever seen. The Princess and King are so taken in by Niki's explanation that they have him appointed their adjutant during their stay in Vienna.

Anna confesses to Niki that she has received her limited knowledge from the royal dictionary and asks him to explain exactly what he did with his eyes when he saw her, and what it means. Niki explains: "When we like someone we smile, but when we want to do something about it, we wink." Anna flashes a quick wink at Niki as she departs.

Anna demands that she be allowed to marry Niki. The King consents after she threatens to marry an American instead. Niki receives word of the proposed marriage while he is breakfasting with Franzi and goes at once to the palace to put an end to the matter. But the King and the Emperor won't be dissuaded: Niki must go through with the marriage.

Niki, however, refuses to consummate the marriage. Matters worsen when the royal family returns to Flausenthurm. Niki spurns Flausenthurmian things and ways; all he can think of is Franzi and Vienna. Escaping from the castle one night, he wanders through the town and suddenly hears the familiar music of Franzi's band. He arranges to have Franzi arrested and they are reunited and Niki returns home in a jovial mood.

Anna soon learns that her husband is "stepping out." She schemes to have Franzi brought before her. A slapping match ensues, but then the two women break down and sob over the fact that they are both in love with the same man. Franzi realizes, however, that "girls who start with breakfast don't usually stay for supper" and decides to teach Anna how to be more appealing to her husband. She advises her how to "dress up her lingerie" and helps to transform the dour Princess into a radiant woman. At first Niki cannot believe the change, but soon he forgets Franzi and happily lives up to his marriage vows.

108

Director:	Ernst Lubitsch
Screenplay:	Ernest Vajda and Samson Raphaelson
Sources:	The operetta, Ein Walzertraum (A Waltz Dream) (1907), by Leopold Jacobson and Felix Doermann [pseud. Felix Biedermann], music by Oscar Straus, from the novel, Buch der Abenteuer (1905), by Hans Müller [pseud. Hans Lothar]
Photography:	George Folsey
Art Director:	Hans Dreier
Music:	Oscar Straus
Lyrics:	Clifford Grey
Editor:	Merrill White
Recording Engineer:	Ernest Zatorsky
Cast:	Maurice Chevalier (Niki), Claudette Colbert (Franzi), Miriam Hopkins (Princess Anna), Charlie Ruggles (Max), George Barbier (King Adolf), Con MacSunday (Emperor), Robert Strange (Adjutant von Rockoff), Hugh O'Connell (Orderly), Elizabeth Patterson (Baroness von Schwedel), Harry Bradley (Count von Halden), Karl Stall (Master of Ceremonies), Werner Saxtorph (Joseph), Janet Reade (Lily), Granville Bates (Bill Collector). Kosmorama (1976) adds: Maude Allen (A Woman), Charles Wasenheim (Officer).
Songs:	"That's the Army," "Live for Today," "Breakfast Table Love," "Jazz Up Your Lingerie"
Production:	Ernst Lubitsch for Paramount
Shooting:	February and March at Paramount's Astoria Studios in Long Island City, New York
Running Time:	88 minutes (Film Daily and several filmographies give 102 minutes)
New York Premiere:	May 22
Released:	August 1

Notes:
Straus' operetta was earlier made as a German silent film, Ein Walzertraum (1925). "Expecting to get back its negative cost out of the foreign market, Paramount has made three versions of The Smiling Lieutenant to supplement the one for domestic use. The versions are silent, one specially for the United Kingdom and the other is French. It is understood that negative cost on the picture was more than $1,000,000" (Film Daily, May 28, p. 7). A print of The Smiling Lieutenant, once

presumed to be a lost film, was discovered in the late 1960s. The film is currently not in circulation, reportedly because of a dispute over the music rights.

Reviews:
    New York Times, May 23, p. 13 and May 31, VIII.5; Variety, May 27, p. 56; Film Daily, May 24, p. 10; Motion Picture Herald, July 11, p. 26; Time, June 1, p. 51; Outlook and Independent, June 3, p. 154; Nation, June 10, p. 646; Life, June 12, p. 20; London Times, July 28, p. 10; Bioscope, July 29, p. 29; New Statesman and Nation, Aug. 1, p. 141; Spectator, Aug. 1, p. 153; Saturday Review, Aug. 8, p. 183; L'Europe Nouvelle, Sept. 5, p. 1209.

Also see:
    Variety, Dec. 3, 1930, p. 4, Dec. 17, 1930, p. 12, Feb. 11, p. 2, Apr. 1, p. 20, June 2, p. 6, June 16, p. 27, July 14, p. 11, Sept. 22, p. 14; Film Daily, Mar. 1, p. 1, p. 5, Mar. 4, p. 5, Mar. 8, p. 5, Mar. 17, p. 6, Mar. 22, p. 5, Apr. 19, p. 5; New York Times, Apr. 12, IX.6.

66   THE MAN I KILLED   (BROKEN LULLABY)
      (1932)

    Paris, November 11, 1919. On the anniversary of Armistice Day, a young Frenchman, Paul, confesses to a priest that he killed a man during the war--a young German soldier who was writing a letter home at the time of his death. The priest says absolution, but the guilt-ridden Paul cannot be satisfied; he feels he must go and beg forgiveness from the family of the man he killed.

    In a small German town, Dr. Holderlin and his wife live with Elsa, the bereaved fiancée of their dead son, Walter. The memory of the departed son is still pressing on the parents' mind and their bitterness against the French is still strong. A young neighbor, Schultz, who hopes to marry Elsa, pays a visit to Dr. Holderlin and callously remarks what a coincidence it is that his own name is Walter, too. Elsa begs the unfeeling Schultz to leave them all alone with their memories.

    On a visit to Walter's grave, Frau Holderlin consoles another grieving mother. Paul watches when she returns home. At dinner that evening, Elsa and the parents attempt to be cheerful, but their overwhelming sadness eventually prevails. The doorbell interrupts dinner, and the maid informs them that a man who said he had come to see Dr. Holderlin quickly left when told the Doctor was dining.

When Elsa goes to place flowers on Walter's grave, Paul is there. A gravedigger nearby confides to her that this stranger has been here before. Then Paul visits Dr. Holderlin in his office. When Dr. Holderlin learns his visitor is a Frenchman, he orders him out. But Elsa appears just at that moment and recognizes Paul as the man who put flowers on Walter's grave. Paul tells them Walter was a friend of his in Paris and describes their last night together. Later, Elsa tells Paul his visit has made all three of them come alive again.

Several days later the townspeople begin to gossip about the romance that has developed between Elsa and the Frenchman. At an inn Schultz and several companions with obviously anti-French feelings discuss Paul and conclude he must be a spy because he keeps a sealed violin case in his room. When Dr. Holderlin arrives at the inn, his friends, many of whom have also lost sons in the war, begin to scorn him, but Dr. Holderlin points out to them French parents lost sons too, and says the responsibility for war is not French or German but universal.

The Holderlins come to think of Paul as their own son. But Paul decides he has to leave them. When he informs Elsa, the two of them admit they love one another but Paul says it can never be. Elsa takes him to Walter's room and reads him the last letter Walter wrote her. Paul recites its conclusion from memory and confesses the truth. He begins to confess to the parents also, but Elsa stops him by saying Paul has decided to make his home with them for good. The parents are overcome with joy.

In private, Elsa chides Paul for his cowardice in wanting to run away. She says they must think only of the parents and Paul must never reveal his secret. Dr. Holderlin brings Walter's violin. Paul begins to play. Elsa accompanies on the piano. The mother and father watch in contentment as the music continues.

Director:	Ernst Lubitsch
Screenplay:	Samson Raphaelson and Ernest Vajda
Source:	The play, <u>L'Homme que j'ai tué</u> (ca. 1925), by Maurice Rostand, and its American stage adaptation by Reginald Berkeley
Photography:	Victor Milner
Art Director:	Hans Dreier
Cast:	Lionel Barrymore (Doctor Holderlin), Nancy Carroll (Elsa), Phillips Holmes (Paul), Louise Carter (Frau Holderlin), Lucien Littlefield

(Schultz), Tom Douglas (Walter Holderlin), Frank Sheridan (Priest),
ZaSu Pitts (Anna), George Bickel
(Bresslauer), Emma Dunn (Frau Mul-
ler), Reginald Pasch (Fritz's Father), Tully Marshall (Gravedigger),
Lillian Elliott (Frau Bresslauer),
Marvin Stephens (Fritz), Joan Standing (Flower Shop Girl), Rodney McLen-
non (War Veteran). Kosmorama (1976)
adds: Torben Meyer (Waiter).

Production:	Ernst Lubitsch for Paramount
Shooting:	September and October 1931 at Para- mount Studios in Hollywood (days of shooting: 43; retakes)
Running Time:	77 minutes (A review of a Hollywood preview in Motion Picture Herald listed the running time as 94 min- utes [Jan. 16, pp. 38-40].)
New York Premiere:	January 19 as The Man I Killed
Released:	February 26 as Broken Lullaby
Other Title:	The Fifth Commandment

Notes:
According to New York Times, the title change was made "because of a feeling that the original title gave a wrong im-
pression of the nature of the story" (Feb. 4, p. 25). There
is a copy of Reginald Berkeley's adaptation of the source play
in the Script Collection at the Library for the Performing
Arts at Lincoln Center.

Reviews:
New York Times, Jan. 20, p. 17 and Jan. 24, VIII.4; Variety, Jan. 26, p. 21; Film Daily, Jan. 20, p. 1, Jan. 24,
p. 10; Motion Picture Herald, Jan. 16, pp. 38-40; New Yorker,
Jan. 30; Time, Feb. 1, p. 48; Outlook and Independent, Feb. 3,
p. 150; Nation, Feb. 17, p. 212; National Board of Review
Magazine, Feb., pp. 16-17; Stage, Mar., p. 42; London Times,
June 13, p. 10; Illustrated London News, May 21, p. 854; Saturday Review, June 18, p. 614; London Mercury, July, pp. 261-
62; Theatre World (London), July, pp. 40,42.

Also see:
Variety, Nov. 12, 1930, p. 11, Nov. 26, 1930, p. 2,
Jan. 14, 1931, p. 11, Jan. 21, 1931, p. 2, Jan. 5, p. 6,
Feb. 9, p. 6, Mar. 1, p. 10, Nov. 8, p. 8; Film Daily, Mar.
17, 1931, p. 6, Mar. 29, 1931, p. 2; Grierson on Documentary,
ed. Forsyth Hardy, rev. ed. (Berkeley: Univ. of California
Press, 1966), pp. 69-70; Eileen Bowser, Film Notes (New York:
Museum of Modern Art, 1969), pp. 81-82.

67 ONE HOUR WITH YOU
    (1932)

Paris, the early 1930s. A police commissioner informs his
men the morale of France is in danger because in the Spring
everyone goes to the parks, rather than to hotels and cafes,
to make love. The policemen go out to clear the parks of
their lovers. One couple found embracing on a park bench
claim to be husband and wife. The policeman doesn't believe
them, of course, and sends them on their way, but later the
man, Dr. André Bertier, turns to the camera and confides that
the woman is indeed his wife, Colette.

After the Bertiers are in bed Colette keeps turning on the
light to continue conversation about her old friend Mitzi,
just back in Paris and coming to visit the following day.

Professor Olivier, Mitzi's husband, has been suspicious of
her for some time and he has engaged a detective to spy on
her. The two of them watch from the window as she gets into
a cab during a rainstorm on her way to visit Colette. By coincidence, the cab is taken and is waiting for its rider,
André, who has gone into a flower shop. The two strangers
agree to share the cab. Professor Olivier and the detective
smile and shake hands.

André buries himself behind his newspaper and ignores Mitzi's insinuations and flirtations. She persists and after
several verbal exchanges with more than a trace of double
meaning, André halts the cab and gets out.

Colette welcomes Mitzi. She tells her friend how happy she
and André are. When André arrives home he is stunned to see
his flirtatious companion from the cab. He turns to the camera and vows not to weaken.

Back at home Mitzi feigns an illness to force Doctor André
to come on a house call. He consents to come only after his
wife insists. Things begin to progress according to Mitzi's
instigations, and when the Professor appears, Mitzi is holding
André's wrist. (In an attempt to cover up, André quickly
switches their wrists and starts taking Mitzi's pulse.)

Shortly before the Bertiers' dinner party, André switches
place cards so he won't be next to Mitzi. Colette sees him,
assumes he does it to be near another woman, Mlle. Martel, and
switches the cards back again. During the party she confides
her suspicions to Mitzi, who to keep her off the track switches the place cards again. Colette is startled and very upset
when she sees the final seating arrangement, but tries to
mask it by flirting with Adolph, a fussy, garrulous middle-
aged friend.

113

After dancing together, André and Mitzi go out onto the terrace. Mitzi undoes André's tie and slips off into the garden. After some hesitation he follows and behind some shrubbery they begin to kiss. Colette and Adolph come into the garden searching for André. André hears them and slips back to the terrace and Colette sees him there with Mlle. Martel, who is tying his tie. Colette is sure her worst fears are confirmed.

As the guests leave, Mitzi whispers to André to meet her outside in a cab. André confides his dilemma in song to the camera. He goes to Colette but she rebuffs him so he goes off to meet Mitzi. Meanwhile, Adolph has stayed after the party and he clumsily professes his love for Colette. She is sympathetic but not responsive and politely asks him to leave.

The Professor has a report on his wife's activities the night before. Mitzi departs with all her belongings. The Professor visits André and informs him he is to be a witness in a divorce case. Colette senses all is not well between the Professor and Mitzi and tries to guess who the man might be. André finally decides to confess he's the other man.

Colette decides to teach André a lesson. With Adolph present she tells André something happened between them. André doesn't believe it but signals Adolph behind her back to concur. Agreeing to trade an Adolph for a Mitzi, the happy couple turn to the camera, ask "What Would You Do?", kiss, and their marital bliss is restored.

Director:	Ernst Lubitsch
Assisted by:	George Cukor
Screenplay:	Samson Raphaelson
Source:	The play, Nur ein Traum (Only a Dream) (1909), by Lothar Schmidt [Goldschmidt]
Photography:	Victor Milner
Art Director:	Hans Dreier
Set Decorations:	A. E. Freudeman
Music:	Oscar Straus
Lyrics:	Leo Robin
Interpolated Music:	Richard A. Whiting
Editor:	William Shea
Costumes:	Travis Banton
Sound Engineer:	M. M. Paggi
Cast:	Maurice Chevalier (Dr. André Bertier), Jeanette MacDonald (Colette Bertier), Genevieve Tobin (Mitzi Olivier), Charlie Ruggles (Adolph), Roland Young (Professor Olivier), Josephine Dunn (Mlle. Martel),

	Richard Carle (Detective), Barbara Leonard (Mitzi's Maid), George Barbier (Police Commissioner)., Charles Judels (Policeman), Charles Coleman (Marcel), Sheila Mannors [later Sheila Bromley] (Collette's Downstairs Maid), Leonie Pray (Colette's Upstairs Maid), George David (Taxi Driver). (From corrected studio cast list of March 25, 1932.) Knowles (1975) adds: Bess Flowers. Kosmorama (1976) adds: Florine McKinney (Girl), Donald Novis (Singer), Eric Wilton (Butler), Bill Elliott (Dancer).
Songs:	"What a Little Thing Like a Wedding Ring Can Do," "We Will Always Be Sweethearts," "Three Times a Day," "One Hour with You," "Mitzi," "What Would You Do?," "It Was Only a Dream Kiss"
Production:	Ernst Lubitsch for Paramount
Shooting:	[December 1931 and January 1932] at Paramount Studios in Hollywood (days of shooting: 44; retakes for a new ending in February at the Astoria studios in New York with Chevalier and MacDonald)
Running Time:	Variously listed as 75 and 80 minutes. Footage count on print at UCLA Film Archive is 6946 [2117m].
Released:	March 25

Notes:
   A musical remake of Lubitsch's The Marriage Circle (1924). Also made in a French-language version, Une heure près de toi; see Films in Review, January 1975, p. 23, for credits. Lubitsch was originally set to supervise this film and Cukor to direct it, but Lubitsch gradually took over direction after shooting had begun. In an unpublished transcript in the University of Illinois Archives, Samson Raphaelson recounts in elaborate detail how this came about: Lubitsch called him to see early Cukor rushes, which they agreed went against the comic conceptions of their original script; shortly after, Lubitsch began to assume direction, though Cukor remained on the set throughout the filming. (Variety reported on Dec. 15, 1931: "Ernst Lubitsch is supervising Chevalier's One Hour with You with his meg in hand. George Cukor, titular director, does considerable sitting out while Lubitsch uses his influence with the French star" [p. 6].) Cukor has given contradictory accounts; see Richard Overstreet, "Interview with

George Cukor," Film Culture, no. 34 (Fall 1964), pp. 13, 15;
Gary Carey, Cukor and Company (New York: Museum of Modern
Art, 1971), p. 25; and Gavin Lambert, On Cukor (New York:
G. P. Putnam's, 1972), pp. 42–44. When it developed that Lubitsch wanted sole director credit, Cukor instituted legal
action (Variety, Mar. 8, p. 4); in a compromise, Cukor was
allowed to go to RKO to make a picture with Constance Bennett,
and he settled for assistant director billing (Variety, Apr.
5, p. 3). In a full-page Variety ad March 22 Lubitsch has
sole billing; in an April 5 ad "assisted by George Cukor" is
inserted. There is an English-language typescript of the
source play in the Theatre Collection of the Library of the
Performing Arts at Lincoln Center.

Reviews:
    New York Times, Mar. 24, p. 17 and Apr. 3, VIII.4; Variety,
Mar. 29, pp. 24–25; Film Daily, Mar. 6, p. 10; Motion Picture
Herald, Apr. 2, pp. 34–35, 38; New Yorker, Apr. 2; Time, Oct.
4, p. 22; London Times, June 29, p. 10; Saturday Review,
July 9, p. 44; Canadian Forum, May, p. 318.

Also see:
    Variety, Apr. 10, 1929, p. 6 (a proposed remake of The Mar-
riage Circle by Alexander Korda), July 28, 1931, p. 2, Aug. 4,
1931, p. 2, Sept. 15, 1931, p. 17, Sept. 29, 1931, p. 2,
Oct. 6, 1931, p. 6, Oct. 13, 1931, p. 3, Nov. 3, 1931, p. 2,
Dec. 8, 1931, p. 6, Feb. 9, p. 10, Feb. 16, p. 5, Mar. 1,
p. 50, Mar. 22, p. 3, Apr. 12, pp. 10, 48, Apr. 19, p. 2,
June 21, p. 14; Photoplay, Feb., p. 128.

68   TROUBLE IN PARADISE
     (1932)

    Venice, the early 1930s. A garbage collector empties cans
into his garbage gondolier, and, as he shoves off down the
canal, gives a rousing rendition of "O Sole Mio." Interior of
a hotel room; a figure leaps over a balcony railing, climbs
down a tree, and removes a disguise. Inside the room a man
staggers and falls to the floor. Outside, two floozies ring
the buzzer. In another room of the hotel, the Baron gives instructions to a waiter for a romantic dinner for two. Meanwhile, a robbery is reported in Room Suite 253-5-7 and 9.
The Countess arrives for dinner with the Baron. M. François
Filiba, occupant of the suite, gives details to the police;
the robber got in by posing as a doctor and asking to see
Filiba's tonsils. The waiter tells the Baron and Countess of
the robbery. After he leaves, the Countess says she knows the
Baron did it. He confesses he's Gaston Monescu, a famous international criminal. She confesses she's Lily, also a swind-
ler and crook. They kiss and fall in love.

116

Paris, a year later. Mariette Colet, a young, rich, beautiful but frivolous widow, owner of Colet and Company, manufacturers of the world's greatest perfumes, tells her Board of Directors to leave salaries where they are even though things are tough in this time of Depression. Then she goes out and buys an expensive handbag. She is besieged by two foolish and stuffy middle-aged suitors, Filiba (the one who was robbed in Venice) and the Major. They accompany her to the opera, where her handbag is stolen. Gaston Monescu, who took it, sees an ad in the paper and returns the handbag for the reward. Madame Colet is much attracted to this urbane and handsome and apparently down-on-his-luck gentleman (who presents himself as M. LeVal) and takes him on as her private secretary. Very soon he is in full control of all her business affairs and is also her frequent personal companion. He in turn takes on a secretarial assistant, Lily, and together they make arrangements to have large sums of cash deposited in Mariette's private safe in her house. Lily soon senses that Mariette has romantic designs on Gaston.

Mariette gives a garden party. All the gossip is about her and her new secretary. M. Filiba is present. He is certain he's seen the man somewhere before. Adolphe Giron, chairman of the Board of Colet and Company and long-time advisor and intimate of the Colets, attempts to arouse Mariette's suspicions about her secretary, but she expresses her continued confidence in Gaston and orders Giron to hand over the company books to him.

Afraid that Filiba will remember him any minute, Gaston makes arrangements for Lily and him to clear out as soon as they have the money from the safe. Mariette accelerates the flirtation and hints at sure results when she comes home from a dinner party that evening at the Major's. While she is out Giron arrives and tells Gaston he knows who he really is; Gaston checkmates him by saying he now knows Giron has been swindling Mariette all these years. Meanwhile, Filiba has been puzzling it over and suddenly at the Major's party he remembers—tonsils. Mariette, feigning insult, rushes home. She plays along with Gaston, but when he realizes she knows, he reveals what he found out about Giron. Gaston confesses he came to rob her but fell in love with her instead. Lily shows up and breaks the spell. Regretfully for both of them Gaston takes leave of Mariette—but with a string of her pearls Lily is especially fond of (and with Mariette's blessing to it).

In a taxicab Gaston looks for the pearls but Lily has picked his pocket. Lily looks for the money in the handbag but Gaston has snitched it. They look at one another and laugh and she throws herself into his arms.

Director:	Ernst Lubitsch
Screenplay:	Samson Raphaelson
Adaptation:	Grover Jones
Source:	The play, The Honest Finder, by Aladar Laszlo
Photography:	Victor Milner
Art Director:	Hans Dreier
Music:	W. Franke Harling
Lyrics:	Leo Robin
Costumes:	Travis Banton
Cast:	Miriam Hopkins (Lily), Kay Francis (Mariette Colet), Herbert Marshall (Gaston Monescu), Charlie Ruggles (The Major), Edward Everett Horton (François Filiba), C. Aubrey Smith (Adolphe J. Giron), Robert Greig (Butler), Leonid Kinskey (Russian who bawls out Mariette). Kosmorama (1976) adds: George Humbert (Waiter), Rolfe Sedan (Salesman), Luis Alberni (Irritated Opera Fan), Hooper Atchley (Insurance Agent), Nella Walker (Mme. Bouchet), Perry Ivins (Radio Announcer), Tyler Brooke (Singer), Larry Steers (Guest), Mary Boland.
Production:	Ernst Lubitsch for Paramount
Shooting:	Begun around July 25 at the Paramount Studios in Hollywood and completed the first or second week in September; approximately eight weeks' shooting
Running Time:	83 minutes
New York Premiere:	November 8
Temporary Production Titles:	The Honest Finder, Finders Keepers, Thieves and Lovers, The Golden Widow, A Very Private Scandal

Note:
    Hungarian playwright Aladar Laszlo's name is transposed on the screen.

Reviews:
    New York Times, Nov. 9, p. 28 and Nov. 13, IX.5; Variety, Nov. 15, p. 19; Film Daily, Nov. 10, p. 6; Motion Picture Herald, Oct. 29, p. 31; Harrison's Reports, Nov. 19, p. 186; New Yorker, Nov. 19; Time, Nov. 21, p. 28; Nation, Dec. 7, p. 576; Vanity Fair, Dec., p. 64; New Outlook, Dec., p. 47; Picture Play, Jan. 1933, pp. 46-47; Life, Jan. 1933, pp. 36-37; London Times, Dec. 15, p. 12; Illustrated London News, Dec. 17,

p. 972; New Statesman and Nation, Dec. 24, p. 833; Saturday Review, Dec. 24, p. 679; Theatre World (London), Jan. 1933, p. 42; Sight and Sound, Winter 1933, p. 121; L'Europe Nouvelle, June 17, 1933, p. 579; Scenario (Milan), Dec. 1933, p. 668.

Also see:
New York Herald Tribune, Nov. 20, VII.3; Photoplay, Apr. 1933, p. 99; Monthly Film Bulletin, Aug. 31, 1938, p. 205; Fifty Famous Films 1915-1945 (London: British Film Institute, 1961), pp. 70-72; Films in Review, Feb. 1964, p. 72; Eileen Bowser, Film Notes (New York: Museum of Modern Art, 1969), pp. 85-86; Richard Koszarski, "On Trouble in Paradise," Film Comment, Fall 1970, pp. 47-48.

69   IF I HAD A MILLION
      (1932)

John Glidden, an eccentric multimillionaire industrialist, is convinced he is going to die. To keep his fortune from falling into the hands of predatory relatives, he dispenses gift checks of a million dollars each to persons chosen at random from the city directory. A series of episodes demonstrates the reactions of the various recipients. (In the episode directed by Lubitsch, Charles Laughton plays Phineas V. Lambert, a lowly clerk in a vast office who, after receiving his check in the mail, calmly tucks it into the pocket of his jacket, rises and walks out slowly past his fellow workers seated at their desks, climbs several flights of stairs, goes through a series of outer doors, and arrives at last at the office of the president of the company. He pauses a moment to straighten his tie, knocks, opens the door, and gives the boss a hearty raspberry.) The last check goes to an elderly lady, Mary Walker, who uses it to restore life, hope, and bustle to the old age home where she resides. At the end John Glidden brushes his doctor aside and goes off to join Mrs. Walker and her elderly companions for a hayride.

Episode	Director	Players
Frame	Norman Taurog	Richard Bennett (John Glidden), Willard Robertson (First Lawyer, Fred)
The China Shop	Norman McLeod	Charlie Ruggles (Henry Peabody), Mary Boland (His Nagging Wife)
The Streetwalker	Stephen Roberts	Wynne Gibson (Violet Smith), Jack Pennick (Sailor)

The Auto	H. Bruce Humberstone	W. C. Fields (Rollo), Alison Skipworth (Emily LaRue)
The Forger	Stephen Roberts	George Raft (Edward Jackson)
The Condemned Man	James Cruze	Gene Raymond (John Wallace), Frances Dee (Mary Wallace), Grant Mitchell (Priest)
The Clerk	Ernst Lubitsch	Charles Laughton (Phineas V. Lambert)
Three Marines	William A. Seiter	Gary Cooper (Steven Gallagher), Jack Oakie (Mulligan), Roscoe Karns (Third Marine), Lucien Littlefield (Zeb), Joyce Compton (Marie)
Old Ladies Home	Edward Sutherland	May Robson (Mary Walker), Dewey Robinson (Cook)

Screenplay:	Claude Binyon, Whitney Bolton, Malcolm Stuart Boylan, John Bright, Sidney Buchman, Lester Cole, Isabel Dawn, Boyce DeGaw, Oliver H. P. Garrett, Harvey Gates, Grover Jones, Ernst Lubitsch, Lawton Mackall, Joseph L. Mankiewicz, William Slavens McNutt, Robert Sparks. Pressbook and most filmographies add: Walter DeLeon, Seton I. Miller, Tiffany Thayer.
Source:	The novel, Windfall (1931, republished in 1940 as If I Had a Million), by Robert D. Andrews
Production:	Paramount Pictures
New York Opening:	December 2
Running Time:	88 minutes

Notes:
  Various filmographies give conflicting director credits; some assign the frame and streetwalker episodes additionally

to Lubitsch. The above credits are based on Kenneth G. Lawrence, "The Academy's Retrospective," Films in Review (Jan.
1970), pp. 17-18, which describes a question-and-answer session with some of the original participants after a showing
of the film, in which several questions were put about the
directorial credits. In the same session it was also revealed
that the Lubitsch-Laughton sequence was shot quickly after the
film was completed to replace the "Condemned Man" episode,
which was eliminated after it got weak preview reactions.
This episode and the streetwalker episode are sometimes missing from the prints. An alternate take sans Bronx cheer was
shot for the British version of the Lubitsch episode. A
shooting script in the Margaret Herrick Library of the Academy
of Motion Picture Arts and Sciences contains additional episodes marked for Thornton Freeland and Lothar Mendes.

Reviews:
    New York Times, Dec. 3, p. 21 and Dec. 11, IX.7; Variety,
Dec. 6, p. 14; Film Daily, Dec. 3, p. 4; Motion Picture Her-
ald, Nov. 12, p. 35; New Yorker, Dec. 10; Time, Dec. 12,
p. 36; Nation, Dec. 21, pp. 624-25; National Board of Review
Magazine, Dec., pp. 9-11; London Times, Jan. 16, 1933, p. 14;
Saturday Review, Jan. 1933, p. 77; Bookman, June 1933, p. 171;
Cinema Quarterly (Edinburgh), Spring 1933, pp. 182-83; Les
Annales Politiques et Littéraires, Apr. 14, 1933, p. 432;
L'Europe Nouvelle, Apr. 22, 1933, p. 371.

Also see:
    Variety, Dec. 18, 1935, p. 7 (shortened reissue version);
Elsa Lanchester, Charles Laughton and I (New York: Harcourt,
Brace, 1938), pp. 108-109; Kurt Singer, The Laughton Story
(Philadelphia: John C. Winston, 1954), pp. 106-107.

70   DESIGN FOR LIVING
     (1933)

    A train bound for Paris, the present. A young woman comes
aboard outside of Marseilles. In her compartment two men are
sleeping. She takes out an artist's pad and begins to sketch
them. Shortly she falls asleep herself. The two wake up delighted to be in the company of such a lovely travelling companion. The three are Gilda Farrell, a commercial artist;
George Curtis, an avant-garde painter ("Lady Godiva on a Bi-
cycle"); and Tom Chambers, a writer of so-far unproduced plays.
The three-hour trip fortifies the interest of the two in Gilda,
and they are crestfallen when she is met in Paris by a fluttery

and rather stuffy looking gentleman who calls her darling. He is Max Plunkett, head of an advertising agency for which Gilda is on assignment. Her current project: sketches of Napoleon wearing a leading brand of underwear.

Max loves Gilda. Tom begins seeing her. Max remonstrates with him. When Tom puts some pompous advice of Max's into his new play--"Immorality may be fun, but it isn't fun enough to take the place of one hundred percent virtue and three square meals a day"--George realizes how it got there and confesses he's been seeing Gilda too. Gilda comes to their apartment and also makes a confession--"a thing happened to me that usually happens to a man": she fell in love with the two of them at the same time. After lengthy consideration by the three of them, Gilda proposes a solution: she will come and live with them, but under a "gentleman's agreement" that they will all forget about sex and concentrate on work. She will inspire them and spur them on to their best efforts.

Gilda pushes Tom to finish his play and brazens her way in to get it read by a London producer. It is accepted and Tom sets out for London. The play is a smash hit. Meanwhile, back in Paris George and Gilda break off the agreement and re-new their affair. They let Tom know by letter, and sadly he sends them good wishes.

One evening Tom sees Max in the audience and learns from him that Gilda and George are fine and George's paintings are the rage of Paris. On impulse Tom decides to run over at once and look them up. George is away on a commission when he ar-rives, and now Tom and Gilda allow their true feelings for one another to come out once again. Next morning George returns unexpectedly to find them having breakfast together, and he socks Tom on the jaw. Gilda goes to pack, presumably to go away with Tom, but actually she goes away alone leaving fare-well notes for each of them. The two old friends settle down and get drunk together. The liquor, Tom declares, is "good for our immortal souls."

Gilda has gone back to New York with Max. When we see them inspecting beds in a store window in New York (Max is measur-ing the width of the beds and then measuring the width of the two of them) we realize she has consented to marry him. Gilda is suffering an unbearably dull life with Max when one day the boys arrive unannounced from China. They pose as policemen and are admitted to a party Gilda and Max are giving for Max's business friends. They hide in Gilda's bedroom and surprise her when she retreats there in desperation to escape the boring games and amateur entertainments of the guests. Soon after the boys join the party and reduce it to a shambles with their pranks. As Max is telephoning to placate his departed client-guests, Gilda, Tom, and George set off in a taxi determined to return to Paris and to resume their "gentleman's agreement."

Director:	Ernst Lubitsch
Screenplay:	Ben Hecht
Source:	The play, <u>Design for Living</u> (1933), by Noel Coward
Photography:	Victor Milner
Art Director:	Hans Dreier
Musical Direction:	Nat Finston
Editor:	Frances Marsh
Costumes:	Travis Banton
Recording Engineer:	M. M. Paggi
Assistant Director:	George Hippard
Cast:	Fredric March (Tom Chambers), Gary Cooper (George Curtis), Miriam Hopkins (Gilda Farrell), Edward Everett Horton (Max Plunkett), Franklin Pangborn (Mr. Douglas, London Producer), Isabel Jewell (Lisping Stenographer), Jane Darwell (Housekeeper), Wyndham Standing (Max's Butler), Harry Dunkinson (Mr. Egelbauer), Helena Phillips (Mrs. Egelbauer), James Donlin (Fat Man), Vernon Steele (First Manager), Thomas Braidon (Second Manager), Armand Kaliz (Mr. Burton), Adrienne d'Ambricourt (Proprietress of Cafe), Nora Cecil (Tom's Secretary), Emile Chautard (Conductor), Mrs. Treboal (Gilda's Landlady), George Savidan (Boy), Cosmo Bellew (Bassington's Voice), Barry Winton (Edgar's Voice). Homer Dickens, <u>Films of Gary Cooper</u> (New York: Citadel, 1970) adds: Grace Hayle (Woman on Staircase), Olaf Hytten (Englishman at Train), Mary Gordon (Theater Chambermaid), Lionel Belmore, Charles K. French (Theater Patrons), Rolfe Sedan (Bed Salesman), Mathilde Comont.

Production:	Ernst Lubitsch for Paramount
Shooting:	Begun in early July at the Paramount Studios in Hollywood and continued through September
Running Time:	90 minutes
New York Opening:	November 22

Notes:

Samuel Hoffenstein is also said to have worked on the script (New York Sun, May 1, p. 27; press interview with Lubitsch and Hecht). Gottfried Reinhardt had his first professional experience in Hollywood as Lubitsch's personal assistant on this picture.

Reviews:

New York Times, Nov. 23, p. 24 and Dec. 3, IX.9; Variety, Nov. 28, p. 20; Motion Picture Herald, Nov. 25, p. 35; Daily Variety, Oct. 23, pp. 3-4; Hollywood Reporter, Oct. 23, p. 3; Film Daily, Nov. 17, p. 11 and Nov. 23, p. 1; New Yorker, Nov. 25; Time, Nov. 27, pp. 30-31; Newsweek, Dec. 2, p. 33; Nation, Dec. 6, pp. 660-61; Literary Digest, Dec. 9, p. 29; New Outlook, Jan. 1934, p. 43; Vanity Fair, Jan. 1934, pp. 45-46; London Times, Jan. 22, 1934, p. 10; Spectator, Jan. 26, 1934, p. 119; Saturday Review, Jan. 27, 1934, p. 107; Monthly Film Bulletin, May 1934, p. 28; Cinema Quarterly (Edinburgh), Spring, 1934, p. 188; Les Annales Politiques et Littéraires, Mar. 23, 1934, p. 331; L'Europe Nouvelle, Apr. 28, 1934, p. 436; Scenario (Milan), June 1934, pp. 330-31.

Also see:

Variety, Mar. 7, p. 3, Mar. 21, p. 8, Apr. 4, p. 11, Apr. 25, p. 3, p. 6, May 2, p. 3, May 9, p. 20, May 16, pp. 2, 25 (interview with Ben Hecht), June 13, p. 6; London Observer, Sept. 24, p. 10 (interview with Lubitsch); New York Sun, Nov. 11, p. 14 (interview with Lubitsch); Village Voice, May 9, 1963, p. 17.

71 THE MERRY WIDOW
(1934)

Marshovia, a central European kingdom so small it can only be seen with a magnifying glass on a map, 1885. Captain Danilo of the Royal Guard, marching at the head of a procession of soldiers, sees a lady in mourning wearing a veil pass in a carriage. Cut to a café with plaintive gypsy violin music playing, as nearby the lady walks in her garden. Captain

Danilo climbs over her garden wall, professes his attraction
to her, and pleads with her to take off the veil. She acts
uninterested and sends him away, but later asks her serving
ladies where he lives and writes about him in her diary. After several sleepless nights she puts off her mourning and
goes to Paris.

A wire from the Marshovian ambassador informs the King that
Madame Sonia is a big hit in Paris; fortune hunters are arriving daily to court her, and he is afraid she may marry a for-
eigner. King Achmed is alarmed because she is the richest
woman in Marshovia and the loss of her taxes would bankrupt
the country. The King decides to send a special envoy to
Paris to marry Sonia and bring her back. When he discovers
that Danilo is having an affair with the Queen, he decides to
send him.

In Paris Sonia hears Danilo singing "I'm Going to Maxim's"
in the street and decides to follow him there. Danilo and the
Marshovian ambassador meet one another after they get into a
scrape over a girl at Maxim's; the ambassador tells him of a
huge ball to be held in Sonia's honor the next evening. When
she arrives at Maxim's, Sonia is mistaken for one of the girls.
She passes herself off to Danilo as "Fifi," and leads him on
so that he admits freely all he wants is one night of love.
Sonia calls in the other girls and, as she leaves, assures him
"there's not a tomorrow among them."

After the ball has begun and Danilo still has not arrived,
the ambassador sends Danilo's orderly out to look for him. As
the orderly and the Maxim's girls are dressing the drunken
Danilo, he discloses the secret mission. Danilo protests to
the ambassador that he cannot carry out the mission because of
his love for another woman, but the ambassador orders him to
go through with it. When they meet, Danilo assures Sonia that
he fell in love with her as Fifi. She tells him Fifi is dead
and refuses to put any stock in what he says. Their argument
is suspended while they dance the "Merry Widow Waltz," as they
had done the night before at Maxim's. Meanwhile, a telegram
arrives from the King saying the secret mission is now public
knowledge, thanks to the Maxim's girls, and that Danilo must
marry the widow tonight before the opposition newspaper pub-
lishes the news. Just as Sonia and Danilo are about to be
reconciled, the ambassador prematurely announces their engagement. Sonia overhears the ambassador talking to Danilo of the
mission and the telegram, and breaks off with Danilo again.
Danilo says publicly the announcement was made without Sonia's

consent or knowledge and there is no engagement. Danilo is taken back to Marshovia under arrest. Sonia resumes her merry life in Paris.

Sonia shows up at Danilo's trial. She testifies he did his patriotic duty--he betrayed her, not his country. Nevertheless, he is convicted and sent to prison. The King and the Queen are packing in anticipation of bankruptcy and exile when word comes that Sonia has requested to visit Danilo in prison. The King orders them locked up together in the cell. They vow that they will not be forced into a reconciliation, but when the gypsies start playing the "Merry Widow Waltz" outside the cell, they cannot resist. A priest appears to marry them through the peephole.

Director:	Ernst Lubitsch
Screenplay:	Ernest Vajda and Samson Raphaelson
Source:	Franz Lehár's operetta, <u>Die lustige Witwe</u> (1905), libretto and lyrics by Victor Leon [pseud. Victor Hirschfeld] and Leo Stein [pseud. Leo Rosenstein]
Photography:	Oliver T. Marsh
Art Director:	Cedric Gibbons (Academy Award)
Associates:	Fredric Hope, Edwin B. Willis, and Gabriel Scognamillo
Music:	Franz Lehár
Musical Adaptation:	Herbert Stothart
Additional Music:	Richard Rodgers
Additional Lyrics:	Lorenz Hart and Gus Kahn
Editor:	Frances Marsh
Costumes:	Ali Hubert
Miss MacDonald's Gowns:	Adrian
Choreography:	Albertina Rasch
Recording Director:	Douglas Shearer
Assistant Directors:	Joe Newman, Joe Lefert
Business Manager:	Eric Locke
Cast:	Maurice Chevalier (Danilo), Jeanette MacDonald (Sonia), Edward Everett Horton (Ambassador), Una Merkel (Queen), George Barbier (King), Minna Gombell (Marcele), Ruth Channing (Lulu), Sterling Holloway (Orderly), Henry Armetta (Turk), Barbara Leonard (Maid), Donald Meek (Valet), Akim Tamiroff (Manager of Maxim's),

126

Herman Bing (Zizipoff), Lucien Prival (Adamovitch). Call Bureau Cast Service List of Aug. 4, 1934, adds: Luana Walters, Sheila Mannors [later Sheila Bromley], Caryl Lincoln, Edna Waldron, Lona Andre (Sonia's Maids), Patricia Farley, Shirley Chambers, Maria Troubetskoy, Eleanor Hunt, Jean Hart, Dorothy Wilson, Barbara Barondess, Dorothy Granger, Jill Bennett, Mary Jane Halsey, Peggy Watts, Dorothy Dehn, Connie Lamont (Maxim's Girls), Charles Requa, George Lewis, Tyler Brooke, John Merkyl, Cosmo Bellew (Escorts), Roger Gray, Christian J. Frank, Otto Fries, George Magrill, John Roach (Policemen), Gino Corrado, Perry Ivins (Waiters), Kathleen Burke [Virginia Field] (Prisoner), George Baxter (Ambassador), Paul Ellis (Dancer), Leonid Kinskey (Shepherd), Evelyn Selbie (Newspaper Woman), Wedgwood Nowell (Lackey), Richard Carle (Defense Attorney), Morgan Wallace (Prosecuting Attorney), Frank Sheridan (Judge), Arthur "Pop" Byron (Doorman), Claudia Coleman (Wardrobe Mistress), Lee Tin (Excited Chinaman), Nora Cecil (Animal Woman), Tom Frances (Orthodox Priest), Winter Hall (Nondescript Priest), Matty Rupert (Newsboy), Ferdinand Munier (Jailer), Dewey Robinson, Russell Powell, Billy Gilbert (Fat Lackeys), Arthur Housman, Johnny "Skins" Miller (Drunks), Hector Sarno (Gypsy Leader), Jan Rubini (Practical Violinist), Jason Robards Sr. (Arresting Officer), Albert Pollet (Head Waiter), Rolfe Sedan (Gabrielovitsch), Jacques Lory (Goatherd). Knowles (1975) adds: Lane Chandler (Soldier). <u>Kosmorama</u> (1976) adds: George Davies, Dorothy Nelson, Erik Rhodes.

Songs: "Girls, Girls, Girls," "Vilia," "Tonight Will Teach Me to Forget," "I'm Going to Maxim's," "Melody of Laughter," "The Merry Widow Waltz," "Widows Are Gay"

Production: Ernst Lubitsch for Metro-Goldwyn-
                               Mayer; Executive Producer Irving
                               Thalberg's name did not appear on
                               the screen, in accord with his usual
                               practice
Shooting: Begun the week of April 9 at MGM
                               Culver City Studios; principal
                               photography completed July 23,
                               after approximately thirteen
                               weeks (days of shooting: 88)
Running Time: Previewed at 110 minutes; released
                               at 99 minutes; English language re-
                               issue version 103 minutes
New York Premiere: October ·11
Other Title: Renamed The Lady Dances by MGM
                               after the 1952 remake

Notes:
   "Four versions of The Merry Widow are being made simultaneously by Ernst Lubitsch at Metro, the most ambitious effort of
any director to date. Film is intended for domestic, English,
French, and Belgium markets with but two languages being dia-
loged. Certain scenes in the picture are being emphasized for
the English speaking audiences and others played down for foreign consumption. Few substitutes being used on account of
lingual difficulties" (Variety, June 19, p. 2). For cast list
and other information on the French-language version, La Veuve
joyeuse, see Ringgold and Bodeen (1973), pp. 122-29. For information on the censorship cuts see Knowles (1975), p. 116.
In Mayer and Thalberg: The Make-Believe Saints (New York:
Random House, 1975, p. 262), Samuel Marx reports that The Merry Widow cost $1,605,000 and showed a loss of $113,000 on
world-wide returns after five years from date of release.

Reviews:
   New York Times, Oct. 12, p. 33; Variety, Oct. 16, p. 12;
Film Daily, Oct. 13, p. 4; Motion Picture Herald, Sept. 8,
p. 34; Daily Variety, Sept. 1, p. 3; Hollywood Reporter,
Sept. 1, p. 3; Harrison's Reports, Oct. 20, p. 166; New
Yorker, Oct. 20; Time, Oct. 22, pp. 42-43; Literary Digest,
Oct. 27, p. 34; New Masses, Nov. 6, pp. 29-30; Nation,
Nov. 14, p. 574; New Republic, Nov. 21, p. 46; Life, Dec.,
p. 34; London Times, Nov. 26, p. 10; Spectator, Nov. 30,
p. 836; Monthly Film Bulletin, Nov., p. 92; Saturday Review,
Dec. 1, p. 477; Theatre World (London), Jan. 1935, pp. 38,
40; Sight and Sound, Winter 1934/35, pp. 165-66.

Also see:
   Variety, June 20, 1928, p. 10 (possible MGM sound version),
Oct. 15, 1930, p. 3, Oct. 22, 1930, p. 3 (a projected

Lubitsch-MacDonald-Chevalier Merry Widow for MGM), Oct. 29, 1930, p. 3, Oct. 20, 1931, p. 3, Jan. 26, 1932, p. 3 (a MacDonald-Ramon Navarro Merry Widow for MGM), July 4, 1933, p. 3, July 11, 1933, p. 3 (Sidney Franklin to direct Chevalier and Mac-Donald in MGM remake), July 25, 1933, p. 3, Sept. 5, 1933, p. 11, Nov. 21, 1933, p. 3, Dec. 19, 1933, p. 2, Dec. 26, 1933, p. 2, Jan. 23, p. 4, Jan. 30, p. 3, Feb. 6, p. 3, Feb. 20, p. 3, Feb. 27, p. 3, Mar. 6, p. 11, Mar. 13, p. 3, Apr. 17, p. 3, July 10, p. 2, July 24, p. 4, Aug. 21, p. 6; New York Herald Tribune, July 8, V.3, Oct. 7, V.3; New York Daily News, July 15, p. 52; Motion Picture Herald, Aug. 25, p. 48; Motion Picture Daily, Oct. 12, p. 2 and Oct. 22, p. 19 (excerpts reviews in nine New York newspapers); Hollywood Reporter, Oct. 13, p. 1; "Ernst Lubitsch Comments on The Merry Widow and Some Movie Problems," New York Sun, Oct. 17, p. 33; Daily Film Renter, Nov. 16, p. 17 and Nov. 29, p. 1 (lists British newspapers that reviewed the picture); Grace Moore, You're Only Human Once (Garden City, N.Y.: Doubleday, Doran, 1944), pp. 199-200; Cinema (Milan), Nov. 15, 1950, pp. 280-81; Bosley Crowther, The Lion's Share: The Story of an Entertainment Empire (New York: E. P. Dutton, 1957), pp. 216-18; Bernard Rosenberg and Harry Silverstein, The Real Tinsel (New York: Macmillan, 1970), pp. 230-31 (gives Lubitsch's views on the direction of the French version of Merry Widow); Cinéma (Paris), Mar. 1972, pp. 148-49; Women's Wear Daily, Sept. 26, 1974, p. 16; Anita Loos, Kiss Hollywood Good-by (New York: Viking, 1974), pp. 166-67.

72   DESIRE
      (1936)

    Paris, the present. At an overseas office of an American automobile company, Tom Bradley, an engineer from Detroit, is granted his request for a vacation and given a company car to take with him. The car is to carry an advertising slogan, "I am happy to drive a Bronson 8." Outside in traffic, Tom's car bumps into another car, which, however, continues on its way.

    The other car pulls up at an exclusive jewelry store, Duvalle and Company. A smart-looking woman emerges and enters the store. Inside she selects a rare and expensive pearl necklace and instructs the jeweler to deliver it that evening to her husband, the renowned psychiatrist, Dr. Maurice Pauquet.

    The woman, who is really Madeleine de Beaupré, a jewel thief, hurries to Dr. Pauquet's office and informs the doctor that her husband, the famous jeweler Duvalle, suffers from hallucinations and has the embarrassing habit of presenting bills to people who do not owe him a cent. When the jeweler arrives, Madeleine takes the pearls from him and sends him in to see the doctor. Duvalle presents the doctor with a bill and the doctor goes to work treating his interesting new patient. Madeleine drives away with the necklace.

On his way to Spain, Tom Bradley gets out of his car and sets up his camera to take a self-portrait. But just as he is about to snap the photograph, a car speeds by and splashes him with mud. Tom chases after the female culprit who ruined his picture. He catches up to her in a small village. It is Madeleine; the horn on her car is stuck; Tom comes to her rescue and fixes it.

At the border, Madeleine places the stolen necklace in Tom's coat pocket as they are passing through customs. She gets through, but Tom is detained for smuggling cigarettes. Madeleine invents car trouble on the road. Tom stops and gives her a lift. After much coaxing, she convinces him to put on his jacket, which he has removed and locked in his suitcase. But Tom returns with a new jacket. When he later goes back to clean off the Bronson 8 sign, Madeleine drives off with the car, leaving him standing dumbfounded in the middle of the road, the suitcase with the pearls in it at his side.

Madeleine abandons the car and takes a train to San Sebastian. Posing as a countess, she checks into an exclusive hotel, where she is visited by her accomplice, "Prince" Carlos Margoli. Newspaper headlines proclaim that the jewel thieves have been traced to Spain. Carlos informs Madeleine they must leave that evening, once they have retrieved the pearls.

A police official arrives and apologizes for disturbing the royal couple, but explains that an American gentleman has made a complaint about a woman who fits the Countess' description taking his car. Madeleine assures the policeman it is no bother and insists on seeing the American. When Tom enters, Carlos pretends to be shocked over his niece's conduct and says he will be forced to punish her. Tom intercedes on her behalf. Tom accepts Madeleine's apology and agrees to take Carlos' check for full restitution. By this time Tom has fallen completely in love with Madeleine, and he eagerly agrees to accompany the royal pair to the country.

In the country Tom dresses for dinner. Lacking formal attire, he dons the sport coat with the necklace in the pocket. Madeleine wears an imitation pearl necklace. When she tries to retrieve the real pearls at dinner, Tom thinks she is flirting with him. After dinner Carlos performs magic tricks. Madeleine removes her necklace and Carlos makes it "appear" in Tom's coat pocket. Taken in by the trick, Tom hands over the real necklace to Carlos. In private, Carlos warns Madeleine not to get emotionally involved.

130

Tom confesses his love to Madeleine while she pretends to sleep. The sound of sirens interrupts him. Madeleine becomes scared and realizes the hopelessness of the life she lives. She recalls Tom's expression of love and the two embrace.

In the morning Carlos awakens Madeleine to tell her Aunt Olga has sent a telegram; he must leave immediately and get rid of Tom in town. But Tom will not be persuaded to leave Madeleine, and Carlos leaves alone. At the breakfast table, Madeleine and Tom talk of love. Aunt Olga, Madeleine's veteran partner in crime, arrives to try to convince Madeleine to leave for Madrid, where they can sell the necklace. When Madeleine refuses, Aunt Olga confesses she once fell in love with a doctor, but realized the impossibility for someone in her situation to be married. Tom is packing for their honeymoon when Madeleine informs him she cannot go through with the marriage. Tom confesses his job is not as important as he led her to believe. Madeleine then owns up to her own past and confesses her love for Tom.

To Carlos' dismay, Madeleine insists that Tom stay for dinner. Tom proposes a toast, first to Madeleine who stole his car and then his heart, and then to Aunt Olga, whose doctor should have stuck by her if he really was in love with her. Intending to flee with the pearls, Carlos pulls a gun, but Tom kicks the table and causes the gun to fall into the fricassee, which is taken away by a servant. Carlos overturns the table and runs but Tom goes after him.

Madeleine is instantly recognized when she and Tom arrive at Duvalle's. However, they ask that they be allowed to return the necklace and that the charges against them be dropped. Duvalle (who is now a patient of Dr. Pauquet's) agrees to take the pearls back, but says Madeleine's debt to the state is another matter.

In a marriage counselor's office, Tom fumbles for their marriage license and pulls out Madeleine's parole papers instead. When the couple are asked to present witnesses, Duvalle and Dr. Pauquet come forth to sanction the marriage.

Director: Frank Borzage
Retakes: Ernst Lubitsch
Screenplay: Edwin Justus Mayer, Waldemar Young, and Samuel Hoffenstein
Source: The play, <u>Die schönen Tage von Aranjuez</u> (apparently unproduced), by Hans Székely and Robert Adolf Stemmle
Photography: Charles Lang
Art Directors: Hans Dreier and Robert Usher
Interior Decoration: A. E. Freudeman

Editor:	William Shea
Costumes:	Travis Banton
Music and Lyrics:	Frederick Hollander and Leo Robin
Special Photographic Effects:	Farciot Edouart and Harry Perry
Sound Recording:	Harry Mills and Don Johnson
Location Photography in Europe:	Eric Locke
Cast:	Marlene Dietrich (Madeleine de Beaupré), Gary Cooper (Tom Bradley), John Halliday (Carlos Margoli), William Frawley (Mr. Gibson), Ernest Cossart (Aristide Duvalle), Akim Tamiroff (Police Official), Alan Mowbray (Dr. Maurice Pauquet), Zeffie Tilbury (Aunt Olga), Enrique Acosta (Pedro), Alice Feliz (Pepi), Stanley Andrews (Customs Inspector). Homer Dickens, Films of Marlene Dietrich (New York: Citadel, 1968) adds: Harry Depp (Clerk), Marc Lawrence (Valet), Henry Antrim (Chauffeur), Armand Kaliz, Gaston Glass (Jewelry Clerks), Albert Pollet (French Policeman), George Davis (Garage Man), Constant Franke (Border Official), Robert O'Connor (Customs Official), Rafael Blanco (Driver of Haywagon), Alden Chase (Clerk in Hotel), Tony Merlo (Waiter), Anna Delinsky (Servant), George MacQuarrie (Clerk with Gun), Isabel LaMal (Nurse), Oliver Eckhardt (Husband), Blanche Craig (Wife), Rollo Lloyd (Clerk in Mayor's Office), Alfonso Pedrosa (Oxcart Driver).
Production:	Ernst Lubitsch for Paramount
Shooting:	Begun September 16, 1935, at the Paramount Studios in Hollywood and completed December 21, 1935
Running Time:	Sources vary from 89 to 99 minutes. First shown at 9700 ft., then cut down to around 8000 ft., then some of the cuts were restored. Library of Congress print is 8585 ft. [2617m].
New York Opening:	April 11
Temporary Production Title:	The Pearl Necklace

Notes:
Of the films made under Lubitsch while he was production head at Paramount, Desire was the one most fully supervised by him. Lubitsch's influence on the subject matter and visual style of the film is quite apparent. Also: "Paramount's rewrite of three sequences of Marlene Dietrich starrer, Desire, to smooth continuity in one spot will require day and a half to shoot. With director Frank Borzage making the Marion Davies picture at Warners and unavailable to handle the job, Ernst Lubitsch will direct added shots" (Daily Variety, Feb. 4, p. 3). It is interesting in light of Hays Office practices at the time to compare the endings in two versions of the script (both in the Margaret Herrick Library at the Academy of Motion Picture Arts and Sciences): in "Final" 11/4/35 Dietrich and Cooper go off free after the jeweler intercedes with the Minister of Justice's wife; in 11/4/35 revisions 11/20/35 Dietrich pays her debt to France, reforms, gets paroled, and marries Tom, as it appears on the screen. Some sources also give a photography credit to Victor Milner.

Reviews:
New York Times, Apr. 13, p. 15 and Apr. 19, IX.3; Variety, Apr. 15, p. 16; Film Daily, Feb. 4, p. 10; Motion Picture Herald, Feb. 8, p. 55; Daily Variety, Jan. 31, p. 3; Hollywood Reporter, Jan. 31, p. 3; Literary Digest, Mar. 7, p. 21; Newsweek, Mar. 7, p. 32; Time, Mar. 9, p. 47; New Republic, Apr. 1, p. 222; New Yorker, Apr. 18; Life, June, pp. 22-23; London Times, Mar. 30, p. 10; Illustrated London News, Apr. 4, p. 600; Spectator, Apr. 3, p. 616; Saturday Review, Apr. 4, p. 448; Monthly Film Bulletin, Apr. 30, p. 64; Theatre World, May, p. 238; Motion Picture Review Digest, Mar. 30, pp. 40-41.

Also see:
Variety, Jan. 29, 1935, p. 4, May 15, 1935, p. 3, Sept. 18, 1935, p. 6, Nov. 13, 1935, p. 4, May 20, p. 2; Hollywood Reporter, July 5, 1935, p. 3, Nov. 4, 1935, p. 4, Feb. 5, p. 1, Feb. 10, p. 1; New York Times, Feb. 9, X.5; Films in Review, Dec. 1965, p. 653; Eileen Bowser, Film Notes (New York: Museum of Modern Art, 1969), pp. 97-98; John Belton, The Hollywood Professionals, Vol. 3: Hawks, Borzage, Ulmer (London: Tantivy; and New York: A. S. Barnes, 1974), pp. 75-76.

73   ANGEL
(1937)

Paris, the 1930s. A lady checks in to a fashionable hotel; though she signs the register as "Mrs. Brown," the name on her passport is Maria Barker. In her handbag is a note that reads "Club de la Russe, 314 rue de la Tour." Cut to a man getting out of a taxi at this address. It is an establishment belonging to the Grand Duchess Anna Dmitrievna—a salon and cocktail lounge and gambling casino where, as we learn, romantic "arrangements" are also made. The gentleman, Anthony Halton, presents his card, and as he waits in the reception room to see the Grand Duchess, Maria Barker arrives and asks to be announced as an "old friend." It becomes clear that she and the Duchess were once closely associated; possibly Maria was one of those for whom the Duchess made arrangements. When the Duchess receives a private telephone call, Maria steps into the next room, where Anthony Halton is waiting. He assumes she is the Duchess; she, finding him interesting, plays along and pretends to misunderstand his wish to have an "amusing time." She suggests the Louvre and the Eiffel Tower and, when he stresses it's companionship he wants, offers to arrange a party for him. He begs her to dine with him. She hesitates but finally accepts and, as she is leaving, confesses she's not the Duchess. When the real Duchess does come in, he says all he wants is to know the name of the lady he just met. The Duchess pretends she doesn't know.

Tony and Maria dine together at a little gypsy cafe. Their principal conversation is over names—he insisting to know who she is and all about her and she resisting. Over champagne in a private dining room she continues to be evasive about herself, and Tony declares he'll call her "Angel." He professes his love for her. Later, in the Bois de Bologne, Maria tells Tony to call for her next Wednesday at the Grand Duchess'. If she comes, she'll go anywhere with him; if she doesn't, he's to forget her. An old flower woman passes and as Tony is purchasing a bunch of violets Maria slips away.

London. Sir Frederick Barker returns from a mission to the League of Nations Conference in Geneva; that it was a great diplomatic success is announced in all the papers. When he arrives at his estate outside London he finds his wife asleep in his bedroom and, not wanting to disturb her, goes to her bedroom to sleep. An important telegram arrives in the middle of the night and is delivered to Lady Barker in Sir Frederick's room. When Frederick wakes up, she tells him a dream she was having—she wanted to kiss him at the League of Nations but he was giving a speech; she went around the world but when she got back he was still talking; finally she took him to Paris and as they walked in a park and started to kiss a knock at the door woke her. It was the telegram; it contains upsetting political news, and Frederick quickly becomes absorbed in its problem. Maria says good night and goes back to her own bed.

Breakfast the following morning. Both the Barkers are absorbed in the morning papers. There are no real complaints in their marriage, but there's no excitement either. After breakfast Maria goes into the salon and plays a tune she heard in

134

the cafe in Paris. She tells Frederick she made it up. He starts to play a tune they associate with a romantic time together in a little hotel in Vienna. Despite the routine they have fallen into in their marriage, clearly Maria still loves her husband.

At the racetrack Maria sees, of all people, Tony. She feigns a headache in order to get away. He is a house guest of Lord Davington, a friend of the Barkers. That Saturday at a get-together for the "boys" at Lord Davington's, Tony introduces himself to Frederick and says he knows him because they had a mutual girl friend in Paris during the war who kept a picture of Frederick in her apartment.

Later, as the Barkers are dressing for the opera, Frederick tells Maria about his new acquaintance, and of his story about the mystery woman he met at the Grand Duchess'. (Frederick puts it all in the sordid light the circumstances imply.) He says Tony is more determined than ever to see her again. Frederick says he's invited the fellow to lunch with them tomorrow.

After lunch next day there is a tense moment when Tony, at the piano, tries to remember a tune he heard in Paris with Angel (the one Maria told Frederick she made up), but Maria heads it off by taking over the piano and playing hers and Frederick's Viennese waltz. She reveals she and Frederick are going to Vienna this week (during the time the Paris rendezvous would have taken place). When Frederick is called from the room, Maria insists it's all to be forgotten, but Tony insists just as strongly he'll never give up. We hear Frederick in the background discussing a political problem on the telephone as Tony, taking his leave, says he'll be at the Grand Duchess' no matter what.

Frederick decides to go to Geneva and this means cancelling the trip to Vienna. This undermines Maria's determination not to go to Paris. She asks if he can drop her off in Paris on his way to Geneva so that she can do some shopping. While he is making arrangements he discovers that Maria chartered a plane to Paris the week before. When Frederick calls Tony at Lord Davington's (presumably to offer to take him to Paris too), he guesses the truth when over the receiver he hears a piano playing Maria's song.

Tony arrives at the Grand Duchess'. Frederick arrives shortly after. Maria enters and is surprised to see Frederick. But she is resolute: she will not go on as before. She goes in to Tony. As she wavers in her decision Frederick enters the room, says the train for Vienna leaves at ten o'clock, and tells her she must say goodbye to Angel forever if she decides to meet him at the station. As he walks toward the entrance hall, Maria catches up to him and they leave together.

Director:	Ernst Lubitsch
Screenplay:	Samson Raphaelson
Source:	The play, Angyal, by Melchior Leng-yel and its English adaptation by Guy Bolton and Russell Medcraft
Photography:	Charles Lang
Art Direction:	Hans Dreier and Robert Usher
Interior Decoration:	A. E. Freudeman
Editor:	William Shea
Costumes:	Travis Banton
Original Music:	Frederick Hollander
Lyrics:	Leo Robin
Musical Direction:	Boris Morros
Special Photographic Effects:	Farciot Edouart
Sound Recording:	Harry Mills and Louis Mesenkop
General Manager:	John Hammell
Assistant Director:	Joseph Lefert
Cast:	Marlene Dietrich (Maria Barker), Herbert Marshall (Sir Frederick Barker), Melvyn Douglas (Anthony Halton), Edward Everett Horton (Graham), Ernest Cossart (Walton), Laura Hope Crews (Grand Duchess Anna Dmitrievna), Herbert Mundin (Greenwood), Dennie Moore (Emma). Homer Dickens, Films of Marlene Dietrich (New York: Citadel, 1968), adds: Ivan Lebedeff (Prince Vladimir Gregorovitch), Lionel Pape (Lord Davington), Phillis Coghlan (Maid in Barker Home), Leonard Carey (First Footman), Eric Wilton (English Chauffeur), Gerald Hamer (Second Footman), Herbert Evans (Butler), Michael S. Visaroff (Russian Butler), Olaf Hytten (Photographer), Gwendolyn Logan (Woman with Maria), James Finlayson (Second Butler), George Davis, Arthur Hurni (Taxi Drivers), Joseph Romantini (Headwaiter), Duci Kerekjarto (Prima Violinist), Suzanne Kaaren (Girl Who Gambles), Louise Carter (Flower Woman). Kosmorama (1976) adds: Gino Corrado (Assistant Manager of Hotel), Major Sam Harris (Man at Club).
Production:	Ernst Lubitsch for Paramount

Shooting: Begun at the Paramount Studios in
                         Hollywood late in March and completed
                         June 14, with location shooting in
                         Europe in June by Harry Perry and
                         Eric Locke (days of shooting: 73)
Running Time: Listed at 89 and 98 minutes
Released: October 29
New York Opening: November 3

Note:
   Frederick Lonsdale worked on the script briefly and is
listed for screenplay contribution in Academy Screen Achieve-
ment Records.

Reviews:
   New York Times, Nov. 4, p. 29; Variety, Sept. 15, p. 13 and
Nov. 10, p. 6; Motion Picture Herald, Sept. 25, pp. 44, 49;
Daily Variety, Sept. 14, p. 3; Hollywood Reporter, Sept. 14,
p. 3; Film Daily, Sept. 17, p. 13; Literary Digest, Oct. 30,
p. 34; New Yorker, Nov. 6; Newsweek, Nov. 8, pp. 22-23; Time,
Nov. 8, p. 48; London Times, Nov. 10, p. 12; New Statesman and
Nation, Nov. 13, p. 795; Spectator, Nov. 26, p. 949; Monthly
Film Bulletin, Nov. 30, p. 244; Theatre World, Dec., p. 294;
Cinema (Milan), Sept. 10, no. 29, p. 161, Nov. 10, no. 33,
pp. 320-21, Jan. 10, 1938, no. 37, pp. 25-26; Les Annales
Politiques et Littéraires, Dec. 25, pp. 684-85; Motion Picture
Review Digest, Dec. 27, pp. 5-6.

Also see:
   Film Daily, Sept. 25, 1936, pp. 1-2; Variety, Aug. 26,
1936, p. 3, June 2, p. 6, Sept. 1, p. 3; New York Times,
Apr. 25, X.3, Nov. 7, XI.6; New York Sun, Aug. 27, p. 6 (press
interview with Lubitsch); Film Society Review, Sept. 1965,
p. 15; Positif, Oct. 1971, no. 131, pp. 64-66; Dossiers du
Cinéma (Paris: Casterman, 1971-   ), Films III, pp. 5-8;
Jugend Film Fennsehen, vol. 17, no. 2 (1973), 107.

74   BLUEBEARD'S EIGHTH WIFE
     (1938)

   The French Riviera, the present. Millionaire Michael Brandon tries to buy only the tops of a pair of pajamas at an elegant department store. The incident is immediately brought to
the attention of the store president, who answers the telephone clad only in a pajama top, becomes indignant, and pronounces it "Communism." A fortunate solution is arrived at,
however, when Nicole de Loiselle, overhearing all the fuss,
offers to purchase only the bottoms of a mutually selected
pair.

When Michael can't fall asleep that night, he follows Nicole's tried-and-true formula, to spell Czechoslovakia backwards, pausing between each letter. It doesn't work. He then asks for quarters in his hotel more conducive to sleep. In the bed in the new room is Nicole's father, the penniless Marquis de Loiselle, wearing the bottoms to Michael's pajamas. The Marquis realizes when Michael receives a phone call that he's the rich American he sent a business proposition to. Michael turns down the offer but realizes that the Marquis is Nicole's father and agrees to purchase an "antique" bathtub from him. He also informs the Marquis he is going to marry Nicole.

Michael finds Nicole on the beach with her garrulous friend and would-be suitor, Albert de Regnier. Michael realizes Albert is an employee of one of his banks and puts him to work as his secretary. Then, in accordance with his motto of always acting spontaneously, Michael asks Nicole to marry him. Though the Marquis is delighted at the financial prospect of the marriage, Nicole is reluctant and only gradually relents.

The de Loiselle relatives assemble for photographs two weeks before the wedding. When rice falls from Michael's pocket, he explains to Nicole that he has been married seven times before. He is divorced from his previous wives but he left them financially well off. Nicole calls off the wedding. The Marquis faints. Finally Nicole is persuaded to go through with it, but only on condition that she receive twice the usual divorce settlement of $50,000.

During their honeymoon in Czechoslovakia, Nicole refuses to orgive Michael for thinking of their honeymoon as a business ɹoposition, and he has to try to spell Czechoslovakia backwards again to fall asleep. She is a wife in name only; the two live in separate sections of their apartment and rarely meet. Nicole buys the book Live Alone and Like It; Michael reads The Taming of the Shrew.

Michael hires a detective to follow Nicole. Aware that she is being watched, Nicole stops the detective one day and forces him to reveal her husband's plan: he is not really going away on business that evening; he will return early and surprise her. Nicole hires a prizefighter to be in her room when Michael returns. Her plans misfire when Albert comes over and the fighter knocks him out cold, but Nicole sees she can use Albert as the alleged other man. Michael arrives home to find the old admirer in Nicole's room.

Newspaper headlines announce the Brandon divorce has been granted. Michael suffers a breakdown from the stress and enters a sanitarium. After Nicole is denied access to the

building where Michael is, the Marquis marches over indignant-
ly, raps at the door, barks loudly, and is ushered in. The
Marquis arranges to buy the sanitarium so Nicole may see Michael. In a strait jacket Michael is no match for Nicole.
She conquers her true lover on her own terms, and the couple
are reunited.

Director:	Ernst Lubitsch
Screenplay:	Charles Brackett and Billy Wilder
Source:	The play, <u>La Huitième Femme de Barbe-bleue</u> (1921), by Alfred Savoir and its American adaptation by Charlton Andrews
Photography:	Leo Tover
Art Directors:	Hans Dreier and Robert Usher
Interior Decoration:	A. E. Freudeman
Editor:	William Shea
Costumes:	Travis Banton
Musical Director:	Boris Morros
Original Music:	Frederick Hollander and Werner R. Heymann
Orchestration:	John M. Leipold
Special Photographic Effects:	Farciot Edouart
Sound Recording:	Harry Mills and Don Johnson
Location Photography in Europe:	Eric Locke
Cast:	Claudette Colbert (Nicole de Loi-selle), Gary Cooper (Michael Brandon), Edward Everett Horton (Marquis de Loiselle), David Niven (Albert de Regnier), Elizabeth Patterson (Aunt Hedwige), Herman Bing (Monsieur Pepinard), Warren Hymer (Kid Mulli-gan), Franklin Pangborn, Armand Cortes (Assistant Hotel Managers), Rolfe Sedan (Floorwalker), Lawrence Grant (Professor Urganzeff), Lionel Pape (Monsieur Potin), Tyler Brooke (Clerk), Tom Ricketts (Uncle Andre), Barlowe Borland (Uncle Fernandel), Charles Halton (Monsieur de la Coste President), Sacha Guitry (Man in Front of Hotel). Call Bureau Cast Service list of January 18, 1938 also gives: Pauline Garon (Woman Customer), Ray de Ravenne (Package Clerk), Sheila Darcy (Maid), Blanche Franke (Cashier), Joseph Romantini (Headwaiter), Alphonse Martell (Ho-tel Employee), Harold Minjir

	(Photographer), Gino Corrado (Waiter Who Carries Horton), Alex Woloshin (First Porter), George Davis (Second Porter), Albert d'Arno (Newsboy), Mariska Aldrich (Nurse), Paul Gustin (Man in Steamship Office), Hooper Atchley (Excited Passenger), John Picorri (Conductor), Albert Petit (Railway Employee), Terry Ray [later Ellen Drew] (Secretary), Joseph Crehan (American Tourist), Wolfgang A. Zilzer (Clerk in Bookstore), Leon Ames (Ex-Chauffeur), Henry Roquemore (Fat Man), Sally Martin (Little Girl on Beach), Olaf Hytten (Valet), Grace Goodall (Nurse), Jimmie Dime (Prizefighter), Eugene Borden (Waiter on Stairs), Jean de Briac (Waiter in Corridor), Harry Lamont (Head Porter), Jacques Vanaire (Manager), Michael Visaroff (Vice-President), Paul Bryar (Radio Announcer), Barbara Jackson, Marie Burton, Joyce Mathews, Paula de Cardo, Gwen Kenyon, Suzanne Ridgway, Lola Jensen, Carol Parker, Dorothy Dayton, Norah Gale, Harriette Haddon, Ruth Rogers, Dorothy White, Gloria Williams (Girls).
Production:	Ernst Lubitsch for Paramount
Shooting:	Begun at the Paramount Studios in Hollywood October 11, 1937 and completed in January 1938, with second unit shooting in Europe for the backgrounds in August 1937 by Eric Locke
Running Time:	80 minutes
New York Premiere:	March 23
Released:	March 25

Notes:
Bluebeard's Eighth Wife, Charlton Andrews' adaptation of the Savoir play, opened on Broadway September 19, 1921; for cast and plot synopsis see Best Plays of 1921-22, p. 421. La Huitième Femme de Barbe-bleue returned to New York in a French-language version on January 26, 1936; see review in New York Times, January 27, 1936, p. 20.

Reviews:
New York Times, Mar. 24, p. 21; Variety, Mar. 23, p. 6 and p. 16; Motion Picture Herald, Mar. 26, pp. 39, 42; Daily

Variety, Mar. 17, pp. 3, 18; Hollywood Reporter, Mar. 17,
p. 3; Film Daily, Mar. 18, p. 4; New Yorker, Mar. 26; News-
week, Mar. 28, pp. 25-26; Time, Mar. 28, p. 38; New Republic,
Apr. 6, p. 275; Photoplay, May, p. 49; Stage, May, pp. 26-27;
London Times, Apr. 25, p. 12; New Statesman and Nation, Apr.
23, pp. 688-89; Spectator, Apr. 29, p. 747; Illustrated London
News, Apr. 30, p. 766; Monthly Film Bulletin, May 31, p. 134;
Motion Picture Review Digest, Apr. 4, p. 12.

Also see:
    Variety, June 30, 1937, p. 5, Aug. 25, 1937, p. 4, Oct. 13,
1937, p. 4; New York Times, Dec. 19, 1937, XI.7, Mar. 20,
XI.4; New York Times Magazine, Mar. 3, 1940, pp. 6, 13; John
Springer, "Charles Brackett," Films in Review, Mar. 1960,
pp. 130-31; Positif, no. 125, Mar. 1971, pp. 65-68; Tom Wood,
The Bright Side of Billy Wilder, Primarily (Garden City, N.Y.:
Doubleday, 1970), p. 61; David Niven, Bring on the Empty
Horses (New York: G. P. Putnam's, 1975), pp. 330-35.

75 NINOTCHKA
(1939)

Paris, the early 1920s. Three Russian trade emissaries--
Iranoff, Buljanoff, and Kopalski--try to decide whether to
check into the plush Hotel Clarence or to go to the cheaper
place where reservations have been made for them. They decide
Lenin would have said to consider the prestige of the Bolshe-
viks, and go to the Clarence. The only safe in the hotel big
enough to accommodate a large suitcase with valuables is in the
Royal Suite. After searching their Party principles once
again, they take it.

Once they are installed in the Royal Suite, Iranoff telephones a jeweler to tell him they have arrived safely with
the jewels confiscated after the Revolution from Grand Duchess
Swana. A room service waiter (who, it turns out, is Russian
emigré Count Rakonin) overhears the call and hurries off to
tell the Duchess, who is living in Paris. Swana is with her
gentleman friend Count Leon d'Algout when Rakonin arrives.
Swana's lawyer says there's probably no chance of confiscation
by the French for political reasons. Leon tells her not to
worry--she can count on him. At their hotel the Russians are
trying to close a deal with the jeweler when Leon barges in,
shows them Swana's Power of Attorney, and says he has filed
for an injunction against the sale of the jewels. Under these
circumstances the jeweler has no choice but to withdraw his
offer. Leon and the Russians have an elaborate luncheon in
the Royal Suite, complete with an orchestra and girls, and
after the comrades get tipsy Leon composes a telegram for them
to their superiors suggesting a fifty-fifty settlement over
the jewels.

Sometime later. The Russians have exchanged their drab business suits and fur hats for formal wear and are living it up in Paris. A telegram comes notifying them of the arrival of a new envoy and cancelling their authority. The replacement envoy is a woman, Nina Ivanovna Yakushova, "Ninotchka," a prim, efficient, drearily loyal Communist. She is outraged at the sumptuous quarters and the comrades' newly acquired tastes.

As she starts off sightseeing, Ninotchka stops a man outside her hotel to ask directions. It is Leon; he follows her to the Eiffel Tower and rhapsodizes over the view. Ninotchka's interest, typically, is prosaically dull. Later, Ninotchka accompanies him home (so she can study him, she says) and Leon begins to make romantic advances toward her. She responds coolly and analytically. She begins to warm up when he kisses her, but the telephone interrupts. It is Buljanoff. Ninotchka overhears, realizes who Leon is, and walks out.

Several days later, Ninotchka takes a break from a conference with her lawyers and goes to have lunch at a workmen's restaurant. Leon is just arriving at the hotel as she leaves and again he follows her. At the restaurant Ninotchka continues to be her cold and formal self until Leon, about to give up in exasperation, turns over in his chair and falls to the floor--at which point Ninotchka explodes with laughter.

Later, at a conference with the lawyers and the three comrades, Ninotchka suddenly bursts into laughter. She is obviously changed--is interested in the birds and weather and is freer with the comrades. After everyone leaves, she tries on her stylish new hat. At Leon's we learn from the butler that Leon too has changed--reading Marx and making his own bed and so on. Ninotchka arrives in her new hat. She confesses to Leon she loves him.

Leon makes reservations at a favorite restaurant. Swana and her party go to the same place. Swana and Ninotchka engage in a barbed repartee. Ninotchka has had her first champagne this evening and it has made her tipsy. She begins making a political speech on the dance floor and tries to organize the workers in the powder room to revolt. Leon takes her home to her hotel. They open the safe and Ninotchka puts on the crown jewels. She falls asleep still wearing them and Leon quietly lets himself out.

Next morning the jewels are missing. Swana comes and tells Ninotchka Count Rakonin took them. She offers to give them back if Ninotchka will clear out at once and leave Leon to her. Later that afternoon Leon begins to confess his love for Ninotchka to Swana, who interrupts to say she can guarantee that at this moment Ninotchka is on her way back to Moscow.

Leon tries to get a visa into Russia but is turned down. Back in Moscow Ninotchka tries to readjust to her bleak, regimented former life. She does give a little party for the three comrades in her crowded quarters, and they reminisce over their good days in Paris. A letter arrives from Leon during the party, but all the text is censored out. "They can't censor our memories, can they?" asks Buljanoff.

Ninotchka's superior informs her she is to be sent on another special mission involving the three comrades. They have been sent to Constantinople on a trade mission, and reports have come back that they are living it up and haven't sold a single piece of fur. Ninotchka is to go and check up on them.

The comrades give Ninotchka a rousing welcome in Constantinople. She says it'll be tough to get them off again, but they explain they've defected for good and have opened a Russian restaurant. Leon suddenly steps in from the balcony: he has engineered it all. Leon vows to fight on if Ninotchka goes back, until he turns every bureaucrat in the Russian system into an Iranoff, Buljanoff, or Kopalski; that being the case, this time, for the good of her country, Ninotchka promises to stay.

Director:	Ernst Lubitsch
Screenplay:	Charles Brackett, Billy Wilder, and Walter Reisch
Source:	Original story by Melchior Lengyel
Photography:	William Daniels
Art Director:	Cedric Gibbons
Associate:	Randall Duell
Set Decorations:	Edwin B. Willis
Editor:	Gene Ruggiero
Gowns:	Adrian
Musical Score:	Werner R. Heymann
Recording Director:	Douglas Shearer
Sound Engineer:	Conrad Kahn
Makeup:	Jack Dawn
Hairstyles for Miss Claire:	Sydney Guilaroff
Assistant Director:	Horace Hough
Cast:	Greta Garbo (Ninotchka), Melvyn Douglas (Leon), Ina Claire (Swana), Bela Lugosi (Razinin), Sig Ruman (Iranoff), Felix Bressart (Buljanoff), Alexander Granach (Kopalski), Gregory Gaye (Rakonin), Rolfe Sedan (Hotel Manager), Edwin Maxwell (Mercier), Richard Carle (Gaston). Call Bureau Cast Service list of August 18, 1939 also gives: Lawrence

143

Grant (General Savitsky), Frank
Reicher, Edwin Stanley (Lawyers),
Dorothy Adams (Swana's Maid), Marek
Windheim (Manager), Mary Forbes
(Lady Lavenham), Alexander Schonberg
(Bearded Man), George Davis (Porter),
Maj. Frederick Farrell (Attendant),
Charles Judels (Père Mathieu), Armand
Kaliz (Headwaiter Louis), George So-
rel, Nino Bellini (Men Guests), Wil-
da Bennett (Lady Guest), Florence
Shirley (Marianne), Albert Pollet
(Waiter), George Tobias (Visa Offi-
cial), Winifred Harris (English
Lady), Lucille Pinson (German Woman
at Railroad Station), Kay Stewart,
Jenifer Gray, Peggy Moran (Cigarette
Girls), Jacques Vanaire (Hotel
Clerk), Hans Joby (Man at Railroad
Station), Wolfgang Zilzer (Taxi
Driver), Tamara Shayne (Anna), Wil-
liam Irving (Bartender), Ellinor
Vanderveer, Sandra Morgan, Bess
Flowers, Emily Cabanne, Symona Boni-
face, Monya Andre (Women Gossips),
Elizabeth Williams (Indignant Woman),
Paul Weigel (Vladimir), Harry Semels
(Bit Spy), Jody Gilbert (Street Car
Conductoress).

Production:	Ernst Lubitsch for Metro-Goldwyn-Mayer; Associate Producer, Sidney Franklin
Shooting:	Begun May 31; days in production: 58
Running Time:	110 minutes
Released:	November 3
New York Premiere:	November 9
Temporary Production Title:	Ninotschka

Notes:

S. N. Behrman wrote a draft of the script. (This 130-page
draft, along with Behrman's earlier notes and subsequent re-
visions, is in the Behrman Collection at Wisconsin Center for
Film and Theatre Research.) Jacques Duval also worked on a
version of the script (New York Times, Apr. 16, 1939, X.5 and
S. N. Behrman papers). For over a decade after its release
Ninotchka was the object of censorship efforts in various
countries because of its unflattering portrait of Communism
(New York Times, Apr. 8, 1940, p. 13, Mexico; New York Times,
May 25, 1941, IX.4, Hungary; Variety, Mar. 12, 1947, p. 24,

Mexico; New York Times, Mar. 31, 1948, p. 31, Apr. 2, 1948, p. 27, Variety, Apr. 14, 1948, p. 5, Italy; New York Times, Feb. 3, 1951, p. 10, Austria). MGM rereleased Ninotchka in 1947 during House UnAmerican Activities Committee hearings. "Several witnesses in the recent probe hearings cited the treatment given Communists in Ninotchka as proof that the industry isn't overridden with subversive elements" (Variety, Nov. 26, 1947, p. 3; also see Variety, Oct. 29, 1947, p. 4 and Nov. 5, 1947, p. 13).

Reviews:
   New York Times, Nov. 10, p. 27 and Nov. 19, X.5; Variety, Oct. 11, p. 13; Motion Picture Herald, Oct. 14, p. 38; Daily Variety, Oct. 7, pp. 3, 5; Hollywood Reporter, Oct. 7, p. 3; Film Daily, Oct. 10, p. 6; Newsweek, Oct. 30, pp. 37-38; New Republic, Nov. 1, p. 370; Commonweal, Nov. 3, p. 47; Time, Nov. 6, pp. 76-77; Daily Worker, Nov. 10, p. 7, Nov. 19, p. 7; New Yorker, Nov. 18; Life, Nov. 20, pp. 44-45; Nation, Nov. 25, p. 587; National Board of Review Magazine, Nov., pp. 11-13; Photoplay, Nov., p. 64; Theatre Arts, Feb. 1940, pp. 119-29; London Times, Feb. 15, 1940, p. 6; Monthly Film Bulletin, Jan. 31, 1940, p. 5; Spectator, Feb. 23, 1940, p. 248; New Statesman and Nation, Feb. 24, 1940, p. 241; Sight and Sound, Winter 1939/1940, p. 133; Sociology and Social Research, Mar. 1940, pp. 397-98; Life and Letters To-Day, Apr. 1940, pp. 71-74; Motion Picture Review Digest, Dec. 25, pp. 71-72.

Also see:
   New York Times, Apr. 16, X.5, Oct. 22, IX.4 (by Lubitsch on Garbo), Nov. 12, IX.4, IX.5, Jan. 4, 1948, II.4 (interview with Melchior Lengyel); New York Sun, Nov. 7, p. 11 (press interview with Lubitsch); New Yorker, June 29, 1940, Aug. 10, 1940; Variety, Nov. 15, p. 15, Sept. 25, 1940, p. 12, Apr. 9, 1941, p. 7, May 21, 1941, p. 4; Best Pictures 1939-1940, eds. Jerry Wald and Richard Macaulay (New York: Dodd, Mead, 1940), pp. 79-128; Motion Picture Herald, Nov. 22, 1947, Product Digest, p. 3942 (review of reissue); L'Écran Français, Mar. 22, 1949, pp. 2, 13; Mercedes de Acosta, Here Lies the Heart (New York: Reynal, 1960), pp. 239-40, 305-306; Films and Filming, Mar. 1962, pp. 21-23, 45; Bosley Crowther, The Great Films: Fifty Golden Years of Motion Pictures (New York: G. P. Putnam's, 1967), pp. 125-29; Salka Viertel, The Kindness of Strangers (New York: Holt, Rinehart and Winston, 1969), pp. 217-18, 242, 247-48; Norman Zierold, Garbo (New York: Stein & Day, 1969), pp. 97-99; Cecil Beaton, Memoirs of the 40's (New York: McGraw-Hill, 1972), pp. 237-39; Garson Kanin, Hollywood (New York: Viking, 1974), pp. 104-105.

76   THE SHOP AROUND THE CORNER
      (1940)

Budapest, the late 1930s. The morning ritual of the opening of Matuschek and Company, a small leather-goods store, begins when Pepi, a smart aleck errand boy for the store, greets
Pirovitch, a middle-aged timid clerk. They are joined by two
other employees, Flora and Ilona. When the head clerk, Alfred
Kralik, arrives, he sends Pepi to the drugstore for bicarbon-
ate of soda. The group are eager to hear about Kralik's dinner the evening before with the Matuscheks. By this time
Vadas, an affected and rather conceited clerk, has joined the
gathering, and immediately instigates trouble by suggesting
perhaps Mrs. Matuschek's goose liver was not good. The discussion is interrupted by the arrival of Mr. Matuschek in a
taxi. Before opening the shop, Matuschek sends Pepi for bi-
carbonate of soda.

As the employees begin their daily duties, Kralik tells
Pirovitch about the most recent letter he has received from
his anonymous "Dear Friend" correspondent. Matuschek interrupts to ask Kralik's opinion of a new item he is especially
taken with, a small box that plays "O Chi Tchornya" when
opened. Kralik advises against stocking the boxes, much to
Matuschek's dissatisfaction.

Klara Novak hesitantly enters the store to ask for a job.
Kralik treats her as a customer and goes through his best
sales tactics. When he learns why she is there, he tells her
there is no opening and she cannot see Matuschek because he is
in a bad mood. Matuschek overhears Kralik saying he can pre-
dict his boss's every action and is annoyed, but still he says
sternly a job for Klara is out of the question. A plump lady
customer looking at the "O Chi Tchornya" box complains she
would have to listen to the tune every time she opened the box
for a piece of candy. Klara sees her chance to prove herself
as a salesgirl and says the box is designed that way to make
people conscious of how much candy they are consuming. The
lady buys the box.

Six months later, during the Christmas season, the employees again gather outside to wait for the opening of the store.
In the window is a special clearance sale display of "O Chi
Tchornya" boxes. Kralik tells Pirovitch he is finally going
to meet his "Dear Friend" that very night. When Klara arrives
for work, Kralik finds fault with the blouse she wore the day
before. The two snipe and quarrel. A taxi pulls up, and
Vadas emerges flaunting a huge wad of money. Matuschek arrives and is displeased with the shop window and tells his employees they must all stay late that night to redecorate it.
Klara confides to Ilona she has a very important engagement

146

that night. Inside, she begins to make up to Kralik and flatter him in an attempt to get out of working late. Kralik is taken in at first, but soon sees through her and they begin to bicker again. Klara and Kralik both ask for the evening off. Matuschek explodes in anger, especially at Kralik, his oldest employee. When Kralik wants to know why he has been treated so unfairly all that week for no reason at all, Matuschek suggests perhaps he has more reason than he thinks. Later Matuschek calls Kralik in and gives him a letter of reference and a month's wages. Kralik says goodbye to his fellow employees, who are shocked by his dismissal. Even Klara admits that although they did not get along, she is sorry he lost his job. After Matuschek receives a telephone call he tells his workers they may leave now and to finish the window the following day.

Soon after everyone is gone, a detective arrives and informs Matuschek his suspicions were correct: Mrs. Matuschek has been seeing one of his employees. But Matuschek is incredulous to learn the other man is Vadas, not Kralik. The detective leaves and Matuschek goes to his office. Pepi returns from an errand and discovers his boss about to commit suicide. There is a struggle, and we hear a shot.

Meanwhile, Pirovitch is with Kralik outside the cafe where the "Dear Friends" are to meet. Unable to keep his appointment because he lost his job, Kralik asks Pirovitch to deliver a note to the woman he finds reading Anna Karenina and using a red carnation as a bookmark. Pirovitch peers through the window and sees Klara with the book and carnation. Kralik is stunned to learn that his enemy of the past six months is also his romantic correspondent.

Klara is anxiously awaiting the arrival of her anonymous suitor, and she becomes upset when Kralik enters and attempts to sit down and join her. They argue and insult one another. Finally, after Klara tells Kralik he is a little, insignificant clerk who wouldn't ever be able to understand the letters written by the man she is expecting, he leaves.

Prompted by a phone call from Pepi, Kralik visits Matuschek in the hospital. Matuschek apologizes for suspecting Kralik of being involved with Mrs. Matuschek and makes him manager of the shop, with instructions to dismiss the real culprit. Pepi seizes the opportunity and convinces Matuschek to promote him to a clerk.

Klara becomes weak and ill after her gentleman fails to show up at the cafe or send a message. While Kralik is visiting her at home, she receives a "Dear Friend" letter. It explains her correspondent didn't appear because he saw her

there with another man and misunderstood. Klara is content
and she assures her new boss she will be able to return to
work the next day.

The day before Christmas turns out to be one of the most
profitable in the history of the shop. Matuschek pays a surprise visit and is delighted with the huge volume of business.
He leaves for an elaborate Christmas Eve dinner at a nearby
restaurant with Rudy, the new delivery boy.

When Klara and Kralik are left alone, she confesses she
fell in love with him when she first stated working in the
shop. He invents a story about how her "Dear Friend" came to
visit him and was a fat, unemployed, depressed man who pla-
giarizes other poets in his letters, then finally confesses he
is her "Dear Friend" suitor after all. Klara is delighted and
the two lovers embrace.

Director:	Ernst Lubitsch
Screenplay:	Samson Raphaelson
Source:	The play, <u>Illatszertar</u> (or <u>Parfume-</u><u>rie</u>), by Nikolaus Laszlo
Photography:	William Daniels
Art Director:	Cedric Gibbons
Associate:	Wade B. Rubottom
Set Decorations:	Edwin B. Willis
Editor:	Gene Ruggiero
Musical Score:	Werner R. Heymann
Recording Director:	Douglas Shearer
Hairstyles for Miss Sullavan:	Sydney Guilaroff
Assistant Director:	Horace Hough
Cast:	Margaret Sullavan (Klara Novak), James Stewart (Alfred Kralik), Frank Morgan (Matuschek), Joseph Schild-kraut (Ferencz Vadas), Sara Haden (Flora), Felix Bressart (Pirovitch), William Tracy (Pepi Katona), Inez Courtney (Ilona), Sarah Edwards (Woman Customer), Edwin Maxwell (Doctor), Charles Halton (Detective), Charles Smith (Rudy). Call Bureau Cast Service list of December 30, 1939 also gives: Grace Hayle (Plump Woman), Charlie Arnt (Policeman), Gertrude Simpson (Woman Customer), William Edmunds (Waiter), Mary Carr (Grandmother), Mabel Colcord (Aunt Anna), Renie Riano, Claire DeBrey, Ruth Warren, Joan Blair, Mira McKin-ney (Customers).

148

Production: Ernst Lubitsch for Metro-Goldwyn-
                               Mayer
Shooting: Begun at MGM Studios in Culver City
                               early in November 1939
Running Time: 97 minutes
Released: January 12
New York Premiere: January 25

Note:
   "It's not a big picture, just a quiet little story that
seemed to have some charm. It didn't cost very much, for such
a cast, under $500,000. It was made in twenty-eight days. I
hope it has some charm" (Lubitsch inverviewed by New York Sun,
Jan. 22, 1940, p. 11).

Reviews:
   New York Times, Jan. 26, p. 13; Variety, Jan. 10, p. 14;
Motion Picture Herald, Jan. 6, p. 42; Daily Variety, Jan. 3,
p. 3; Hollywood Reporter, Jan. 3, p. 3; Film Daily, Jan. 8,
p. 4; New Yorker, Jan. 27; Newsweek, Jan. 29, p. 34; Commonweal, Feb. 2, p. 328; Time, Feb. 5, pp. 62-63; New Republic,
Feb. 19, p. 247; National Board of Review Magazine, Feb.,
pp. 21-22; Photoplay, Mar., p. 63; London Times, May 27,
p. 4; Monthly Film Bulletin, Mar. 31, pp. 42-43; Spectator,
May 31, p. 749; Sight and Sound, Spring, p. 15; New Statesman
and Nation, June 1, p. 700; Illustrated London News, June 8,
p. 790.

Also see:
   Variety, Oct. 4, 1939, p. 2, Feb. 14, p. 27.

77   THAT UNCERTAIN FEELING
     (1941)

   New York, about 1940. Beautiful Park Avenue socialite Jill
Baker has an irritating problem--hiccups; they come and go.
Her friends recommend she take her problem to Dr. Vengard, a
fashionable Freudian psychologist. Dr. Vengard implants the
idea that Jill's marriage may be the cause of her problem, and
she begins to look at her husband, Larry, an insurance executive, with a critical eye. She concludes he is wrapped up in
his own routines and concerns and takes her pretty much for
granted.

   Jill visits Dr. Vengard again. In his waiting room she
meets Alexander Sebastian, a concert pianist who is seeking a
cure for "inhibitions." He is arrogant, outspoken, and obnox-
iously self-satisfied, but he is such a contrast to her husband that Jill is fascinated with him. She invites him to a
dinner party her husband is giving for Hungarian clients.

Just as Larry is about to conclude an agreement with the Hungarians, Sebastian starts a loud and lengthy piano recital that almost torpedoes the deal.

With her new friend and his music and their mutual interest in art, Jill's hiccups disappear and she takes a new lease on life. Larry, fearing for their marriage, concocts a scheme he hopes will bring Jill to her senses and eventually save it--he will offer her a divorce and a generous settlement. He enlists the aid of Jones, his friend and attorney, in the scheme. The divorce plans hit a snag over the problem of a co-respondent; Jill will be mortified if her friends think another woman stole Larry from her, and Larry won't agree to let her be discovered in compromising circumstances with Sebastian. A compromise is reached--they will stage a fight, with Jones's secretary as witness, and use cruelty as the grounds for divorce. After great effort and several stiff drinks, Larry strikes Jill and stalks out. Jill is touched because he had to get drunk to do it.

Larry is installed in bachelor quarters at the Carleton Hotel. Sebastian is a regular visitor at Jill's. Larry is seen with another woman. Sebastian gets to be hard to take in large doses. Jill's hiccups return. In a remorseful mood she goes to see Larry at his hotel; she is humble and Larry conciliatory. Larry pretends there is a girl in his bedroom. Jill is amused and delighted when she discovers the ruse; she doesn't let on she knows. Finally, they embrace.

Sebastian announces himself loudly at Jill's and begins to pound at the piano. Larry comes out of the bedroom in his pajamas, asks him to play more softly, and puts Sebastian's picture outside the bedroom door before closing it. Sebastian gathers up all his photographs of himself and departs. Larry comes out, locks the door, and, with a kick and a jump, heads back into the bedroom.

Director:	Ernst Lubitsch
Screenplay:	Donald Ogden Stewart
Adaptation:	Walter Reisch
Source:	The play, Divorçons (Let's Get a Divorce) (1880) by Victorien Sardou and Émile de Najac
Photography:	George Barnes
Art Director:	Alexander Golitzen
Set Interiors:	A. E. Freudeman
Music:	Werner R. Heymann
Editor:	William Shea
Miss Oberon's Gowns:	Irene
Miss Oberon's Jewelry:	Flato
Sound Technician:	Arthur Johns

150

Production Manager:	Barney Briskin
Assistant:	John Sherwood
Assistant Director:	Horace Hough
Second Assistant Director:	Lee Sholem
Cast:	Merle Oberon (Jill Baker), Melvyn Douglas (Larry Baker), Burgess Meredith (Sebastian), Alan Mowbray (Dr. Vengard), Olive Blakeney (Margie Stallings), Harry Davenport (Attorney Jones), Sig Ruman (Mr. Kofka), Eve Arden (Sally), Richard Carle (Butler), Mary Currier (Maid), Jean Fenwick (Nurse).
Production:	Ernst Lubitsch, in association with Sol Lesser; released through United Artists
Shooting:	October to December 1940
Running Time:	84 minutes
Released:	April 20
New York Opening:	May 1
Temporary Production Title:	Divorces

Notes:
    A remake of Lubitsch's Kiss Me Again (1925). "Lubitsch is philosophical about stories and their originality, and in seeking one that would protect him against charges of plagiarism he turned back to 1925 when he filmed Kiss Me Again for Warners with Marie Prevost and Monte Blue. The property was owned by Paramount in the form of Divorçons, a French play by Victorien Sardou, which that studio produced in 1918 as Let's Get a Divorce. He bought the rights from Paramount, including four adaptations, for $27,000 and then ignored them all--a not unusual procedure" (New York Times, Dec. 15, 1940, X.7). The story file on Divorçons in the Paramount Collection at the Margaret Herrick Library of the Academy of Motion Picture Arts and Sciences contains these various adaptations and other information on the source play.

Reviews:
    New York Times, May 2, p. 25; Variety, Mar. 19, p. 16; Film Daily, Mar. 14, p. 10; Motion Picture Herald, Mar. 22, pp. 36, 39; Daily Variety, Mar. 27, pp. 3, 11; Hollywood Reporter, Mar. 27, p. 3; Time, Mar. 31, pp. 70-71; Newsweek, Apr. 28, pp. 67-68; Commonweal, May 2, pp. 38-39; New Yorker, May 10; London Times, June 11, p. 6; Spectator, June 20, p. 654; New Statesman and Nation, June 21, p. 627; Monthly Film Bulletin, June 30, p. 73.

Also see:
    <u>Variety</u>, July 3, 1940, p. 19, July 10, 1940, p. 5, Sept. 4,
1940, p. 3, Feb. 12, p. 7; Chicago <u>Daily News</u>, Jan. 4, p. 19
(on the set with Lubitsch); New York <u>Morning Telegraph</u>, Jan.
26, p. 3; New York <u>Herald Tribune</u>, May 4, VI.3; Eric Bentley,
ed., <u>'Let's Get a Divorce!' and Other Plays</u> (New York: Hill
and Wang, 1958), p. 347.

78   <u>TO BE OR NOT TO BE</u>
     (1942)

    Warsaw, August 1939. Adolf Hitler walks down a Warsaw
street and pauses in front of a delicatessen; a crowd gathers.
To see how he came to be there (says the voiceover) we must go
to Gestapo headquarters in Berlin. Hitler enters to his salut-
ing underlings and "Heils" himself--at which point the producer stops the play we have been watching. It is <u>Gestapo</u>, a
satire on the Nazis, being rehearsed by a troupe of Polish
"hams." As an experiment to see how believable the Hitler
character looks, the actor goes out into the streets as we saw
him; out of the crowd at the delicatessen comes a little girl,
who calls the actor by name and asks for his autograph.

    The stars of the troupe are Joseph and Maria Tura, lumina-
ries of the Warsaw Theater. Maria has a secret admirer who
sends her flowers. She loves her husband but is flattered at
the attentions of this person, a young Polish aviator, Lieutenant Sobinski. She grants him permission to come to her
dressing room while her husband is on stage; the cue will be
the first line of his "To be or not to be" soliloquy in <u>Hamlet</u>.
Maria agrees to go for a ride in his bomber the next day.
When Joseph comes in he is despondent; the worst thing that
can happen to an actor has happened to him--someone walked out
during his big scene. Next day for political reasons the Foreign Office forbids the playing of <u>Gestapo</u>. <u>Hamlet</u> is quickly
substituted for that evening. At the same point in the soliloquy the young aviator walks out again. That same evening
the Germans invade Poland and bomb and occupy Warsaw. The
theaters are closed.

    England, the headquarters of the Polish squadron of the
RAF. Professor Siletsky, a double agent for the Nazis, manip-
ulates the exiled Polish fliers into sending messages through
him to their relatives in Warsaw. Lieutenant Sobinski's suspicions are aroused when Siletsky doesn't recognize the recip-
ient of his message, Maria Tura, the most famous actress in
Poland. He alerts military intelligence. If the information
gets to the Nazis it will mean the virtual elimination of the
Polish Underground. Sobinski is parachuted into Warsaw with
instructions to upset the Professor's scheme. The Turas are

part of the Underground; Maria Tura hides the Lieutenant in their apartment. Maria is summoned to see the Professor to receive the message--"To be or not to be." She overhears him making arrangements to deliver his information to a Nazi officer, Colonel Ehrhardt. To prevent him from accomplishing his mission, the actors get out the Gestapo set and costumes and Joseph Tura poses as the Nazi colonel. When Tura is overly curious about the message from the flier to Maria, the Professor guesses the truth and is shot while trying to escape. Now Joseph Tura has to play the Professor for the meeting with the real Colonel Ehrhardt. After the Nazis have found Professor Siletsky's body, Tura-Siletsky seeks an appointment with the Colonel. He has just managed to persuade the Nazis that the real Professor was the fake, and has arranged safe transport out of the country, when the actor Nazis arrive to rescue him by showing he was the fake after all and taking him into custody.

The real Hitler arrives in Warsaw and attends the opera. Once he is in his box the stage Hitler impersonates him and commandeers his airplane and the actors escape to England. (Meanwhile, the railroad station is blown up; the Underground has been saved.) Joseph Tura is a hero, and his fondest wish is granted--to play Hamlet in the country of Shakespeare. As he begins his "To be" soliloquy, however, a different young officer gets up and walks out.

Director:	Ernst Lubitsch
Screenplay:	Edwin Justus Mayer
Source:	Original story by Melchior Lengyel and Ernst Lubitsch
Photography:	Rudolph Maté
Production Design:	Vincent Korda
Interior Decoration:	Julia Heron
Associate Art Director:	J. MacMillan Johnson
Editor:	Dorothy Spencer
Miss Lombard's Costumes:	Irene
Musical Score:	Werner R. Heymann
Makeup:	Gordon Bau
Special Effects:	Lawrence Butler
Sound:	Frank Maher
Casting Director:	Victor Sutker
Production Manager:	Walter Mayo
Assistant Directors:	William Tummel and William McGarry
Technical Supervisor:	Richard Ordynski
Cast:	Carole Lombard (Maria Tura), Jack Benny (Joseph Tura), Robert Stack (Lt. Stanislav Sobinski), Felix Bressart (Greenberg), Lionel Atwill (Rawitch), Stanley Ridges (Professor Siletsky), Sig Ruman (Colonel

	Ehrhardt), Tom Dugan (Bronski), Charles Halton (Producer Dobosh), George Lynn (Actor-Adjutant), Henry Victor (Captain Schultz), Maude Eburne (Anna), Armand Wright (Makeup Man), Erno Verebes (Stage Manager), Halliwell Hobbes (General Armstrong), Miles Mander (Major Cunningham), Leslie Dennison (Captain), Frank Reicher (Polish Officer), Peter Caldwell (William Kunze), Wolfgang Zilzer (Man in Bookstore), Olaf Hytten (Polonius in Warsaw), Charles Irwin (Reporter), Leland Hodgson (Second Reporter), Alec Craig (Scottish Farmer), James Finlayson (Second Farmer), Edgar Licho (Prompter), Robert O. Davis (Gestapo Sergeant), Roland Varno (Pilot), Helmut Dantine, Otto Reichow (Co-Pilots), Maurice Murphy, Gene Rizzi, Paul Barrett, John Kellogg (Polish RAF Flyers).
Production:	Ernst Lubitsch, in association with Alexander Korda, for Romaine Film Corporation; released through United Artists
Shooting:	Begun at Samuel Goldwyn Studios in Hollywood November 6, 1941 and completed December 23, 1941 (days in production: 42)
Running Time:	99 minutes
Released:	March 6

Notes:

Lubitsch was originally scheduled to make To Be or Not To Be in association with Walter Wanger, but Korda came in when Wanger's busy production schedule wouldn't permit it. United Artists later argued in tax court that To Be or Not To Be had been a "salvage operation," owing to the changes in production arrangements, Miss Lombard's death in an air crash shortly before the film's release, and the film's unmarketability because of its lighthearted treatment of the Nazis (United Artists files, Wisconsin Center for Film and Theatre Research).

Reviews:

New York Times, Mar. 7, p. 13, Mar. 22, VIII.3, Mar. 29, VIII.3 (Lubitsch's rebuttal); Variety, Feb. 18, p. 8; Motion Picture Herald, Feb. 21, p. 36; Daily Variety, Feb. 18, p. 3; Hollywood Reporter, Feb. 18, p. 3; Film Daily, Feb. 19, p. 8; Newsweek, Mar. 2, p. 50; Life, Mar. 9, pp. 63-66; Commonweal,

Mar. 13, p. 513; New Yorker, Mar. 14; Time, Mar. 16, p. 90; New Republic, Mar. 23, p. 399; National Board of Review Magazine, Mar., pp. 5-6; London Times, Apr. 30, p. 6; New Statesman and Nation, May 2, p. 288; Spectator, May 8, p. 442; Monthly Film Bulletin, May 31, p. 63; Sight and Sound, Summer, pp. 15-16.

Also see:
Variety, June 25, 1941, p. 6, Aug. 13, 1941, p. 5, Oct. 8, 1941, p. 4, Jan. 21, p. 2; Film Daily, Aug. 8, p. 10; New York Times, Dec. 7, 1941, X.9, Jan. 25, IX.5, Mar. 1, VIII.4; Cahiers du Cinéma, Jan. 1962, pp. 54-57; Image et Son, Summer 1962, no. 153-54, pp. 43-44, 49; Graham Petrie, "Theater Film Life," Film Comment, May/June 1974, pp. 38-43; Robin Wood, "Acting Up," Film Comment, Mar./Apr. 1976, pp. 23-24; Tino Balio, United Artists: The Company Built by the Stars (Madison: Univ. of Wisconsin Press, 1976), pp. 172-74.

79   HEAVEN CAN WAIT
(1943)

Hell, 1942. Henry Van Cleve, age 70, has just died and (voiceover) as his soul "passed over the Great Divide, he realized that it was extremely unlikely that his next stop could be Heaven, and so, philosophically, he presented himself where innumerable people had so often told him to go." His Excellency, Satan, grants him an interview and asks him to name some outstanding crime he committed on earth. Henry replies he can't think of one, but can safely say his whole life has been one continuous misdemeanor. Henry's story is told in flashbacks set on his birthdays.

The Van Cleves' Fifth Avenue home, New York, 1872. Mother (a society lady) and grandmother dote over the infant Henry.

Central Park, 1874. A nurse flirts with an Irish policeman as Henry squalls in his carriage.

The same, 1881. Nine-year-old Henry's first lesson in the ways of the opposite sex: little Mary accepts a beetle from him as a gift and then charms and beguiles him out of a second one.

The Fifth Avenue house, 1887. Mrs. Van Cleve engages a French maid and pays her extra to tutor Henry in French. On Henry's birthday he is in bed with a strange sickness. It comes out it's nothing more than a common hangover, he and Mademoiselle slipped out and went carousing the night before. Mademoiselle is discharged.

The same, Sunday morning of Henry's twenty-sixth birthday, 1898. The older Van Cleves are concerned over Henry, who throws away his money gambling and running around with showgirls. Henry rhapsodizes privately to his mother he's finally found the girl for him though he's seen her only once and doesn't know her name. That evening Henry's stuffy cousin Albert brings his fiancée, Martha, and her parents, the E. F. Strabels, the meat packers of Kansas City, to Henry's party. Martha, it turns out, is Henry's special girl; he followed her into a bookstore the day before and pretended to be a clerk in order to talk to her. Later, when Martha has to excuse herself during someone's song to sneeze, she goes into the library and Henry is there. He kisses her and begs her to marry him. To the astonished stares of all those assembled, Henry carries her out of the house to elope. Mr. Strabel vows to disinherit her. Grandfather Van Cleve is delighted and sends money for a honeymoon.

The Van Cleve house the morning of Henry's birthday, 1908. Henry and Martha have an eight-year-old son, Jackie. At breakfast Mrs. Van Cleve says how wonderful it would be if Henry's father had lived long enough to see Henry settle down. Henry says it's all Martha's influence. About that time a telegram comes from Martha saying she's left him.

The Strabel home in Kansas. The Strabels are at breakfast when Albert Van Cleve arrives and says he ran into Martha on the train and she's right outside in a carriage. The Strabels are cool to Martha at first but finally they give in and tearfully welcome her home. That evening Henry and Grandfather are secreted in Martha's room when she retires. She says she knows Henry has continued his philandering; what she can't take is his constant maneuvering to cover it up--like on the present occasion, when he gives her a bracelet for an anniversary gift and at home she has seen a jeweler's bill for two bracelets. Finally she wavers and the three of them creep out downstairs past Albert, reading at a desk, and Mr. Strabel, snoring loudly in his chair.

New York, 1922. On his fiftieth birthday Henry pays a visit to Peggy Nash, a beautiful Ziegfeld Follies girl. He tries to turn on the charm, but has the wind taken out of his sails when she calls him a retired Casanova with a tummy. He pays her off to get her to stop seeing his son, Jack. He is crestfallen when she correctly guesses his age. Martha sees through him too and guesses what he's been up to. Jack comes in to say he's already given Peggy Nash up for another showgirl. Martha tells Henry not to worry--Jack is just a chip off the old block.

The Van Cleve house, 1923, during Henry and Martha's twenty-fifth anniversary party. In the library Henry insists on knowing whom a telephone call Martha just received was from. Martha finally confesses she's been seeing a doctor. They dance in the hall, and Henry's voice on the soundtrack tells us it was their last anniversary together.

An insert of the photograph of Henry's sixtieth birthday party; Henry informs us the total age of the assembled group was over fourteen hundred years. One day later that year Henry tells Jack (now in charge of the family business) he needs a bigger allowance to hire a reading companion. (He confesses she is twenty-four years old.)

Henry's bedroom, the day after his seventieth birthday. Henry is sick in bed from too much celebrating. A homely nurse wakes him up from a beautiful dream of dancing the "Merry Widow Waltz" with a gorgeous blonde. Shortly after, the day nurse is replaced by the night nurse, a gorgeous blonde. She closes the door to Henry's room and from outside we hear the strains of the "Merry Widow Waltz."

His Excellency's office. Henry says what a wonderful way it was to go. His Excellency says regretfully they can't give his class of people accommodations here. If he'll try the other place, he may not get into the Main Building at once, but he should be patient, as there are doubtless many inside who will be willing to plead his case. Elevator Boy: Down? Excellency: No--up. (The original plan called for Henry to get married again in his late fifties to a young, blonde, golddigging manicurist, whose whole crude family moves into the Fifth Avenue mansion; Jack was finally to kick them out when he came back on his father's sixtieth birthday and saw how cruelly they were taking advantage of the old man.)

Director:	Ernst Lubitsch
Screenplay:	Samson Raphaelson
Source:	The play, <u>Szuletesnap</u> (<u>Birthday</u>) (1934) by Laszlo Bus-Feketé
Photography:	Edward Cronjager
Art Directors:	James Basevi and Leland Fuller
Set Decorations:	Thomas Little
Associate:	Walter M. Scott
Music:	Alfred Newman
Technicolor Color Director:	Natalie Kalmus
Editor:	Dorothy Spencer
Costumes:	Rene Hubert

Makeup:	Guy Pearce
Special Photographic Effects:	Fred Sersen
Sound:	Eugene Grossman and Roger Heman
Assistant Director:	Henry Weinberger
Cast:	Gene Tierney (Martha), Don Ameche (Henry Van Cleve), Charles Coburn (Hugo Van Cleve), Marjorie Main (Mrs. Strabel), Laird Cregar (His Excellency), Spring Byington (Bertha Van Cleve), Allyn Joslyn (Albert Van Cleve), Eugene Pallette (E. F. Strabel), Signe Hasso (Mademoiselle), Louis Calhern (Randolph Van Cleve), Helene Reynolds (Peggy Nash), Aubrey Mather (James), Michael Ames (Jack Van Cleve), Leonard Carey (Flogdell), Clarence Muse (Jasper), Dickie Moore (Henry Van Cleve, age 15), Dickie Jones (Albert Van Cleve, age 15), Trudy Marshall (Jane), Florence Bates (Mrs. Craig), Clara Blandick (Grandmother), Anita Bolster (Mrs. Cooper-Cooper), Nino Pipitone, Jr. (Jack as a Boy), Claire Du Brey (Miss Ralston), Maureen Rodin-Ryan (Nurse), Frank Orth (Coachman). Call Bureau Cast Service list of August 9, 1943 also lists: Alfred Hall (Albert's Father), Grayce Hampton (Albert's Mother), Gerald Oliver Smith (Smith), Charles Halton (Clerk in Brentano's), James Flavin, Arthur Foster (Policemen), Libby Taylor, Bernice Pilot (Maids), Michael McLean (Henry, age 15 months), Edwin Maxwell (Doctor), Scotty Beckett (Henry, age 9), Marlene Mains (Mary), Gerald Pierce (Elevator Boy), Doris Merrick (Nurse). Several filmographies also list: Claire James, Rose-Anne Murray, Marian Rosamond, Adele Jurgens, Ruth Brady (Ziegfeld girls).
Production:	Ernst Lubitsch for 20th Century-Fox
Shooting:	Begun at the 20th Century-Fox Westwood Studios on February 1 and completed April 10
Running Time:	112 minutes
New York Premiere:	August 11
Released:	August 13
Temporary Production Title:	Birthday

Reviews:
   New York Times, Aug. 12, p. 15; Variety, July 21, p. 22;
Motion Picture Herald, July 24, Production Digest Section,
p. 1441; Daily Variety, July 21, pp. 3-4; Film Daily, July 21,
p. 11; Hollywood Reporter, July 21, p. 3; Time, July 19, p. 96;
Newsweek, Aug. 9, pp. 84-85; Commonweal, Aug. 13, p. 421; New
Yorker, Aug. 14; New Republic, Aug. 30, p. 284; Life, Aug. 30,
pp. 61-62, 64; Nation, Sept. 4, p. 275; Photoplay, Sept.,
p. 32; London Times, Sept. 3, p. 6; Spectator, Sept. 10,
p. 239; New Statesman and Nation, Sept. 11, p. 168.

Also see:
   Variety, Dec. 16, 1942, p. 7; Hollywood Reporter, Feb. 16,
p. 6 (Ziegfeld sequence), Aug. 16, p. 16 (excerpts reviews in
New York papers); New York Herald Tribune, Feb. 28, VI.5; New
York Sun, Aug. 2, p. 15 (press interview with Lubitsch); Sat-
urday Evening Post, Feb. 9, 1946, p. 50; Cahiers du Cinéma,
Jan. 1962, pp. 54-57; Dossiers du Cinéma (Paris: Casterman,
1971-   ), Films I, pp. 33-36.

80   A ROYAL SCANDAL
     (1945)

   The Imperial Court of Catherine the Great, St. Petersburg,
the second half of the eighteenth century. His Excellency the
Chancellor, a wily court politician, is trying to convince the
Czarina of the need for a defense alliance with the French.
The French Ambassador is due at any moment, but her royal
highness is with her current lover, Variatinsky, Commander of
the Palace Guard. Fortunately the Czarina gets into a violent
quarrel with Variatinsky at just the right time and kicks him
out. In double entendres from political language the Chancellor coaches the French Ambassador on how to deal with the
amorous Czarina and is about to show him in when a young officer bursts in and insists on being allowed to see her majesty.
He is Lieutenant Alexei Chernoff, fiancé of one of Catherine's
ladies-in-waiting, Countess Anna. He forces his way into the
Czarina's presence and tells her he has ridden three days and
nights from the Western front to warn her that two of her most
trusted generals are plotting against her. The Chancellor assures the Czarina he already knows of the plot and has had it
defused. The Czarina is impressed with the devotion and especially the good looks and physical prowess of her young subject. She promotes him to captain, cancels her audience with
the French Ambassador and the banquet in his honor, and commands Alexei to come to her at 10:00 that evening with a report on the state of things in the Western garrison. The
Chancellor makes a gift to Alexei of a magnificent stallion
and suggests he use it to return to the front. Alexei ignores
the advice.

That evening the Czarina brushes aside the matter of the report and asks Alexei whether he has ever been in love. Alexei confesses he is in love with someone now. The Czarina orders him back to the front. But when he mentions the Chancellor's gift and advice the Czarina is enraged at the Chancellor for presuming to interfere in her personal life. She promotes Alexei to major and orders him to stay. Alexei swears his undying loyalty to his sovereign. She is moved and permits him to kiss her. Alexei kisses her again and admits the experience has emboldened him. After fortifying himself with champagne he goes to her on her bed--and begins to read his 35-page report.

Next day Alexei is a colonel and Commander of the Palace Guard. The Czarina listens to his grand scheme for national reform and sends him off to work on it. By accident she happens to learn the other woman is Anna. She summons her at once, tells her she's pale and obviously needs a rest, and commands her to take a vacation. Anna refuses to go and warns her defiantly that Alexei is only temporarily infatuated with the mystique of the throne and one day will return to her.

General Ronsky is ringleader of a plot to overthrow the Czarina. To win Alexei (now a general) over, he gets him to a banquet and has Variatinsky take him aside and make unpleasant revelations about the Czarina. Alexei attacks Variatinsky furiously and as he storms out pauses to overturn the banquet table to the astonishment of the assembled generals. He goes to Catherine and confronts her with Variatinsky's story and demands to know whether it's true. She denies it and is enraged because his attack on Variatinsky has probably started talk that will spread all over Europe about a royal scandal. But his suspicions linger and his trust in her is further shaken when he finds one of his edicts for peasant reform tossed away in a wastebasket.

Alexei goes over to Ronsky and the generals. The Chancellor appears too, explaining to the plotters he always makes sure he ends up on the winning side. Alexei goes to Catherine in her bedchamber to tell her the revolt has taken place and she no longer reigns. She is on her knees pleading with him to save her when shouts of jubilation are heard and the Chancellor appears with Ronsky in custody to inform her majesty the revolt has been suppressed. Alexei is stripped of his rank and thrown into prison.

Anna goes to the Czarina to plead on Alexei's behalf but loses her temper and throws a vase. The Czarina pronounces her banished to the Crimea; the Chancellor points out that Russia doesn't own the Crimea yet. Private Alexei is called before the Czarina and told he is to be sentenced to death for

treason. The Czarina offers him a way out and pleads with him
to take it: if he will humble himself before her, even the
least little bit, she will commute the sentence. He refuses:
his idol on a pedestal has been destroyed for him and he would
rather die than give in to her again. She gives him an hour
to think it over.

The Czarina confesses to the Chancellor she is downhearted
and lonely. The Chancellor manages to get the French Ambassador admitted at last. He flatters the Czarina extravagantly
and arouses her romantic interest. The Chancellor asks about
what to do with Alexei; the Czarina tears up the death warrant
she is still clutching in her hand. He asks too about Anna;
the Czarina tells him not to bother her with such trifles, as
she is too busy with the affairs of state; handle it as he
will. She confides to the Ambassador that for all the pomp
and power around her she is still the loneliest person on
earth. The Ambassador confesses he is lonely too. The Chancellor beats a hasty retreat.

Director:	Otto Preminger
Screenplay:	Edwin Justus Mayer
Adaptation:	Bruno Frank
Source:	The play, The Czarina (1913), by
	Lajos Biró and Melchior Lengyel
Photography:	Arthur Miller
Art Directors:	Lyle R. Wheeler and Mark Lee Kirk
Set Decorations:	Thomas Little
Associate:	Paul S. Fox
Costumes:	Rene Hubert
Music:	Alfred Newman
Orchestral Arrangements:	Edward Powell
Editor:	Dorothy Spencer
Makeup:	Ben Nye
Special Photographic Effects:	Fred Sersen
Sound Technicians:	Alfred Bruzlin and Roger Herman
Assistant Director:	Tom Dudley
Cast:	Tallulah Bankhead (The Czarina, Catherine II), Charles Coburn (Chancellor Nicolai Illytch), Anne Baxter (Countess Anna Jaschikoff), William Eythe (Lt. Alexei Chernoff), Vincent Price (Marquis de Fleury, the French Ambassador), Mischa Auer (Captain Sukov), Sig Ruman (General Ronsky), Vladimir Sokoloff (Malak-off), Mikhail Rasumny (Drunken General), Grady Sutton (Boris), Don Douglas (Variatinsky), Egon Brecher (Wassilikov), Eva Gabor (Countess

Demidow). Call Bureau Cast Service list of May 1 also gives: Frederick Ledebur, Paul Baratoff, George A. Gleboff, Fred Nurney, Leonid Sneg- off, Henry Victor, Wilton Graff, Michael Visaroff, General Sam Savit- sky, Eugene Beday, Nestor Eristoff, Richard Ryen, Eugene Sigaloff (Rus- sian Generals), Virginia Walker, Renee Carson, Sandra Poloway, Rox- anne Hilton, Dina Smirnova, Martha Jewett, Ann Hunter (Ladies in Wait- ing), John Russell (Guard), Feodor Chaliapin, Mario Gang, George Shdan- off (Lackeys), Fred Essler, Marek Windheim, Torben Meyer, Victor Del- insky (Stooges), Harry Carter (Foot- man), Leo Bulgakov (Majordomo), Maurice Brierre, William H. O'Brien (Servants), Arno Frey (Captain). Weinberg (1968) also lists Lubitsch in an unspecified bit role.

Production:	Ernst Lubitsch for 20th Century-Fox
Shooting:	Begun at the 20th Century-Fox West- wood Studios the week of September 14, 1944 and completed on November 25 (days of shooting: approx. 60)
Running Time:	94 minutes
New York Opening:	April 11
Alternate Title:	The Czarina

Notes:
A remake of Lubitsch's Forbidden Paradise (1924). Lubitsch prepared the script but Preminger was called in when Lubitsch's doctor advised him against directing the film. "Not yet strong enough...to expose himself to a full day on the set, Mr. Lu- bitsch...directs only the rehearsals" (New York Times, Oct. 8, 1944, II.3). Preminger has talked about how he came in and how his approach to the comedy material differed from Lubitsch's to: Peter Bogdanovich, On Film (New York), vol. 1, no. zero (ca. 1970), pp. 38-39, and Gerald Pratley, The Cinema of Otto Preminger (New York: Castle Books, 1971), pp. 70-72; also see Willi Frischauer, Behind the Scenes of Otto Preminger (New York: William Morrow, 1974), pp. 114-15; and Preminger: An Autobiography (Garden City, N.Y.: Doubleday, 1977), pp. 84-89.

Reviews:
New York Times, Apr. 12, p. 19; Variety, Mar. 21, p. 10; Motion Picture Herald, Mar. 24, Product Digest Section, p. 2373; Daily Variety, Mar. 21, p. 3; Film Daily, Mar. 26, p. 6; Hollywood Reporter, Mar. 21, pp. 3, 10; Nation, Apr. 7, p. 396; Time, Apr. 9, pp. 94, 96; Commonweal, Apr. 13, p. 649;

Newsweek, Apr. 16, pp. 102, 104; New Yorker, Apr. 21; New
Movies, Apr., p. 7; London Times, May 15, p. 8; Spectator,
May 25, p. 474; Monthly Film Bulletin, May 31, p. 60.

Also see:
    Hollywood Reporter, Apr. 16, p. 7 (excerpts reviews from
New York papers); New York Motion Picture Critics' Reviews,
Apr. 16, pp. 406-407 (reprints reviews of New York papers).

81   DRAGONWYCK
      (1946)

        An American Jane Eyre but with Rochester as a real villain.

        Greenwich, Connecticut, 1844. Abigail Wells, wife of a
humble farmer, receives a letter from a distant relation,
Nicholas Van Ryn, a wealthy landowner, offering to let one of
her daughters come to live at Dragonwyck, his estate on the
Hudson River in the Catskills, as a companion to his eight-
year-old daughter, Katrine. Miranda Wells, 18, beautiful, and
a romantic dreamer, sees it as a fulfillment of one of her
cherished fantasies and begs to be permitted to go. Her mother is not opposed but her strict, religious father is. She
persists, however, and after a passage selected at random in
the Bible turns out to involve a journey, he takes it as a
sign and gives his consent.

        Nicholas Van Ryn is a descendant of the original Dutch
patroon who received his land with manorial privileges by
grant from the old Dutch government of New York. In a time
of agitation for reform, he still manages his lands in the
old way, by leasing them out to tenant farmers but retaining
ownership of them. Miranda is entranced with his wealth and
aristocratic bearing and fails to see his darker traits--his
arrogance, effeteness, and tyrannical disposition. His wife,
Johanna, is a mindless twit and a glutton. Katrine is the
kind of child whose natural buoyancy has given way to a kind
of resigned listlessness as a result of constant parental indifference and neglect. The servants whisper of skeletons in
the Van Ryn closet involving a maternal ancestor whose portrait hangs on the wall. A century ago she swore a curse on
the line after her husband, whose only interest was in a male
heir, mistreated her. She died not long after the child was
born, some say a suicide, but her presence is still strong in
the house, they say, and sometimes at night the Van Ryn de-
scendants can hear her playing her harpsichord. Shortly after
Miranda's arrival a young doctor, Jeff Turner, becomes interested in her, but she is bedazzled by the trappings of wealth
and aristocracy and she rejects him for what she thinks are
better things. At rent day one of Nicholas' farmers protests

his not being able to own his own land and tries to set off a
strike by refusing to pay his annual rent. Nicholas coldblood-
edly orders the man off his land and this frightens the others
into submission. Next day at a ball hosted by the Van Ryns
the young ladies of patroon families make fun of Miranda's
humble origins. Nicholas tries to make amends by dancing with
her.

Miranda has not been at Dragonwyck long when Johanna dies
mysteriously of what Dr. Turner had diagnosed as only a common
cold. That same evening Nicholas tells Miranda Johanna had
been incapable of giving him another child, confesses that he
loves her, and says it was fated for them to be together. As
Miranda is leaving to go back home, Jeff stops her carriage
and asks if he may come to see her in Connecticut. Again Miranda gives him no hope.

It is obvious to everyone in the Wells family that something is wrong with Miranda. She doesn't eat or sleep and
daydreams half the time. She perks up suddenly, however, when
her father receives a note from Nicholas saying he has come to
Connecticut to see him on a matter of great urgency. Nicholas
asks for Miranda's hand, she prevails on her father to consent, and the marriage takes place the following day.

Back at Dragonwyck the Van Ryns announce a ball but as a
snub to Miranda practically everyone declines. Nicholas returns from New York and is displeased because Miranda has
taken on a crippled Irish maid, Peggy. He says the sight of
deformity displeases him and makes cruel jokes about her.
Miranda is shocked at his impiety, they quarrel, and in his
anger Nicholas confesses to her that despite what he has led
her to believe he really doesn't believe in God after all.
Miranda is her father's daughter and she is practically distraught at this revelation. In her upset she blurts out that
she's pregnant and asks if that's enough to earn her the right
to keep Peggy. A few months later, and a new governor of the
state has been elected. There is also a new law guaranteeing
tenant farmers the right to purchase their land. Nicholas'
farmers are gathered at a tavern to celebrate and they are
mimicking their patroon's magisterial behavior when he enters
in search of Jeff Turner to come and deliver Miranda's baby.
The child is born with a malformed heart and he lives just
long enough to receive baptism.

Nicholas becomes depressed and reclusive and spends most
of his time brooding alone in the tower room. When Miranda
goes to him he taunts her for her religious beliefs, says he
believes only in himself, and reveals he's become addicted to
drugs. Miranda's growing disillusion with him has begun to
strengthen her and she tells Nicholas boldly she thinks the

drugs and the whole posture of superiority are just attempts to run away from things he can't face or control. Meanwhile, Peggy has become alarmed over the state of things and she goes to Jeff Turner to tell him her fears. When she mentions by chance that Nicholas has moved a strange plant into Miranda's bedroom, suddenly Jeff comprehends the cause of Johanna's death and realizes Nicholas is now trying to kill Miranda in the same way. Back at Dragonwyck Miranda too has begun to suspect the cause of Johanna's death. Jeff and Peggy arrive and Jeff confronts Nicholas with what he has learned. There is a struggle and Jeff knocks Nicholas out cold. Nicholas is now almost totally insane, and when he regains consciousness he goes wandering and gives a mighty speech of defiance from his patroon's platform to the empty night. When Jeff and Miranda arrive with a crowd of farmers to arrest him, Nicholas pulls a gun and fires and is shot dead himself.

Jeff arrives just as Miranda is about to leave Dragonwyck for good, taking with her only the single suitcase she came with. She tells him she now realizes the wisdom of her mother's warning, "You can't marry a dream." As her carriage pulls away she reminds Jeff Connecticut isn't so far away, perhaps he can come to visit her there sometime.

Director:	Joseph L. Mankiewicz
Screenplay:	Joseph L. Mankiewicz
Source:	The novel, <u>Dragonwyck</u> (1944), by Anya Seton
Photography:	Arthur Miller
Art Direction:	Lyle Wheeler and J. Russell Spencer
Set Decorations:	Thomas Little
Associate:	Paul S. Fox
Editor:	Dorothy Spencer
Costumes:	Rene Hubert
Music:	Alfred Newman
Orchestral Arrangements:	Edward B. Powell
Makeup:	Ben Nye
Special Photographic Effects:	Fred Sersen
Dances Staged by:	Arthur Appel
Sound:	W. D. Flick and Roger Heman
Assistant Director:	F. D. Johnston
Cast:	Gene Tierney (Miranda), Walter Huston (Ephraim Wells), Vincent Price (Nicholas Van Ryn), Glenn Langan (Dr. Jeff Turner), Anne Revere (Abigail Wells), Spring Byington (Magda, a Servant), Connie Marshall (Katrine), Henry Morgan (Klaus Bleecker), Vivienne Osborne (Johanna), Jessica Tandy (Peggy O'Malley),

165

Trudy Marshall (Elizabeth Van Bord-
en), Reinhold Schunzel (Count de
Grenier), Jane Nigh (Tabitha Wells),
Ruth Ford (Cornelia Van Borden),
Scott Elliott (Tom Wells), Boyd Ir-
win (Tompkins), Keith Hitchcock (Mr.
McNab), Maya Van Horn (Countess de
Grenier), Francis Pierlot (Dr.
Brown). Call Bureau Cast Service
list of April 19, 1946 also gives:
Arthur Thompson, Al Winter, Larry
Steers, Wallace Dean, Tom Martin
(Servants), Edwin Davis, Shelby Ba-
con (Dancers on Deck of Boat), Ruth
Cherrington, Elizabeth Williams
(Dowagers), John Chollot (French
Count), Nenette Vallon (French Count-
ess), Virginia Lindley (Helena),
George Ford, Alexander Sacha, Nestor
Eristoff, Ted Jordan, William Carter
(Bit Men), Mickey Roth (Nathaniel),
Jaime Dana (Seth), R. Buzz Henry
(Messenger Boy), Dudley Dickerson,
J. Louis Johnson (Porters), Walter
Baldwin, Harry Humphrey, Robert Mal-
colm, Clancy Cooper, Trevor Bardette,
Arthur Aylsworth, Tom Fadden, Addi-
son Richards (Farmers), Jane Louise
Porter (Little Girl), Betty Fairfax
(Mrs. McNab), Michael Garrison (Zack
Wilson), Grady Sutton (Hotel Clerk),
Walter Tetley (First Bell Hop), Bud-
dy Gorman (Second Bell Hop), Ger-
trude Astor (Nurse), Charles Waldron
(Minister), Steve Olsen (Vendor),
Douglas Wood (Mayor). Press sheet
and various filmographies list David
Ballard (Obadiah); this character is
alluded to in the film but doesn't
appear and the part was probably
shot but cut later.

Production: Ernst Lubitsch for 20th Century-Fox;
Executive Producer, Darryl F. Zanuck
Shooting: Begun at the 20th Century-Fox West-
wood Studios early February 1945 and
completed May 1945, with several
days' location shooting at Sherwood
Forest the first week of April
Running Time: 103 minutes
New York Opening: April 10

166

Notes:
   "Apparently Lubitsch, who produced it, had thought of directing it himself, but when he was prevented by illness he assigned it to Mankiewicz.... Lubitsch, for many years Mankiewicz's close friend and 'sponsor,' was the greatest external influence on his work. Although Mankiewicz had rejected Dragonwyck when offered it earlier by the studio, he felt that 'under Lubitsch' he could find no more masterful guidance for his first directorial effort"--John Russell Taylor, Joseph L. Mankiewicz: An Index to His Work (London: British Film Institute, [1960]), p. [3]. Lubitsch's name does not appear in the credits in either of the two prints the authors screened.

Reviews:
   New York Times, Apr. 11, p. 35; Variety, Feb. 20, p. 8; Motion Picture Herald, Feb. 23, Product Digest Section, p. 2857; Daily Variety, Feb. 18, p. 3; Film Daily, Feb. 28, p. 5; Hollywood Reporter, Feb. 18, p. 3; Life, Mar. 18, pp. 121-24; Time, Apr. 1, p. 96; Commonweal, Apr. 5, pp. 623-24; New Yorker, Apr. 13; Newsweek, Apr. 22, pp. 94, 96; Cosmopolitan, May, pp. 70, 185-86; Photoplay, May, p. 22; London Times, May 20, p. 8; Sight and Sound, Autumn, pp. 97-98.

Also see:
   New York Times, Mar. 4, 1945, II.1, II.3; Hollywood Reporter, Apr. 15, p. 12 (excerpts reviews in New York papers); New York Motion Picture Critics' Reviews, Apr. 15, pp. 578-80 (reprints reviews of New York papers).

82   CLUNY BROWN
     (1946)

   London, a Sunday, June 1938. Hilary Ames's sink is stopped up on the day of his cocktail party. At first he mistakes a caller, Professor Adam Belinski, who has come there to meet one of the guests, for a plumber. Then Cluny Brown, pretty young niece of the real plumber, arrives in her uncle's place because the uncle was out when Ames's desperate phone call came. While fixing the sink, Cluny tells of going once to have tea at an elegant restaurant and says her uncle always tells her she doesn't know her place. Belinski replies that her place is where she wants to be; if she wants to "feed squirrels to the nuts" rather than "nuts to the squirrels," who is to stop her? Cluny has martinis with Ames and the Professor, becomes tipsy, and lies down on a couch babbling nonsense. Her uncle arrives, misconstrues the situation, and vows he will send his niece into service.

   During the cocktail party socialite Andrew Carmel and his friends see Belinski napping on Ames's bed and recognize him

at once as a famous Czech liberal and writer who had to flee
Prague when the Nazis invaded. He and the others somewhat
overdramatically offer their protection, and the Professor
graciously accepts their offer, their money, and their invitation to be an extended house guest with Andrew's parents in
the country.

By coincidence, Cluny Brown is being sent into service as a
maid for the Carmels. She runs into Colonel Duff Graham, a
neighbor of the Carmels, at the railroad station. He assumes
she is the Carmels' guest and gives her a lift. The Carmels
in turn think Cluny is a friend of the Colonel and invite her
to tea. But they are very gracious to her when they discover
their error. At dinner the first evening Cluny drops a serving platter when she sees Belinski at the table. He intercedes to save her job. Later, Belinski comes to Cluny's room
and tells her he would like to be her friend and maybe, one
day, something more. Cluny objects, saying it would be out of
place.

Cluny begins to spend time with the local pharmacist, Wilson, a pompous, insufferable petit bourgeois who lives with
his mother, a Dickensian character who never speaks but constantly clears her throat loudly. They become romantically
inclined. Belinski dislikes the fellow and begins to harass
and play tricks on him. Cluny goes to the Wilsons for Mrs.
Wilson's birthday dinner and, hopefully, an announcement of
her engagement. But when there is a noise in the plumbing
during dinner and Cluny volunteers to fix it, the Wilsons and
their friends are shocked, and the engagement is off.

Meanwhile, Andrew has arrived from London, very annoyed to
find that his girl friend, Betty Cream, with whom he is temporarily on the outs, is his mother's house guest for the
weekend. Belinski goes to Betty's room late in the evening,
apparently on Andrew's behalf and with the intention of pro-
voking an incident that will bring Betty and Andrew together,
but when he becomes overly insistent, Betty screams and wakes
up the house. After, when she and Lady Carmel are alone,
Betty assents that she does indeed intend to marry Andrew.
Lady Carmel advises her to tell him as soon as possible. Next
morning, after the engagement is announced, Andrew calls Belinski inside with the intention of giving him a drubbing, but
ends up giving him a loan. Betty says how fortunate it was
Belinski came to her room, since it brought her and Andrew
together.

Belinski brings farewell gifts for the servants. He is
told that Cluny is indisposed as a result of the birthday
party. He leaves a message for her that concludes with "squirrels to the nuts." Shortly after Cluny takes out after him

and catches up to him at the train station. They take the train together. Belinski says he's giving up his plan to write Morality and Expediency and will begin to write murder mysteries so he can support her.

Sometime later, in America, Cluny and Belinski look in a window of a Fifth Avenue bookstore filled with copies of his The Nightingale Murder. Cluny faints; sometime later, in the same window, we see a display of the sequel, The Nightingale Strikes Again, written to support a new addition to the family.

Director:	Ernst Lubitsch
Screenplay:	Samuel Hoffenstein and Elizabeth Reinhardt
Source:	The novel, Cluny Brown (1944), by Margery Sharp
Photography:	Joseph La Shelle
Art Directors:	Lyle Wheeler and J. Russell Spencer
Set Decorations:	Thomas Little
Associate:	Paul S. Fox
Editor:	Dorothy Spencer
Costumes:	Bonnie Cashin
Music:	Cyril Mockridge
Musical Direction:	Emil Newman
Orchestral Arrangements:	Maurice de Packh
Makeup:	Ben Nye
Special Photographic Effects:	Fred Sersen
Sound:	Arthur L. Kirbach and Roger Heman
Assistant Director:	Tom Dudley
Technical Advisor:	Capt. Harry Lloyd Morris
Cast:	Charles Boyer (Adam Belinski), Jennifer Jones (Cluny Brown), Peter Lawford (Andrew Carmel), Helen Walker (Betty Cream), Reginald Gardner (Hilary Ames), Reginald Owen (Sir Henry Carmel), Sir C. Aubrey Smith (Col. Duff Graham), Richard Haydn (Wilson), Margaret Bannerman (Lady Alice Carmel), Sara Allgood (Mrs. Maile), Ernest Cossart (Syrette), Florence Bates (Dowager), Una O'Connor (Mrs. Wilson), Queenie Leonard (Weller), Billy Bevan (Uncle Arn), Michael Dyne (John Frewen), Christopher Severn (Master Snaffle), Rex Evans (Guest Piano Player), Ottola Nesmith (Mrs. Tupham), Harold de Becker (Mr. Snaffle), Jean Prescott (Mrs. Snaffle), Clive Morgan (Waiter), Charles Coleman (Constable

Birkins), George Kirby (Latham),
Whit Bissell (Dowager's Son), Philip
Morris (Policeman), Betty Fairfax
(Woman in Chemist's Shop), Norman
Ainsley (Mrs. Tupham). Second re-
vised cast list of Feb. 14, 1946 also
lists: Mira McKinney (Author's
Wife). Call Bureau Cast Service
list of June 19, 1946 also lists:
Al Winters (Rollins), Bette Rae
Brown (Girl at Party), Brad Slaven
(English Boy on Bike), Billy Gray
(Boy in Shop).

Production: Ernst Lubitsch for 20th Century-Fox
Shooting: Begun at the 20th Century-Fox West-
wood Studios in December 1945 and
completed in early February 1946
(days of shooting: approx. 60)

Running Time: 100 minutes
Released: June
New York Premiere: June 1

Note:
Margery Sharp's 1944 novel was an international best seller.
It was serialized in Ladies' Home Journal (as "Be Good, Sweet
Maid"), was both a Book of the Month Club and Dollar Book Club
selection, and was serialized in comic strip form in over 100
newspapers.

Reviews:
New York Times, June 3, p. 27 and June 9, II.1; Variety,
May 1, p. 8; Motion Picture Herald, Apr. 27, Product Digest
Section, p. 2961; Daily Variety, May 1, p. 3; Film Daily,
May 1, p. 6; Hollywood Reporter, May 1, pp. 3, 19; Newsweek,
May 6, p. 90; Time, May 20, p. 90; Life, May 27, pp. 125-28;
Nation, June 8, p. 701; Commonweal, June 14, p. 216; New York-
er, June 15; Theatre Arts, June, pp. 349-50; Cosmopolitan,
June, pp. 69, 163; Woman's Home Companion, June, pp. 10-11;
New Republic, July 29, p. 103; Forum, Aug., p. 177; Photoplay,
Aug., p. 4; London Times, July 29, p. 8; Monthly Film Bulle-
tin, May 31, p. 62; New Statesman and Nation, July 27, p. 64;
Spectator, Aug. 2, p. 115; Sight and Sound, Autumn, pp. 97-98.

Also see:
New York Times, Dec. 16, 1945, II.3; Variety, Feb. 13,
p. 7, June 16, 1948, p. 15; Hollywood Reporter, June 7, p. 9
(excerpts reviews in New York papers); Positif, Oct. 1971,
no. 131, pp. 64-66.

83   THAT LADY IN ERMINE
      (1948)

The Principality of Bergamo, in southeastern Europe, 1861.
In the castle of Bergamo an old head servant, Luigi, bids
goodnight to the ancestral paintings on the wall as a voiceover identifies them. Especially striking is Francesca, the
barefoot lady in ermine who saved the castle from invaders
three hundred years ago. Francesca is especially happy tonight, for her great, great, great, great granddaughter and
look-alike, Angelina, is to be married tomorrow to Baron Mario.

After the wedding ceremony Mario carries his bride over the
threshold. His vanity is wounded because Angelina had the superior position in the ceremony and had to raise his rank and
make him a Bergamo for them to marry. As she soothes and woos
him, guns are heard in the distance, and Luigi comes with the
news that Hungarian invaders have broken through the lines and
are on their way to the castle. Mario flees for his life.

Midnight, the gallery. The figures in the paintings come
to life and urge Francesca to save the castle, as she did in
the past. From the tower Francesca sees through a spyglass
the approach of a handsome Hungarian colonel, and, in song,
promises she'll take care of him.

The Hungarians enter the castle and the Colonel is in-
trigued by the beauty of Francesca and the mystery of the bare
feet. The lady of the castle sends word she has already retired and does not wish to be disturbed. There is a scream in
the gallery and one of the women swears she saw the lady in
the painting move. The Colonel starts upstairs to see about
the Countess when the lady in ermine smiles at him.

Next morning the Colonel is at the painting again when Angelina comes down. She is mockingly gracious and solicitous.
The Colonel learns from her of her bridegroom's abrupt departure and taunts her about it until she begins to cry. He
softens up and confesses he is in love with her ancestor in
the painting.

The Colonel entreats Luigi to tell him the story of Francesca. The scene fades back three hundred years when (as now)
the castle has been captured by an invader, the Duke of Raven-
na. The Duke orders the castle destroyed. Alberto, the ruler
of Bergamo, entreats him to reconsider, but he remains un-
moved. Francesca makes a final try, in her ermine coat (signifying dignity) and bare feet (signifying humility). Francesca and the Duke go into his tent, and some time later the
Duke comes out to say the castle will be spared and the people
are free. He returns to his tent and collapses, stabbed to

171

death with a dagger in his back. Some say (Luigi tells the Colonel) she killed the man who had fallen in love with her simply because he was the enemy; others say she was afraid of herself because she was falling for him; still others say it was because she couldn't bear the thought of any other woman having him.

That night Mario comes to Angelina's room disguised as a gypsy. He is infuriated when the Colonel stops to tell Angelina goodnight. Soldiers overhear his talking and come to search the room. The Colonel comes and dismisses them. Mario exits via the balcony. Shortly after, Angelina hears the Colonel underneath her balcony. (He finds Mario's gypsy earring and guesses the truth.)

Next day Mario, still disguised as a gypsy, is caught and brought before the Colonel. Without letting Mario know, the Colonel tells Angelina he'll spare her husband's life if she will bare her feet, wear an ermine coat, and dine with him that evening. Angelina does not show up for the dinner and around midnight the Colonel, who has been drinking, falls asleep. Francesca appears to the Colonel, as in a dream, as Angelina. They kiss and exchange confessions of love. Francesca vows this time the lover will live. Ecstatically the Colonel picks her up and carries her up the stairs as the ancestors look on.

Next morning the Colonel is exceedingly pleasant with his men. Angelina appears to plead for Mario's life, and the Colonel orders the gypsy freed despite his Major's warning that he is an enemy officer. The Colonel tells Angelina how magnificent she was the night before, vows his eternal love, and orders the Major to make preparations to leave the castle immediately. Mario boasts how he fooled the Colonel. Angelina produces the earring to show he wasn't fooled at all. Mario wants to know what then she had to do to save his life. She explains it was the dream. A scream is heard; it's the same lady saying this time she saw the lady in ermine smile. The Colonel has become extremely irritable; all the men understand it's Angelina. One evening after he has fallen asleep on a sofa Angelina arrives escorted by Luigi and falls asleep herself as she waits. In his dreams the Colonel is dancing with Francesca when she stabs him in the back and he wakes up. Angelina explains that Mario wouldn't believe her that nothing happened between them and walked out; the marriage has been annulled. She has brought a priest with her and she and the Colonel are to be married at once.

In a final scene Francesca leads the ancestors in a dance as they all sing, "Ooh, what she'll do to that wild Hungarian!" (Lubitsch's original plan called for a final scene where

Francesca pours herself a glass of wine, remembers her beautiful dream with the Colonel, and finally takes off the ermine coat to reveal what she wore to the Duke's tent. This was eliminated by Preminger.)

Directors:	Ernst Lubitsch and Otto Preminger
Screenplay:	Samson Raphaelson
Source:	The operetta, <u>Die Frau im Hermelin</u> (1919), by Rudolf Schanzer and Ernest Welisch and its English-language adaptations
Photography:	Leon Shamroy
Art Directors:	Lyle Wheeler and J. Russell Spencer
Set Decorations:	Thomas Little and Walter M. Scott
Lyrics and Music:	Leo Robin and Frederick Hollander
Musical Direction and Incidental Music:	Alfred Newman
Vocal Direction:	Charles Henderson
Orchestral Arrangements:	Edward Powell, Herbert Spencer, and Maurice de Packh
Technicolor Color Director:	Natalie Kalmus
Associate:	Leonard Doss
Editor:	Dorothy Spencer
Wardrobe Direction:	Charles LeMaire
Costumes:	Rene Hubert
Choreography:	Hermes Pan
Makeup:	Ben Nye; George Lane and Frank Prehoda
Special Photographic Effects:	Fred Sersen
Sound:	Arthur L. Kirbach and Roger Heman
Production Manager:	A. F. Erickson
Assistant Director:	Tom Dudley
Cameraman:	Bud Mantino
Script Supervisor:	Doris Drought
Hair Stylists:	Marie Brasselli and Esperanza Corona
Grip:	Roger Murphy
Still Man:	Anthony Ugrin
Cast:	Betty Grable (Angelina and Francesca), Douglas Fairbanks, Jr. (Colonel Ladislaus Karoly Teglash and Duke of Ravenna), Cesar Romero (Mario), Walter Abel (Major Horvath and Benevenuto), Reginald Gardiner (Alberto), Harry Davenport (Luigi), Virginia Campbell (Theresa), Whit Bissell (Giulio), Edmund MacDonald (Captain Novak), David Bond (Gabor), Harry Cording, Belle Mitchell, Mary Bear, Jack George, John Parrish, Mayo

	Newhall (Ancestors), Lester Allen (Jester). Call Bureau Cast Service list of August 25, 1948 also lists: Harry Carter, Thayer Roberts, Don Haggerty (Staff Officers), Robert Karnes (Lieutenant), Duke York (Sergeant), Ray Hyke (Albert's Knight), Jimmy Ames (Bit Guard), Joe Haworth (Soldier), Francis Pierlot (Priest).
Songs:	"This Is the Moment," "Ooh, What I'll Do (To That Wild Hungarian)," "Jester's Song," "The Melody Has To Be Right" (Some sources list an additional song, "It's Always a Beautiful Day," attributed to Lubitsch and Leo Robin.)
Production:	Ernst Lubitsch for 20th Century-Fox
Shooting:	Begun October 20, 1947 at the 20th Century-Fox Westwood Studios and completed January 5, 1948 (days in production: 62)
Running Time:	89 minutes
Released:	August
New York Premiere:	August 24
Temporary Production Titles:	This Is the Moment, The Lady in Ermine

Notes:
   "As a posthumous gesture of respect, Ernst Lubitsch will be given screen credits as producer and director of This Is the Moment, which he was making at 20th-Fox at the time of his death [November 30]. Otto Preminger, who took over the half-finished production, asked that Lubitsch be given all the credit" (Variety, Dec. 17, 1947, p. 2). Preminger took over shooting on December 5 and shot 26 days. Of the 50 set-scene stills in the 20th Century-Fox Set-Stills book (in the Cinema Library at the University of Southern California) 36 have Lubitsch's name on them and 14 have Preminger's. The Lady in Ermine, "a musical play in three acts; book by Frederick Lonsdale and Cyrus Wood from the book by Rudolph Schanzer and Ernest Welisch; music by Jean Gilbert and Alfred Goodman; lyrics by Harry Graham and Cyrus Wood" opened on Broadway October 2, 1922 and ran until spring; for a plot synopsis, see Best Plays of 1922-23, p. 468.

Reviews:
   New York Times, Aug. 25, p. 31; Variety, July 14, p. 12; Motion Picture Herald, July 17, Production Digest Section, pp. 4241-42; Daily Variety, July 14, pp. 3, 8; Film Daily, July 15, p. 5; Hollywood Reporter, July 14, p. 3;

Commonweal, Sept. 3, p. 499; New Yorker, Sept. 4; Newsweek, Sept. 6, pp. 74-75; Life, Sept. 27, pp. 90-91; Good Housekeeping, Sept., pp. 118-19; London Times, July 16, 1949, p. 7; Spectator, July 22, 1949, p. 109.

Also see:
    Hollywood Reporter, June 3, 1942, p. 5, Aug. 4, 1942, p. 1, Feb. 25, 1943, pp. 1-2 (proposed version with Irene Dunne and Charles Boyer), Mar. 26, 1943, p. 4, June 10, 1943, p. 8, Sept. 5, 1944, p. 8 (Jeanette MacDonald to star); Aug. 27, p. 7 (excerpts reviews from New York papers); Time, Aug. 23, pp. 40-44 (cover story on Betty Grable); New York Sun, Aug. 24, p. 13.

IV. Writings about
Ernst Lubitsch, 1920-1977

1920

84 ANON. "New Film Record Set by <u>Passion</u>." <u>New York Times</u>, December 23, p. 28. Reprinted in Pratt (1966).

Report on the phenomenal success of <u>Madame Dubarry</u> (retitled <u>Passion</u> for U.S. release), the film that broke the blockade in effect from World War I against American importation of German films and launched the so-called "German invasion." The success of this film with American audiences opened the way for other previously unseen German films such as <u>Cabinet of Dr. Caligari</u> and Lubitsch's <u>Anna Boleyn</u> and ultimately for the importation of German directors and stars. The sequence of the "German invasion" is summarized in the <u>New York Times</u>, Feb. 4, 1923, VII.3, and can be traced through <u>Moving Picture World</u>, a representative trade journal of the time: Sept. 11, pp. 181, 205, Oct. 9, p. 759, Oct. 16, p. 908, Oct. 30, pp. 1209, 1214, Nov. 27, pp. 469, 513; (1921) Jan. 8, p. 161, Jan. 29, p. 537, Apr. 30, p. 989, May 7, pp. 31, 40; May 14, p. 190, May 21, p. 321, June 16, p. 328, Sept. 24, p. 428, Oct. 1, pp. 510-12, 574, Oct. 8, p. 629, Oct. 29, pp. 1010-12, Dec. 24, p. 949.

<u>Also see</u>:
<u>New York Times</u>, Oct. 3, VII.2, Oct. 10, VI.2, Oct. 24, VI.2, Jan. 30, 1921, VI.2; <u>Variety</u>, (1921) Apr. 15, p. 45, May 13, p. 2, p. 47, May 20, pp. 1-2, June 17, pp. 1, 37, Nov. 25, p. 44, Dec. 16, p. 39; (1922) Jan. 27, p. 45, Feb. 3, p. 46, July 28, p. 2; and Alfred B. Kuttner, "The Foreign Invasion," <u>Exceptional Photoplays</u>, Nov. 1921, pp. 1-2.

1921

85 ANON. "How Lubitsch Works." <u>Wid's Daily</u>, December 28, pp. 1, 4.

When Lubitsch visited America in December to make distribution arrangements for his unreleased films and to

study American studio methods, he was widely interviewed by
the press. Favorite topics of the interviewers were Lubitsch's working methods and his impressions of American
films. Other press interviews worthy of note include:
Sumner Smith, "Ernst Lubitsch Describes Novel Method of
Preparing a Picture for Production," Moving Picture World,
Jan. 7, 1922, pp. 53-54; John Walker Harrington, "Lubitsch,
Master of Mobs," New York Times, Jan. 8, 1922, VII.4; Ludwig Lewisohn, "Ernst Lubitsch," Nation, Jan. 18, 1922,
p. 76; Russell Holman, "How Lubitsch Works," Filmplay,
Apr. 1922, pp. 33, 56; Frederick James Smith, "The Photoplay in Stagnant Waters," Motion Picture Classic, Apr. 1922,
pp. 34, 77.

1922

86   HOWE, HERBERT. "The Film Wizard of Europe." Photoplay, De-
     cember, pp. 28-29, 96, 98-99. Substantial excerpt in Pratt
     (1966).
         A visit with Lubitsch on the set of Die Flamme in Ber-
     lin. The director comments on his work in the cutting room
     as well as on the set.

87   MILNE, PETER. "Ernst Lubitsch: German Director," in Motion
     Picture Directing: The Facts and Theories of the Newest
     Art. New York: Falk Publishing Company, pp. 195-204.
         In this early critical assessment, Lubitsch is praised
     for his handling of actors and his genius at understate-
     ment, but the author complains that Lubitsch's films are
     not properly edited and says he is a lesser director of
     spectacles than Griffith because of his inattention to in-
     dividual characters and details.

1923

88   ANON. "Lubitsch on Directing." New York Times, December 16,
     IX.5. Reprinted in Pratt (1966).
         With The Marriage Circle completed, Lubitsch is in New
     York looking for story material. He speaks of his recent
     transition from spectacle to "intimate drama," praises A
     Woman of Paris, and talks about the difficulty of finding
     good material.

89   CARR, HARRY. "The 'No' Man Comes to Hollywood." Motion Pic-
     ture, July, pp. 27-28, 86.
         Concerning Lubitsch and his early collaborators at the
     Pickford-Fairbanks Studio. Lubitsch talks at length on
     his Faust project, which was later abandoned for Rosita.

90 _____. "The Directors Who 'Bring 'Em In.'" Classic, November, pp. 24-25, 89-90.
In this brief survey of the top directors of the day,
Lubitsch is called "a von Stroheim trying to behave" and
"in many ways...the finest director of all of them." Other
director survey articles of the time with material of in-
terest on Lubitsch include: Alison Smith, "Movies and the
Melting Pot," Motion Picture Classic, Mar. 1924, pp. 38-39,
78; Harry Carr, "How the Great Directors Work," Motion
Picture, May 1925, pp. 52-53, reprinted in Pratt (1966);
Harry Carr, "The Status of the Directors," Motion Picture
Classic, Nov. 1925, pp. 20-21, 80; Terry Ramsaye, "What
Makes a Director?" Photoplay, Dec. 1925, pp. 50-51, 92, 94;
Matthew Josephson, "Masters of the Motion Picture," Motion
Picture Classic, Aug. 1926, pp. 24-25, 66, 83.

1924

91 LICHT-BILD-BÜHNE. Luxusnummer. 30 Jahre Film. Berlin:
"Licht bildbühne."
This anniversary number of the German trade periodical
includes short contributions by Lubitsch and two of his
principal German collaborators. In "Wie das Deutsche
Licht spieltheater enstand" (pp. 7-10), producer Paul Davidson outlines the history of film theaters in Germany and
relates a few anecdotes from his twenty-year career in
films, including how Lubitsch first came to direct comedies
and his later reluctance to take on more serious subjects,
and how the author boosted the film careers of Ossi Oswalda
and Pola Negri. In "Wie mein erster Grossfilm entstand"
(pp. 13-14), Lubitsch outlines the steps in his transition
from short comedies to the giant costume epics that made
him internationally famous, but confesses that his real
preference is for small, intimate dramas (Kammerspiele)
like Rausch, Die Flamme, and The Marriage Circle. In "Vom
Notizbuch zum Liebhaberdruck" (pp. 33-34), Hans Kraly
traces the changing function of the writer in films, from
the days when improvisation was the rule and a scenario was
a few notes "on the cuff," down to the time of this writing,
when a scenario was more likely to be a totally conceived
dramatic work setting down in intricate detail precisely
what is to happen in the film. A copy of this rare item
may be found in the Library of the Museum of Modern Art.

92 NEGRI, POLA. "The Autobiography of Pola Negri. Part II."
Photoplay, March, pp. 56-57, 86, 118-20.
In this installment of her autobiography, Lubitsch's
foremost actress in Germany tells of her "discovery" of Lubitsch and of their work together in Germany. They made
one film together in America, Forbidden Paradise, which

she talks about with Harry Carr in "The Mystery of Pola Negri," <u>Motion Picture</u>, Apr. 1925, pp. 34-35, 108-109.

<u>Also see</u>:
   Robert Florey, <u>Pola Negri</u> (Paris: Publications Jean-Pascal, 1926), and entry 166 on Miss Negri's memoirs (1970).

1926

93   BARRY, IRIS. <u>Let's Go to the Pictures</u>. London: Chatto & Windus, pp. 203-204, 227-29.
       Apt critical overview of Lubitsch's first American films.

94   FLOREY, ROBERT. <u>Deux ans dans les studios américains</u>. Paris: Publications Jean-Pascal. Première partie, 28-30, 119-22; deuxième partie, 158-63.
       Reflections and reminiscences of the French emigré film-maker. He tells of Lubitsch's arrival in Hollywood and paraphrases their conversations about contemporary films. Of special importance is Florey's detailed notebook of the first two days of shooting on <u>Rosita</u>. Florey later greatly expanded his accounts of Lubitsch's relationship with Mary Pickford and of the shooting of <u>Rosita</u> in "En regardant tourner Lubitsch," <u>La Lanterne Magique</u>, no. 6, Documents de Cinéma (La Cinémathèque Suisse-Lausanne, 1966), pp. 83-90.

95   GREEN, ELEANOR. "Mr. and Mrs. Lubitsch." <u>Motion Picture</u>, January, pp. 34, 116.
       A rare glimpse of the first Mrs. Lubitsch.

96   TULLY, JIM. "Ernst Lubitsch." <u>Vanity Fair</u>, December, p. 82.
       An unsympathetic and condescending interview article, but with good moments, as when Lubitsch is asked: "Why is it you are satisfied to direct light comedy when you might do another <u>Passion</u>?"

1927

97   BRATZ, CARL. "Carl Bratz an Lubitsch." <u>Licht-Bild-Bühne</u>, May 28, p. 11.
       A speech given in praise of Lubitsch during intermission at a festival of his films in Berlin. Lubitsch is present on the occasion. According to the editorial notes, <u>Lady Windermere's Fan</u> was especially well received.

98   GROSVENOR, ROBERT. "Ernst Lubitsch Looks at Life and the Cinema." <u>Cinema Art</u>, October, pp. 16-17, 45.
       Lubitsch on German vs. American audiences, on Chaplin

("one of the greatest artists in the world"), and on his oft-repeated theme that he would like to be making serious pictures.

99   NEDOBROVO, VLADIMIR. <u>Ernst Liubich</u>. Moscow: Kinopechat', 16 pp.
      <u>Carmen</u>, <u>Madame Dubarry</u>, <u>Anna Boleyn</u>, <u>Die Austernprinzessin</u>, and <u>The Marriage Circle</u> are among the films discussed in this semi-popular Marxist tract. The author is not unsympathetic to Lubitsch as a director, but is sarcastic about the system under which he works, commercial cinema in the non-Communist world, and its bad effects on his art. A copy of this rare item may be found in the Library of the Museum of Modern Art.

1928

100   SACHS, HANNS. "Film Psychology: <u>Drei Frauen</u>, by Lubitsch." <u>Close Up</u>, November, pp. 14-15.
      Freudian interpretation of an incident in <u>Three Women</u> in which a woman pulls at a man's tie. Reprinted (in French) in <u>Positif</u>, no. 74, March 1966.

1929

101   WEINBERG, HERMAN G. "Lubitsch Views the Movies." <u>Movie Makers</u>, September, pp. 570-71.
      Lubitsch and the author discuss contemporary films. Lubitsch talks at length about his reactions to Dreyer's <u>La Passion de Jeanne d'Arc</u>, Russian films, and Vidor's <u>The Crowd</u>.

1930

102   ANON. "Lubitsch Appointed Supervising Director in East." <u>Film Daily</u>, August 29, pp. 1, 6.
      Announcement of Paramount's ambitious venture to transfer a major portion of its production schedule to its Astoria Studios in Long Island City. Lubitsch was assigned to supervise all Astoria productions, and seventeen features were put on the schedule for the first year. Lubitsch's own <u>The Smiling Lieutenant</u> was made at Astoria in this period. The eastern studio operation was a disappointment and announcement was made in May 1931 that the venture was being abandoned.

      <u>Also see:</u>
      <u>Variety</u>, Sept. 3, pp. 1, 6, Oct. 1, pp. 4, 5, Oct. 15, pp. 2, 3, Nov. 12, p. 11, Dec. 3, p. 4, Dec. 31, p. 8;

(1931) Mar. 25, p. 4, Apr. 1, p. 7, May 27, p. 5, June 2, pp. 7, 21, 43; and Film Daily, Sept. 7, pp. 1-2, Oct. 19, p. 5; (1931) May 28, pp. 1, 7.

103 BEAUMONT, BEVERLY. "Soup and Fish." Rob Wagner's Script, July 5, p. 28.
Social column report on a dinner Lubitsch gave in Hollywood in honor of Sergei Eisenstein.

104 CASTLE, HUGH. "This Thrilling Instalment." Close Up, August, pp. 130-39.
General discussion of screen comedy. Lubitsch is called "one of the very few men who have ever come near to filmic comedy."

105 HUBERT, ALI. Hollywood: Legende und Wirklichkeit. Leipzig: Verlag E. A. Seemann.
A personal memoir of Hollywood by Lubitsch's perennial costume designer. Includes many anecdotes and details of Lubitsch, Jannings, Kraly, and the author in Hollywood. Of special interest are lengthy accounts of one day's work on The Patriot, from shooting of a scene with Jannings in the morning to screening rushes in the evening, and of the problems the author encountered meeting the costuming schedule and requirements for The Student Prince. Lengthy excerpts appeared in French as "Lubitsch au travail: Les Coulisses d'un grand film," Revue du Cinéma, no. 10, pp. 10-22.

1931

106 ANON. "'Patchwork' Films Not Wanted Abroad, Says Lubitsch." Film Daily, April 28, pp. 1, 6.
"Unless American producers make first-class product for the foreign market they had better abandon this field, said Ernst Lubitsch in an exclusive interview...yesterday." Lubitsch also comments negatively on the future of widescreen.

107 LEJEUNE, C. A. Cinema. London: Alexander Maclehose and Company, pp. 63-69.
Nominates Lubitsch "laureate to the cinema" because of his incredible consistency and versatility. A compelling summation of Lubitsch's achievements.

108 WHITE, KENNETH. "Movie Chronicle: The Style of Ernst Lubitsch." Hound & Horn, January/March, pp. 273-76.
Makes two important critical points: that Lubitsch's chief contribution to the musical was the successful integration of music and action, and that the Lubitsch style is more dependent on mise en scène than on montage.

1932

109   ANON. "A Chat with Mr. Lubitsch." New York Times, February
       28, VIII.6.
             In New York for the opening of One Hour with You, Lu-
       bitsch discusses playwriting and his plans for a stage pro-
       duction in the near future. (See Unrealized Projects, en-
       try 288.)

110   ANON. "Lack of Varied Roles Kills Stars Early, Says Lubitsch."
       Film Daily, March 1, pp. 1, 7.
             Interview remarks by Lubitsch on type-casting and on
       proper uses of music in pictures.

111   ANON. "Lubitsch's Analysis of Pictures Minimizes Director's
       Importance." Variety, March 1, pp. 2, 17.
             The interviewer summarizes Lubitsch's reflections on
       such topics as percentage payment to film directors, film
       as business vs. film as art, and film "cycles." Much more
       to the point on Lubitsch as a director working in Hollywood
       than most Lubitsch press interviews.

112   BURNETT, R. G., and E. D. MARTELL. The Devil's Camera: Men-
       ace of a Film-Ridden World. London: Epworth Press, pp. 29-
       34.
             In the view of these authors, The Smiling Lieutenant is
       dangerously immoral because it glamorizes illicit sex. Of
       interest for its brief mention of the film's censorship
       problems in England.

1933

113   ANON. "Fans Abroad Want Films in Own Tongue--Lubitsch."
       Film Daily, January 14, pp. 1-2.
             "If American producers want to retain their prominent
       position in the foreign market, they must produce dialogue
       pictures directly for audiences there, declared Ernst Lu-
       bitsch in an exclusive interview...yesterday, following his
       return...from a vacation in Europe."

114   ANON. "Lubitsch Sees Gloomy Prospects Abroad...." Variety,
       January 24, p. 6.
             Lubitsch warns that American films are losing ground in
       foreign markets because not enough native language produc-
       tions are being made.

115   ANON. "Lubitsch Says Films Must Reflect Times." Film Daily,
       November 9, pp. 1, 4.
             "It is unfair to criticize producers for the type of
       stories they make," says Lubitsch, because they are only

giving the public what it wants. He also raves about Walt
Disney ("the greatest screen artist") and says he hopes
musicals won't be killed off through overproduction because
they are a good "meal ticket" for the studios.

116   HECHT, BEN. "Lubitsch in a Nutshell." New York World Tele-
      gram, November 21, p. 17.
          From a Paramount publicity release. A typical bit of
      Hechtian leg-pull. Discussed in Weinberg (1968), pp. 249-
      51.

117   HERRING, ROBERT. "Fan Males." Close Up, March, pp. 40-46.
          Relates how Lubitsch discovered Jeanette MacDonald.

118   HUTCHISON, BARNEY. "Hollywood Still Leads...says Ernst Lu-
      bitsch." American Cinematographer, March, pp. 8, 38.
          Back from a vacation in Europe, Lubitsch is interviewed
      on the state of European film production. He compares and
      contrasts American procedures and techniques with those in
      the European studios, and extols the superiority of Ameri-
      can technicians and laboratories.

119   LEE, SONIA. "Four Directors Tell What's Wrong with the Mov-
      ies." Motion Picture, September, pp. 42, 90-92.
          Lubitsch criticizes the supervisory system in the stu-
      dios and the procedure of assigning many writers to one
      story--ironically, two practices he was later to defend as
      head of production at Paramount.

120   MACDONALD, DWIGHT. "Notes on Hollywood Directors." The Sym-
      posium, April, pp. 168-72.
          Macdonald distinguishes between Lubitsch as a director
      of sophisticated comedies and a Reinhardt-trained director
      of pretentious historical dramas, and says "His vital qual-
      ities are called into play only in comedy." He discusses
      Trouble in Paradise as the epitome of Lubitsch comedy. Re-
      printed in Dwight Macdonald on Movies (Englewood Cliffs:
      Prentice-Hall, 1969).

121   QUIRK, MAY ALLISON. "'All Women Are Sirens at Heart.'" Photo-
      play, August, pp. 58, 96.
          "How is it that every actress acquires unsuspected sex
      allure under your direction?" Lubitsch answers such ques-
      tions about Pola Negri, Mary Pickford, Florence Vidor,
      Jeanette MacDonald, and Miriam Hopkins. Reprinted in The
      Talkies, ed. Richard Griffith (New York: Dover, 1971),
      pp. 164, 338.

1934

122   CHEATHAM, MAUDE. "'They Have Something Different'--Ernest
      [sic] Lubitsch." Silver Screen, August, pp. 23, 64-65.
         Brief remarks by Lubitsch on many of the performers who
      have worked with him.

123   SENNWALD, ANDRE. "A Word with Ernst Lubitsch." New York
      Times, October 14, X.5.
         Account of an interview with Lubitsch at the time of
      the New York opening of The Merry Widow, in which Lubitsch
      speaks out against the rigidity of the Motion Picture Pro-
      duction Code. A crackdown on enforcement of the Code came
      in the late stages of production of The Merry Widow, Franz
      Lehár's risqué operetta full of taboo boudoir incidents.
      There were Hays Office objections to The Merry Widow, and
      accommodations had to be made. (See especially New York
      Times, Nov. 25, IX.4; and also Hollywood Reporter, Aug. 10,
      p. 4, Aug. 15, p. 2, Aug. 25, p. 2, and Variety, Aug. 28,
      p. 2 and Sept. 4, p. 4.) Other Lubitsch interviews in the
      same vein appeared in Film Daily, Oct. 10, pp. 1, 8 and New
      York Sun, Oct. 17, p. 33. Martin Quigley, trade publisher
      and advocate for the Legion of Decency, condemned Lubitsch
      and defended the Code in a front-page reply in Motion Pic-
      ture Daily, October 19. (Also see "A Reader Answers Mr.
      Lubitsch," New York Times, Oct. 28, IX. 4.) Lubitsch re-
      plied to Quigley in Hollywood Reporter (Oct. 22, p. 1),
      saying: "No industry that lives from drama can exist if
      not permitted to deal with the urgent problems of the times,
      and it should not be forced to treat such problems in an
      unbelievable, fairy-tale manner."

1935

124   ANON. "Cohen Quits Post with Paramount." New York Times,
      February 6, p. 23.
         Announcement of Lubitsch's being elevated to production
      head at Paramount. He held this position until February
      1936, when he was replaced by William LeBaron. For what-
      ever reasons, production lagged and costs soared during
      Lubitsch's tenure as production head. For highlights of
      Lubitsch's term in the post, see Variety, Feb. 5, pp. 1,
      5, Feb. 12, pp. 4, 5, 7, Feb. 20, pp. 5, 25, Feb. 27,
      p. 4, Mar. 13, p. 5, Mar. 20, pp. 3, 4, Mar. 27, p. 5,
      Apr. 10, p. 5, Apr. 24, p. 5, May 22, p. 5, May 29, p. 1,
      June 5, pp. 1, 50, June 12, pp. 3, 29, pp. 5, 29, June 19,
      pp. 5, 79, July 31, p. 4, Aug. 7, p. 3, Oct. 9, p. 5,
      Nov. 13, pp. 4, 6, Nov. 20, pp. 2, 6; (1936) Feb. 5, p. 5,
      Feb. 12, p. 5, Feb. 26, p. 5, Mar. 18, p. 6; and Hollywood
      Reporter, (1935) Feb. 12, p. 1, Mar. 8, p. 1, Mar. 15,

p. 3, Mar. 19, p. 3, Mar. 26, pp. 1, 3, June 3, p. 8,
June 5, pp. 1-2, June 7, p. 1, June 11, pp. 1-2, June 13,
pp. 1, 10, June 14, p. 3, June 15, p. 1, June 17, pp. 1-2,
June 18, p. 1, June 22, pp. 1, 3, June 26, p. 1, June 27,
p. 2, Aug. 2, p. 6, Oct. 24, p. 4, Nov. 5, p. 1; (1936)
Jan. 31, pp. 1, 6, Feb. 3, p. 1, Feb. 4, pp. 1-2, Feb. 8,
pp. 1-2, Feb. 21, p. 1.

Also see:
   The following feature articles: "Lubitsch Named Produc-
tion Head...," Motion Picture Herald, Feb. 9, p. 39; "Lu-
bitsch for Cohen," Time, Feb. 18, p. 72; "Lubitsch at the
Helm," New York Times, Mar. 31, XI.4; Idwal Jones, "Side
Glance at Lubitsch," New York Times, Sept. 22, X.4. His
exit as head of production is covered in New York Times,
Feb. 9, 1936, II.6 and Mar. 1, 1936, IX.5.

125   ANON. "The Famed 'Lubitsch Touch.'" Cue, July 27, pp. 3, 7,
      11, 13.
         From a studio publicity release; includes many biograph-
      ical details.

126   FIELDING, ADELAIDE. "Head Ladies' Man out of Circulation."
      New York Daily News, August 4, p. 50.
         Essentially a gossip column written shortly after Lu-
      bitsch's second marriage, this story mentions numerous rare
      details and prints several persistent rumors concerning Lu-
      bitsch's personal life.

127   JONES, GROVER. "Movie Magician." Collier's, September 21,
      pp. 26, 33.
         Career sketch by an old screenwriting hand who has
      adaptation credit on Trouble in Paradise. There are many
      revealing anecdotes, including several on Lubitsch's early
      professional years in Germany, which appear to have come
      from Lubitsch himself.

128   PAVOLINI, CORRADO. "Lucio D'Ambra, precursore di Lubitsch."
      Scenario (Rome), January, pp. 17-20.
         Outlines the contributions of this early Italian scen-
      arist and director of comedies (he was most active between
      1916 and 1921) to the art of the film, and enumerates sev-
      eral parallels between his cinematic conceptions and inno-
      vations and those of Lubitsch. "In Lubitsch's comedies
      today one sees resonances of D'Ambra's early poetry."

                              1936

129   ANON. "Lubitsch in Moscow." Variety, May 6, p. 4.
         Report on Lubitsch's first trip to the USSR. The visit
      was hosted by B. Z. Shumyatsky, head of Central Adminis-

tration of the Soviet Film Industry. On his return to
the United States Lubitsch commented: "I visited the
studios over there and I was astonished....In the matter of
technique they have introduced nothing new, nothing that we
don't know in Hollywood. But their method of story treatment is changing. They are realizing that strict propaganda
must give way to story films, to humor, and pictures por-
traying this new slant are now engaging their attention....
I saw one film over there called Circus, which turned out to
be Soviet Russia's idea of an American musical comedy. It
was done very well, too. When I left they were discussing
plans to build studios in the Crimea, a sort of a south Russian Hollywood" (New York World-Telegram, May 23, p. 4B).

Also see: New York World-Telegram, May 26, p. 19.

1937

130   ANON. "Paramount." Fortune, March, pp. 86-96, 194-98, 202-
      12.
          Corporate profile of the studio where Lubitsch spent one
      of the most productive periods of his career. Includes in-
      formation on Lubitsch's performance as head of production.

131   CREELMAN, EILEEN. "Hans Drier [sic], Paramount Set Designer,
      Talks of the Sets for Lubitsch's Angel." New York Sun,
      September 10, p. 31.
          At the time of the interview Dreier is just beginning to
      do preliminary sketches for Bluebeard's Eighth Wife. He
      describes how he goes about designing a production such as
      this one and how he and Lubitsch work together on it. He
      also recalls details of his work on Angel, which is about
      to be released.

1938

132   STULL, WILLIAM. "Camera Work Fails True Mission When It Sinks
      Realism for Beauty." American Cinematographer, February,
      pp. 56, 59-60.
          Hollywood cinematographers and other craftsmen are too
      often committed to the pursuit of technical perfection for
      its own sake, Lubitsch charges to this interviewer. As a
      consequence, Hollywood films are not convincingly realistic
      in the way such recent European films as La Grande Illusion
      and Pépé le Moko are. (Veteran cameraman Victor Milner,
      who worked on several of Lubitsch's Paramount films, re-
      plied to this charge in the March issue of American Cine-
      matographer, pp. 94-95. He remarks at one point that Lu-
      bitsch himself doesn't practice what he preaches.) See
      the 1923 article by Lubitsch in the same magazine for some
      very different remarks on American cinematographers.

1939

133   ANON. "New Group Plans $3,000,000 Films." New York Times,
       March 29, p. 21.
         Announcement that Lubitsch and veteran independent pro-
       ducer Sol Lesser had formed their own production company,
       with an arrangement for their films to be released through
       United Artists. A deal to star Eddie Cantor in their first
       picture never materialized (Film Daily, Apr. 16, 1940, p. 2).
       Eventually only one picture came out the the Lubitsch-
       Lesser venture, That Uncertain Feeling. Sol Lesser wrote
       the present authors (July 27, 1976) that it was Lubitsch
       who called off their agreement, "because he missed, in my
       limited environment, contact at lunch with the stars and
       other professionals that he associated with at MGM and
       other glamorous studios, and of course I gave him his re-
       lease readily." Lubitsch also made his next film, To Be
       or Not To Be, for United Artists release, with Alexander
       Korda as executive producer.

       Also see:
         New York Times, Jan. 16, 1940, p. 19, and June 18, 1941,
       p. 25. A detailed account of the organization, history,
       and current state of the company around the time Lubitsch
       was associated with it is given in "United Artists," For-
       tune, Dec. 1940, pp. 94-102, 170-78.

134   JACOBS, LEWIS. The Rise of the American Film: A Critical
       History. New York: Harcourt, Brace, pp. 305-308, 354-61.
         An influential early assessment of Lubitsch's achieve-
       ment. Lubitsch is remembered for past triumphs and inno-
       vations, especially in the Warners comedies and the early
       sound musicals, but his continued tendency to work almost
       exclusively in upper-class comedy of manners, Jacobs feels,
       has prevented him from "keeping abreast with the swiftly
       changing times," and caused him to rely more and more on
       safe comic formulas, which resulted in a loss of his crea-
       tive vitality. "The leadership he enjoyed during the pre-
       talkie era has been lost; his influence today is of minor
       proportions." Impeccably researched for its time.

1944

135   TYLER, PARKER. "To Be or Not To Be; or, The Cartoon Trium-
       phant," in his The Hollywood Hallucination. New York:
       Creative Age Press. Reprinted New York: Simon & Schuster,
       1970, pp. 208-21.
         Tyler gives reasons why he thinks the film is a failure;
       it is an uneasy mixture of various Hollywood styles and
       genres, its approach to its subject is ambiguous, and Jack
       Benny is inadequate for the role.

1947

136   ANON. "E. Lubitsch Dead; Film Producer, 55." <u>New York Times</u>,
       December 1, p. 21.
              Lubitsch died on November 30, 1947, in Hollywood. No-
       tices appeared in <u>Variety</u> on December 3, p. 6. An account
       of the funeral appears in <u>Los Angeles Examiner</u>, Friday,
       Dec. 5. The will was probated on Dec. 22, and this was re-
       ported in <u>Variety</u> on Dec. 31, p. 2. Lubitsch's paintings,
       prints, art objects, and furniture were sold at a New York
       auction gallery in 1952; a brief description of these col-
       lections appears in <u>New York Times</u>, June 8, 1952, p. 79.

137   CHEVALIER, MAURICE. <u>Ma route et mes chansons</u>. Paris: René
       Julliard, II, 154-57, 186-89, 196-97.
              A highly selective account of Chevalier's involvement
       with Lubitsch on their Paramount pictures. Chevalier's
       <u>The Man in the Straw Hat</u> (New York: Thomas Y. Crowell,
       1949) and <u>With Love</u>, as told to Eileen and Robert Mason
       Pollock (Boston: Little, Brown, 1960), both contain addi-
       tional material on <u>The Merry Widow</u> and new material on the
       Paramount films, but the French volume is the most inter-
       esting for the actor's attitudes toward Lubitsch.

138   HUFF, THEODORE. An Index to the Films of Ernst Lubitsch."
       <u>Sight and Sound Index Series</u>, no. 9, January, 31 pp.
              A pioneering filmography, much copied by later writers
       such as Weinberg (1968). Unfortunately the information is
       derived principally from printed sources such as pressbooks
       and is often inaccurate for the films as released.

139   KRACAUER, SIEGFRIED. <u>From Caligari to Hitler: A Psychologi-
       cal History of the German Film</u>. Princeton, N.J.: Prince-
       ton University Press, pp. 47-58.
              Lubitsch's costume epics are analyzed for submerged
       political content. The author sees them as cynical, nihil-
       istic, anti-progressive, and anti-democratic, and thinks
       these traits are linked to the mass feelings of a defeated
       nation.

140   MERRICK, MOLLIE. "25 Years of the 'Lubitsch Touch' in Holly-
       wood." <u>American Cinematographer</u>, July, pp. 238-39, 258.
              During production on <u>That Lady in Ermine</u>, Lubitsch
       talks about how he works with his cameramen and about the
       problems of handling fantasy in this film.

141   SCHEUER, PHILIP K. "Lubitsch Looks at His 'Oscar.'" <u>Los
       Angeles Times</u>, April 6, pp. 1, 3.
              Lubitsch is interviewed shortly after he received his
       special career achievement Academy Award. He tells why he
       stopped making musical comedies, lists his favorites among

his own films (he calls Shop around the Corner "the best
picture I ever made"), and talks about his preference for
art of "simple depiction" over art of thematic pretension--
a Cézanne still life over a painting of the Crucifixion,
Miracle of Morgan's Creek over a film with a "big theme"
and "message." Includes quotations from Mervyn LeRoy's
speech presenting the Oscar.

1948

142 POZZI, GIANNI. "Parere su Lubitsch." La critica cinematogra-
fica (Parma), May, p. 12.
     Calls Lubitsch undoubtedly the best European director
working in America and characterizes the typical Lubitsch
film as "a well constructed and harmonious whole whose lim-
pid exterior conceals the ironies of a conventional world."
The author does not care much for Ninotchka, which has just
been released in Italy. He says its political message
"ought to be taken lightly," and its chief merit is its vi-
vacious dialogue.

143 La Revue du Cinéma, no. 17, September, pp. 2-48.
     Special Lubitsch section with two lengthy critical arti-
cles, a tribute, and a filmography. In "Les origines du
'style Lubitsch,'" Lotte H. Eisner attempts to trace the
main features of Lubitsch's comic style to his Berlin origins. In "Lubitsch ou l'idéal de l'homme moyen," Mario Verdone discusses Lubitsch's handling of actors, the atmosphere of elegance in his films, his affinities with Lucio
D'Ambra and René Clair, the broad appeal of his comedies
(from intellectuals to the common man), and Heaven Can Wait
as an autobiographical testament. Jean George Auriol's
"'Chez Ernst'" is an affectionate personal view of Lubitsch
comedy. The brief filmography is by Jean Mitry (with Amable
Jameson).

144 Screen Writer, January, pp. 15-20.
     "Ernst Lubitsch: A Symposium." Contains tributes and
recollections by some of Lubitsch's close associates--
Chevalier, Brackett and Wilder, Jeanette MacDonald, Kraly,
Raphaelson, Steffie Trondle (his personal secretary), and
Darryl Zanuck. A separate tribute by Brackett and Wilder
in Hollywood Reporter (Dec. 3, 1947, p. 2) is reprinted by
Tom Wood in The Bright Side of Billy Wilder, Primarily (New
York: Doubleday, 1970), pp. 38-39.

145 WOLLENBERG, H. H. "Two Masters: Ernst Lubitsch and Sergei M.
Eisenstein." Sight and Sound, Spring, pp. 46-48.
     On the fundamental differences in their approaches to
film: Lubitsch's "pictorial" composition versus the
"documentary" appearance of Eisenstein's films, Lubitsch's
reliance on the camera as the storytelling instrument versus

Eisenstein's reliance on montage. After screening <u>Potemkin</u>, Lubitsch is said to have remarked: "but this film isn't pictorial. It looks like news-reel."

<u>Also see</u>:
　　Two other items by Wollenberg, both 1948--"Ernst Lubitsch" (<u>Penguin Film Review</u>, no. 7, Sept., pp. 61-67), a general survey with special emphasis on his major German films (reprinted in Whittemore and Cecchettini, 1976), and <u>Fifty Years of German Film</u> trans. Ernst Sigler (London: Falcon Press), which mentions Lubitsch briefly in the general context of German films.

1949

146　CASTELLO, GIULIO CESARE. "Contributo alla storia della 'Sophisticated Comedy.'" <u>Bianco e nero</u>, September, pp. 33-50.
　　The first five pages of this general essay stress Lubitsch's fundamental importance to the evolution of this American genre. <u>Trouble in Paradise</u> and <u>Design for Living</u> are discussed as special landmarks in this evolution. The rest of the essay is devoted to Capra, Hawks, and others.

1951

147　JANNINGS, EMIL. <u>Theater, Film--das Leben und Ich</u>. Berchtesgaden: Verlag Zimmer und Herzog, pp. 115-32, 157-91.
　　Like many star autobiographies, Jannings' is disappointingly brief on the production details and creative trials that lie behind his films. But one is grateful for whatever information can be had on Lubitsch's early films in Germany, and Jannings' conceptions of his roles and his opinions of the films in which he appeared are of interest.

148　STERN, ERNST. <u>My Life, My Stage</u>. Translated from the German manuscript by Edward Fitzgerald. London: Victor Gollancz, pp. 160-61, 178-87.
　　Max Reinhardt's famous set designer recalls details of his work on two Lubitsch films, <u>Die Bergkatze</u> and <u>Das Weib des Pharao</u>. Some sketches for the two films are reproduced.

1955

149　PICKFORD, MARY. <u>Sunshine and Shadow</u>. Garden City, N.Y.: Doubleday, pp. 250-55.
　　Mary Pickford imported Lubitsch from Germany to direct her in a film that would be a departure from her standard juvenile image. The outcome was <u>Rosita</u> (1923). Miss

Pickford's version of her tempestuous relationship with
Lubitsch on <u>Rosita</u> is given in her autobiography. She later
embellished this story in an interview with Kevin Brownlow
for <u>The Parade's Gone By</u> (New York: Ballantine, 1968). Miss
Pickford now detests <u>Rosita</u> and has persistently refused to
let it be shown. As late as 1976 she told one of her employees: "If you ever restore that film, I'll not only fire you,
I'll sue you" (<u>Variety</u>, Apr. 14, 1976, p. 33). From press
accounts through the 1920s about impending Pickford-Lubitsch
projects and about Miss Pickford's continued high regard for
Lubitsch, one wonders when her extreme bitterness toward Lubitsch really began; <u>see</u> especially <u>Moving Picture World</u>,
Sept. 8, 1923, p. 189; Mar. 1, 1924, p. 31; July 19, 1924,
p. 176.

<u>Also see</u>:
   Jack Spears, "Mary Pickford's Directors," <u>Films in Review</u>,
Feb. 1966, pp. 89-90; Raymond Lee, <u>The Films of Mary Pickford</u>
(New York: Barnes, 1970); and Robert Windeler, <u>Sweetheart:</u>
<u>The Story of Mary Pickford</u> (New York: Praeger, 1973).

1957

150 RIESS, KURT. <u>Das Gab's nur Einmal</u>. Hamburg: Verlag der
     Sternbücher, 1956. Second, expanded edition, 1957, pp. 80-
     85, 93-110, 132-36, 156-67.
        Lubitsch's life and career occupy a substantial portion
     of this gossipy, informal history. Many startling inci-
     dents and details are reported here without documentation,
     and many of them do not appear to be substantiated else-
     where in print. Most of the German portion of the criti-
     cal essay in Weinberg (1968) is taken from this book.

1958

151 PAOLELLA, ROBERTO. "Ernst Lubitsch, regista del tempo per-
     duto." <u>Bianco e nero</u>, January, pp. 1-19.
        A general overview of Lubitsch's career. <u>Anna Boleyn</u>
     is held to be his most important German film, because of
     its incipient realism. Lubitsch is undoubtedly the Euro-
     pean director who profited most from going to work in
     America, the author says, for immediately in his American
     films one sees a decided movement away from the excesses
     of his German films and an ever-increasing simplicity in
     motive and <u>mise en scène</u>. Lubitsch continued to improve
     throughout the silent years and reached his height in four
     films of the 1930s--<u>Trouble in Paradise</u>, <u>Design for Living</u>,
     <u>Desire</u>, and <u>Angel</u>. <u>Bluebeard's Eighth Wife</u> marks the be-
     ginning of his decline, though there were still masterpieces

192

like Ninotchka to come. The advent of World War II did not
materially affect him; aesthetically he remained most fully
committed to the values of the "Belle Époque" of the late
nineteenth century. Heaven Can Wait was his last great
comedy. Includes an abbreviated filmography.

1959

152 Film Journal (Australia), no. 13, June.
     Special issue, "The Films of Ernst Lubitsch." Contains:
     the Eisner and Auriol items from Revue du Cinéma (Sept.
     1948), translated into English by Ingrid Burke; Ian Klava,
     "The Sound Films of Ernst Lubitsch," a well-researched but
     rambling and derivative attempt to cover a great deal of
     ground; and the Theodore Huff filmography, annotated by
     Ian Klava.

153 IHERING, HERBERT. Von Reinhardt bis Brecht; vier Jahrzehnte
     Theater und Film. Berlin: Aufbau-Verlag; vol. II (1924-
     1929), 1959, vol. III (1930-1932), 1961.
     German reviews of six of Lubitsch's American films by
     the Berlin theater critic, written at the time they played
     in Germany. In vol. II, Rosita (Aug. 31, 1924), The Mar-
     riage Circle ("Ehe im Kreise," Sept. 2, 1924), The Patriot
     (Feb. 28, 1929); in vol. III, The Love Parade (Nov. 25,
     1930), The Smiling Lieutenant ("Die Schauspieler und der
     Tonfilm," Sept. 15, 1931), and The Man I Killed ("Ernst
     Lubitsch," Nov. 15, 1932).

1964

154 BAUM, VICKI. It Was All Quite Different. New York: Funk and
     Wagnalls, pp. 326-39.
     Contains information on two treatments Miss Baum pre-
     pared specifically for Lubitsch in the early 1930s. The
     first was a doomed attempt to duplicate her success with
     Grand Hotel, transferring the action from a hotel to a de-
     partment store. The other was an Oscar Straus operetta to
     star Maurice Chevalier--probably an early treatment of One
     Hour with You. (She does not mention the early treatments
     of The Merry Widow she did for Irving Thalberg.) Also of
     general interest as a fascinating account of how treat-
     ments were prepared in the studio system.

155 VERDONE, MARIO. Ernst Lubitsch. Premier Plan no. 32. Lyon:
     SERDOC, 78 pp.
     Verdone's introductory essay is essentially a reworking
     of his article in the 1948 special Lubitsch issue of Revue

du Cinéma, with a few new passages added. The volume also includes French translations of Lubitsch's 1937 article in Cinema on American actors and his 1947 letter to Herman Weinberg printed in Film Culture (1962); Jean George Auriol's "'Chez Ernst,'" reprinted from the 1948 Lubitsch Revue du Cinéma issue; and an abbreviated filmography.

1966

156   PRAGER, MICHAEL. "4 x Lubitsch: Die Komödie als Zeitkritik." Action (Vienna), no. 1, pp. 11, 14.
      Four comedies shown at the 1965 Venice Festival--Die Austernprinzessin, Die Puppe, Kohlhiesels Töchter, and Die Bergkatze--are analyzed for sociopolitical content and implications.

157   PRATT, GEORGE C. Spellbound in Darkness. Rochester, N.Y.: University of Rochester, pp. 267-81. Another edition with photographs, Greenwich, Conn.: New York Graphic Society, 1973, pp. 307-24.
      Excellent selection of contemporary documents (many from New York Times) illustrating the reception of Lubitsch's silent films in America.

1967

158   Action!, November/December, pp. 14-15.
      "A Tribute to Lubitsch (1892-1947)" by various filmmakers--Walter Reisch, Lewis Milestone, Billy Wilder, William Wyler, Andrew Marton, Henry Koster, Frank Capra, King Vidor, Alfred Hitchcock, and H. C. Potter.

1968

159   Cahiers du Cinéma, no. 198, February, pp. 10-45, 68-71.
      Special Lubitsch feature. Includes two new pieces, "Lubitsch était un prince," by François Truffaut and "L'homme de partout" by Jean Domarchi; French translations of Lubitsch's brief essay on film directing from Winchester (1933) and of several brief testimonies on Lubitsch from Weinberg (1968); a filmography by Patrick Brion; and brief commentaries on the films by numerous hands. Brion's filmography adds much new information on Lubitsch, especially obscure material such as minor character players in the films.

160 EISENSCHITZ, BERNARD. "Lubitsch (1892-1947)." Anthologie du Cinéma. Paris: L'Avant-Scène du Cinéma and C.I.B. vol. III, 113-68.
A well-researched general survey of Lubitsch's career, with good biographical information. Especially interesting remarks on Lubitsch's German origins, his association with Max Reinhardt, and his Warners features. The filmography adds some minor Lubitsch credits and other new information.

161 THOMPSON, HOWARD. "Glow of 'Lubitsch Touch' Is Rekindled Here." New York Times, November 15, p. 39.
Late in 1968 the Museum of Modern Art presented one of the most complete retrospective showings of Ernst Lubitsch ever held. A number of rarely seen films were included. Published program notes on the retrospective include: Calvin Green, "Lubitsch: The Trouble with Paradise," Film Society Review, Dec., pp. 18-33, Jan. 1969, pp. 19-34; Leonard Maltin, "Lubitsch," Film Fan Monthly, no. 90, pp. 3-5; and Bond (1977). Weinberg's The Lubitsch Touch was published in conjunction with the retrospective.

162 WEINBERG, HERMAN G. The Lubitsch Touch: A Critical Study. New York: E. P. Dutton, 344 pp. Revised edition with minor changes. New York: E. P. Dutton, 1971, 344 pp. Third enlarged edition with many textual additions and corrections and thirty-five new photographs. New York: Dover, 1977, 366 pp. In Spanish as El toque Lubitsch, translated by Ernesto Mayans. Barcelona: Editorial Lumen, [1973], 375 pp. French-language edition in preparation.

Reviews:
Robert Joseph, Action, May/June 1969, p. 39; Dick Adler, Book World, Feb. 23, 1969, p. 3; Cinéaste, Winter 1968/69, p. 19; Robert Joseph, Cinema (Los Angeles), vol. 5 no. 1, n.d., 46-47; Richard Dyer MacCann, Cinema Journal, Feb. 1969, p. 56; Frank Manchel, Film Comment, Fall 1969, p. 83; R. A. Haller, Film Heritage, Winter 1969/70, pp. 31-32; William K. Everson, Film Library Quarterly, Spring 1969, pp. 40-42; A. D. Malmfelt, Film Society Review, Jan. 1969, pp. 44-45; Sheridan Morley, Films and Filming, Mar. 1969, p. 72; International Film Guide 1970, p. 399; Publishers' Weekly, Sept. 30, 1968, p. 62; Glen Hunter, Take One, Nov./Dec. 1968, pp. 26-27.

A pioneering and indispensable work. Not the model of film scholarship it is sometimes called: the biographical and historical material is often paraphrased or borrowed outright from secondary sources without attribution, the criticism is essentially a cataloguing of Lubitsch "touches" accompanied by fulsome praise, and both the filmography and bibliography are unsystematic and largely unselective

gatherings of masses of information, much of it printed
without any indication of source or attempt at verification. Perhaps this book would be more justly described as
a devoted and highly partisan tribute to a favored subject.
It is like a lengthy expansion of one of the author's
"Coffee, Brandy, and Cigars" columns in a well-known film
magazine--uncritical, unhurried, discursive and unabashedly
opinionated. But it contains a treasure of miscellaneous
information gathered over a lifetime's interest in its subject, and despite its shortcomings by contemporary stand-
ards, will remain one of the essential starting points for
anyone seriously interested in Lubitsch.

1969

163   EISNER, LOTTE H. L'Écran démoniaque. Paris: Editions André
      Bonne, 1952. Revised French edition, Paris: Le Terrain
      Vague, 1965. Published in English as The Haunted Screen,
      translated by Roger Greaves, Berkeley: University of Cali-
      fornia Press, 1969; paperback edition, 1973.
            Chapter 4, "Lubitsch and the Costume Film," includes re-
      marks about Lubitsch's "Berliner mentality" (essentially a
      condensation of her lengthy piece in Revue du Cinéma, 1948)
      and a brief illustration of how Lubitsch's costume epics
      are indebted to Max Reinhardt. Her offhand comments on Lu-
      bitsch through the book are variations on her theme that he
      is outside the mainstream of German expressionist cinema.

*164 MATRAY, ERNST. Article in Pens Personal Bulletins (London),
      April 25.
            Not located. Cited in Horak (1975), p. 15.

1970

165   DURGNAT, RAYMOND. The Crazy Mirror: Hollywood Comedy and the
      American Image. New York: Horizon Press. Delta paper-
      back, 1972, pp. 109-14, 180-82.
            On Lubitsch's "sophisticated" comedies and their rela-
      tion to the moods of their times.

166   NEGRI, POLA. Memoirs of a Star. Garden City, N.Y.: Doubleday,
      pp. 112-248.
            Miss Negri elaborates from the perspective of fifty
      years on certain aspects of her involvement with Lubitsch.
      Especially interesting when compared with her remarks on
      the same topics in the series of memoirs she published in
      1924 (see entry 92).

167 WEINBERG, HERMAN G. "Ernst Lubitsch: A Parallel to George
     Feydeau." Film Comment, Spring, p. 62.
         Relates several coincidental parallels. Reprinted in
     the author's Saint Cinema, 2d. rev. ed. (New York: Dover),
     pp. 315-18.

1971

168 BARRY, JOHN K. "Ernst Lubitsch and the Comedy of the Thir-
     ties." Mise-en-Scène, no. 1, n.d., pp. 7-10.
         Random observations. Weak.

169 BAXTER, JOHN. "Some Lubitsch Silents." The Silent Picture,
     Summer/Autumn, no page numbers.
         Notes on Madame Dubarry, Die Puppe, Rosita, and The
     Student Prince in preparation for a British retrospective.

170 BERGMAN, ANDREW. We're in the Money: Depression America and
     Its Films. New York: New York University Press, pp. 57-
     59.
         A socio-historical view of three Lubitsch comedies (One
     Hour with You, Trouble in Paradise, and Design for Living)
     in the context of the Depression.

171 SARRIS, ANDREW. "Lubitsch in the Thirties." Film Comment,
     Winter 1971/72, pp. 54-57; Summer 1972, pp. 20-21.
         A series of critical insights, some of them splendid, on
     the state of Lubitsch criticism and on Lubitsch's place
     among the major directors working in the 1930s.

172 WEINBERG, HERMAN G. Review of The American Film Institute
     Catalog: Feature Films, 1921-1930. Film Quarterly, 25
     (Winter 71/72), 59-65.
         Proffers corrections for the Lubitsch entries.

1972

173 BEHRMAN, S. N. People in a Diary: A Memoir. Boston: Little,
     Brown, pp. 145, 152-53, 155-57, 162-65.
         The playwright, one of Lubitsch's friends, tells several
     interesting stories about their association, including the
     one about his involvment in the pre-Lubitsch first draft of
     Ninotchka.

174 BOGDANOVICH, PETER. "Hollywood." Esquire, November, pp. 82,
     86.
         Fond and insightful overview of Lubitsch comedy. Re-
     printed in the author's Pieces of Time (New York: Delta
     Books, 1973), pp. 219-25.

175 BRACKETT, CHARLES, BILLY WILDER, and WALTER REISCH. <u>Ninotch-</u>
<u>ka</u>. The MGM Library of Film Scripts. New York: Viking,
114 pp.
   The shooting script, annotated to indicate important
changes in the completed film. "Minor variations that do
not affect plot or characterization have not been document-
ed." A release script of the film was published in 1975.

176 ISRAEL, LEE. <u>Miss Tallulah Bankhead</u>. New York: G. P. Putnam's Sons, pp. 239-43.
   On the actress' involvement in <u>A Royal Scandal</u>. Of
special interest for its detailed portraits of Lubitsch and
his relations with his associates in the later years when
his illnesses were beginning to take their toll.

177 PATALAS, ENNO. "Ernst Lubitsch." <u>Süddeutsche Zeitung</u> (Munich), no. 23, January 29/30, Magazine Section, page unnum-
bered.
   A brief tribute on the eightieth anniversary of Lubitsch's birth. Of interest chiefly for a few precise descriptions of incidents in rare Lubitsch films--including
one from the long-lost <u>Die Flamme</u> in which the composer's
mother serves him coffee and cookies. Also reprints Howe
(1922) in German.

178 VITOUX, FRÉDÉRIC. "Ernst Lubitsch, le maître." <u>Positif</u>, no.
137, April, pp. 57-63.
   Brief reappraisal of <u>One Hour with You</u> and <u>The Merry</u>
<u>Widow</u>. Lubitsch is associated with Roman Jakobson's theory
of metaphor and metonymy.

                              1973

179 DUFOUR, FERNAND. "Lubitsch: l'être et le paraître." <u>Cinéma</u>
(Paris), no. 177, June, pp. 74-78.
   Analytic program note occasioned by a French television
retrospective.

180 MAST, GERALD. "The 'Lubitsch Touch' and the Lubitsch Brain,"
in his <u>The Comic Mind: Comedy and the Movies</u>. Indianapo-
lis: Bobbs-Merrill, pp. 206-24.
   Principally on recurring plot motifs and dramatic de-
vices in the Warners and early Paramount comedies. Some
may feel that Mast generalizes too quickly and that his
analyses are somewhat overly schematic. But his Lubitsch
essay is full of striking insights that ought to be carefully considered. For instance: "[The] later Lubitsch

films make their moral questions quite specific--love and
politics (Angel, Ninotchka), art and politics (To Be or Not
To Be), class differences and international politics (Cluny
Brown). A sign of Lubitsch's painfully overt moral and social consciousness is that beginning with Angel, Lubitsch
maintains that human beings grow.... The earlier Lubitsch
films imply continuing human foolishness, not recognitions,
reconciliations, and conversions. This moral consciousness
led to the dampening, softening, and sweetening of Lubitsch's sharp, hard wit."

181   RINGGOLD, GENE, and DEWITT BODEEN. Chevalier: The Films and
      Careers of Maurice Chevalier. Secaucus, N.J.: Citadel
      Press.
          Contains more factual information than other star pro-
      files in this series. Includes extremely elaborate film-
      ographies, many production details not reported elsewhere,
      and reproductions of rare advertisements and sheet music
      for the five Lubitsch-Chevalier pictures: The Love Parade,
      Paramount on Parade, The Smiling Lieutenant, One Hour with
      You, and The Merry Widow.

                              1974

182   BOURGET, JEAN-LOUP. "Muted Strings: Ernst Lubitsch's Broken
      Lullaby." Monogram (Brighton Film Review), no. 5, pp. 24-
      26.
          An examination of visual and dramatic strategies in The
      Man I Killed, and an attempt to relate the styles and con-
      cerns of this film to Lubitsch's comedies. Ineffectively
      written, sometimes evasive of genuine critical issues, and
      given to somewhat extravagant interpretations, the essay is
      of interest nevertheless as one of the rare efforts to pay
      careful attention to Lubitsch's only fully "serious" sound
      film.

183   CORLISS, RICHARD. Talking Pictures: Screenwriters in the
      American Cinema, 1927-1973. Woodstock, N.Y.: Overlook
      Press.
          The organization, idiom, and method of Andrew Sarris'
      The American Cinema: Directors and Directions, 1929-1968
      applied to screenwriters. The major Hollywood writers are
      grouped in categories of relative achievement, and a samp-
      ling of their work is examined for themes and other charac-
      teristic traits that may be attributable to them. Among
      the Lubitsch scripts considered are Design for Living (Ben
      Hecht), Desire (Edwin Justus Mayer and Waldemar Young),
      Ninotchka (Charles Brackett, Billy Wilder, and Walter
      Reisch), and three by Samson Raphaelson--Trouble in Para-
      dise, Angel, and The Shop around the Corner. Raphaelson is

singled out for special praise; in his work with Lubitsch, the author asserts, he created "the most highly polished and perfectly sustained comedy style of any Hollywood screenwriter."

184   GOLD, HARRIET. "Restoration Comedy and Trouble in Paradise." Macguffin [University of Illinois, Urbana], Summer, pp. 3-7. On similarities in character types and plot motifs.

185   HASKELL, MOLLY. From Reverence to Rape: The Treatment of Women in the Movies. New York: Holt, Rinehart and Winston. Penguin paperback edition, pp. 96-102.
    Lubitsch "created women characters of depth and complexity whose originality was glossed over in the general designation of 'Continental sophistication.'" He respected the wisdom that "the multiplicity of a woman's roles [is] a primary condition of her being" and as a consequence he was extremely successful at exploring and defining the conditions of a successful male-female relationship in his films. Three of his love-triangle films--Trouble in Paradise, Design for Living, and Angel--are examined to illustrate these themes.

186   HOCHMAN, STANLEY. American Film Directors. New York: Ungar, pp. 279-90.
    Brief reprints and excerpts of criticism and commentary on Lubitsch, selected at random from 1923 to 1971.

1975

187   ANOBILE, RICHARD J., ed. Ninotchka. The Film Classics Library. New York: Darien House, 256 pp.
    Script edition with over 1500 frame enlargements and dialogue transcribed from the screen. An edited shooting script of the film was published in 1972.

188   HIGHAM, CHARLES. Warner Brothers. New York: Charles Scribner's Sons, pp. 18-28.
    The fullest account in print of Lubitsch's Warner Brothers period. Many (undocumented) behind-the-scenes anecdotes and details, presumably from the author's interviews with such Lubitsch associates in the 1920s as Irene Rich, Henry Blanke, Robert Florey, Harold Grieve, and Charles Van Enger. Reports in trade journals of the time do not always square with Higham's versions.

189   HORAK, JAN-CHRISTOPHER. "The Pre-Hollywood Lubitsch." Image (Rochester), December, pp. 19-29.
    A lengthy extract from the author's 1975 Master's thesis "Ernst Lubitsch and the Rise of Ufa, 1917-1922" (Boston

University). The extract outlines Lubitsch's activities
from the beginning of 1919 to the end of 1920 and Anna
Boleyn, and is rich in production and release details.
The thesis alternates between two topics, a corporate history of the German film industry in a crucial five-year period, and Lubitsch's production activity in these same
years. The arguments are sometimes inadequately developed
and the research methods are inconsistent, as is often the
case with such efforts, but this is a pioneering and important work nevertheless for its extended coverage of an
inadequately known phase of Lubitsch's career and for its
use of previously untapped mines of information such as
German trade periodicals of the time.

190   ISAACS, NEIL D.   "Lubitsch and the Filmed-Play Syndrome."
      Literature/Film Quarterly, 3 (Fall), 299-308.
          An attempt to show how Lubitsch's roots are in theater,
      and how he transformed and transcended the theatrical in
      his films. The examples considered are Trouble in Paradise,
      Design for Living, and To Be or Not To Be. Lacks scope and
      convincingness.

191   KNOWLES, ELEANOR.   The Films of Jeanette MacDonald and Nelson
      Eddy. London: Tantivy; New York: A. S. Barnes, pp. 32-39,
      48-57, 86-95, 115-28.
          Includes elaborate filmographies, production details,
      and music notes on the four musicals Jeanette MacDonald
      made with Lubitsch--The Love Parade, Monte Carlo, One Hour
      with You, and The Merry Widow.

192   KREUGER, MILES, ed.   The Movie Musical from Vitaphone to 42nd
      Street. New York: Dover, 367 pp.
          The early sound musical as seen through the pages of
      Photoplay. Reprints material on the four Lubitsch Para-
      mount musicals--The Love Parade, Monte Carlo, The Smiling
      Lieutenant, and One Hour with You--and Paramount on Parade:
      production stills, reviews, advertisements, production sto-
      ries, and features on Chevalier and Jeanette MacDonald.

193   SCHWARTZ, NANCY.   "Lubitsch's Widow: The Meaning of a Waltz."
      Film Comment, March/April, pp. 13-17.
          A critical analysis of The Merry Widow which combines
      close critical scrutiny and careful historical research.
      Includes many details of the production history and an in-
      terview with Samson Raphaelson, the screenwriter.

1976

194   BAXTER, JOHN.   "The Continental Touch." American Film, Sep-
      tember, pp. 17-21; October, pp. 61-66.

Brief geographical profiles of European emigration to Hollywood in the 1920s and 1930s. Part One deals with the Hungarians and Viennese, among whom were such names associated with Lubitsch's as the Hungarian writers Vajda, Lengyel, and Bus-Feketé, and Max Reinhardt. Part Two, on the Germans, calls Lubitsch "the most influential of all the European artists who came to Hollywood in the twenties." See entry 195 for additional information on the same topics.

195 _____. The Hollywood Exiles. New York: Taplinger, pp. 27-57.
Lubitsch's association with Max Reinhardt, behind-the-scenes corporate maneuvering during the "German invasion" of the early 1920s, and the emigration to Hollywood of Emil Jannings, Pola Negri, Hans Dreier, and Lubitsch himself, are among the topics considered in this general study of the European presence in Hollywood. Should be used in conjunction with the author's two 1976 articles in American Film, which contain material not in the book.

196 FEIN, IRVING. Jack Benny: An Intimate Biography. New York: G. P. Putnam's Sons, pp. 86-88.
Contains several anecdotes about the comedian's involvement in To Be or Not To Be.

Also see:
American Film Institute Discussion of June 4, 1971, in which Jack Benny recalls in rich detail his involvement in the film and talks at length about how Lubitsch worked with the actors. This is Transcript 111 in the Charles K. Feldman Library at the American Film Institute (Beverly Hills); it has recently been made available on microfilm with the other American Film Institute Seminars by Microfilm Corporation of America.

197 Kosmorama (Copenhagen), no. 129, Spring, pp. 39-64.
Special Lubitsch feature. Contains: Steen Lassen and Henning B. Hansen, "Lubitsch' stumfilm: Fra slapstick til nonchalance"; Jørgen Stegelmann, "Figurer hos Lubitsch nogle portraetter"; Henrik Lundgren, "Det sublimerede lystspil"; and a well-researched filmography by P[er] C[alum]. Also includes several rare production stills from the collection donated to the Danish Film Museum by Nicola Lubitsch.

198 LUFT, HERBERT G. "Ernst Matray: A Career of More Than 65 Years." Films in Review, January, pp. 25-31.
Career article on a Lubitsch associate from the Reinhardt and early film days. The claims are made that Matray

introduced Lubitsch to motion pictures and that he later
introduced Lubitsch and Jannings to producer Paul Davidson.

199   MILLS, ROBERT WILLIAM. "The American Films of Ernst Lubitsch:
      A Critical History." Ph.D. dissertation, University of
      Michigan, 213 pp. Summarized in Dissertation Abstracts In-
      ternational, September, p. 1270-A.
         "The purpose of this study is to designate Lubitsch's
      stature as a figure of great and somewhat neglected impor-
      tance in the history of the American cinema through an
      evaluation of his contributions, both artistic and techni-
      cal, to that art form." In fact, this study is a sketchy
      general survey of Lubitsch's entire career which consists
      principally of paraphrases of secondary sources (especially
      Huff's 1947 index and Weinberg, 1968) and lengthy quota-
      tions from reviews and general film histories. An inade-
      quately researched, inconsequential effort.

200   PARISH, JAMES ROBERT. The Jeanette MacDonald Story. New York:
      Mason/Charter, pp. 37-45, 47-48, 57-61, 71-77.
         Contains biographical and production information per-
      taining to the four films in which Miss MacDonald was di-
      rected by Lubitsch: The Love Parade, Monte Carlo, One Hour
      with You, and The Merry Widow. Most interesting is the
      lengthy behind-the-scenes view during the making of The
      Love Parade.

201   WHITTEMORE, DON, and PHILIP ALAN CECCHETTINI, eds. "Ernst Lu-
      bitsch," in their Passport to Hollywood: Film Immigrants:
      Anthology. New York: McGraw-Hill, pp. 148-69.
         A general introduction that is not always on firm ground,
      followed by reprints of Wollenberg's 1948 article from
      Penguin Film Review and reviews of Ninotchka from The New
      Republic, Time, and Nation.

                              1977

202   BOND, KIRK. "Ernst Lubitsch." Film Culture, no. 63-64,
      pp. 139-53.
         Belated appearance of a lengthy commentary on the 1968
      Museum of Modern Art Lubitsch retrospective. Critically
      eccentric, but of value for its detailed notes on several
      rarely seen Lubitsch films. See entry 161.

203   BYRON, STUART, and ELISABETH WEIS, eds. The National Society
      of Film Critics on Movie Comedy. New York: Grossman/Vik-
      ing, pp. 70-75.
         Reprints brief excerpts from books by four well-known
      writers: Richard Schickel (The Movies), Arthur Knight (The

Liveliest Art), Andrew Sarris (The American Cinema), and
Richard Corliss (Talking Pictures).

204   EPHRON, HENRY. We Thought We Could Do Anything. New York:
      W. W. Norton, pp. 18-32.
         A husband-and-wife playwriting team at work on their
      first screenwriting assignment, Lubitsch's unmade World War
      II comedy on the WACs, All-Out Arlene (see Unrealized Proj-
      ects, entry 307). A richly detailed account of Lubitsch
      working with his writers, with a fascinating side glimpse
      of the director recuperating at his home in Bel Air from
      the heart attack that forced him to give up the project.

205   POAGUE, LELAND A. The Cinema of Ernst Lubitsch: The Holly-
      wood Films. London: Tantivy; New York: A. S. Barnes,
      180 pp.
         Close "readings" of thirteen of Lubitsch's American
      films in the manner of literary new criticism. The films
      are discussed in complementary or contrasting pairs or
      groups. The Marriage Circle and The Shop around the Corner
      are considered first to illustrate the author's underlying
      theme, that Lubitsch was a humanist at heart all along and
      that the visual razzle-dazzle and the cynical posturings of
      the earlier films were eventually supplanted by a profound
      sympathy for his characters. In the body of the book,
      three groups of films are discussed in terms of what the
      author sees as their essential concerns: personal inclina-
      tion versus social responsibility in Lady Windermere's Fan,
      The Student Prince, and The Merry Widow; appearance versus
      reality in One Hour with You, Trouble in Paradise, and To
      Be or Not To Be; and the nature of the love relationship in
      So This Is Paris, The Love Parade, and Ninotchka. In the
      final chapter two late films, Heaven Can Wait and Cluny
      Brown, are presented as complex, rich, and wholly success-
      ful manifestations of Lubitsch's deeply felt compassion
      and humanity. One objection to this book might be that it
      is insufficiently aware of the films as films. Another
      could be that its interpretations are often too solemn and
      earnest and even relentless for the incidents discussed.
      ("The initial rendezvous between Gaston and Lily provides
      a magnificent triple perspective on the games rich people
      play. That is, Gaston and Lily are poor people [their as-
      sets are their abilities, not their bank accounts], who
      pretend to be rich people, who in turn are pretending to be
      Hollywood movie stars [Miriam Hopkins and Herbert Marshall,
      perhaps]. The scene is thus an hilarious parody to the
      third power; and our laughter is all the more intense, and
      all the more pointed, as we realize that the Baron is a
      thief and the Countess a pickpocket.") Another would be
      that in making Lubitsch into a consistent humanist the au-
      thor too much disregards his gifts and achievements as a

satirist. Perhaps the chief virtue of the book is its attempt to show that the films of Lubitsch's last decade are
as worthy of our attention (though on different grounds)
as those of the twenties and early to middle thirties.

206   ZOLOTOW, MAURICE. <u>Billy Wilder in Hollywood</u>. New York: G. P.
       Putnam's, 1977, pp. 61-66, 75-86.
          Background information on Wilder's involvement in the
       scripting of <u>Bluebeard's Eighth Wife</u> and <u>Ninotchka</u>. Es-
       pecially interesting on the politics and political circum-
       stances behind <u>Ninotchka</u>.

206a   GILLETT, JOHN. "Munich's Cleaned Pictures." <u>Sight and Sound</u>,
       Winter 1977/78, pp. 37-39.
          On the week-long retrospective of September 1977 marking
       the opening of the new quarters of the Munich Film Museum,
       and the meticulous restoration efforts of Munich Curator
       Enno Patalas and his staff. Among the films shown were two
       long-lost Lubitsch titles, <u>Ein fideles Gefängnis</u>, a short
       comedy from his middle German years, and <u>Das Weib des
       Pharao</u>, the next-to-last of his German features. The au-
       thor describes a scene in the comedy in which "the dis-
       traught wife seeking her missing husband goes to the tele-
       phone and, in a great <u>coup de théâtre</u>, the camera suddenly
       and most obligingly pans downwards to reveal him quietly
       sloshed under the desk"--an early example of the "Lubitsch
       touch." The print of <u>Das Weib des Pharao</u> was reconstructed
       according to the script from cans of assorted material
       found in Gosfilmofond in Moscow, newly titled, and is re-
       portedly about three-fourths complete. "Despite some holes
       in the narrative," the author writes, "this reconstruction
       fills an important gap, for here we see Lubitsch's full
       mastery in handling big crowd scenes (including one stun-
       ning shot of a man clambering up a rock pit with hundreds
       of figures seen in deep focus far below), as well as the
       persistent Reinhardt influence making itself felt in gran-
       diose interior design and intense, ritualistic acting."
       Future plans at Munich include work on Lubitsch's <u>Die
       Flamme</u>, which exists at present only in a thirty-minute
       fragment.

V. Writings, Performances and Other Film Related Activity

STAGE PERFORMANCES

1. Productions for Max Reinhardt (Verified)

> Following is a list of Max Reinhardt stage productions in which Lubitsch appeared as an actor. Each entry includes (as known or appropriate): title of the work as it was performed, an English title, author; the adaptor or translator of this production, the director of this production, the theater it was performed in (the three Reinhardt theaters were the Deutsches, the Kammerspiele, and the Volksbühne), the opening date, and the number of performances in its run; and Lubitsch's role in the production. Cast lists for many Reinhardt productions have not yet been determined, and it is likely that Lubitsch appeared in many more Reinhardt productions than are listed here--including some of those in the next section, Productions for Max Reinhardt (Unverified).

1911

207 DER FETTE CASÄR ("Fat Caesar") by Friedrich Freksa. Directed by Felix Holländer.
      Opened at Deutsches Theater August 26 and ran for three performances. Lubitsch's role is unknown.

208 VERTAUSCHTE SEELEN ("Souls Exchanged") by Wilhelm von Scholz. Directed by Eduard von Winterstein.
      Opened at Kammerspiele October 5 and ran for eight performances. Lubitsch played two roles, Hosenschlitz and first slave.

1912

209 DER ZORN DES ACHILLES ("The Wrath of Achilles") by Wilhelm Schmidtbonn. Directed by Felix Holländer.

Opened at Deutsches Theater January 13 and ran for
three performances. Lubitsch's role is unknown.

210 GEORGE DANDIN by Molière. German by Karl Vollmöller. Directed by Max Reinhardt.
Opened at Deutsches Theater April 13 and ran for 29 performances. Lubitsch played Colin, George Dandin's valet.

211 DON JUAN by Carl Sternheim. Directed by Felix Holländer.
Opened at Deutsches Theater September 13 and ran for two
performances. Lubitsch's role is unknown.

212 KÖNIG HEINRICH IV, I ("King Henry IV, Part I") by Shakespeare.
Directed by Max Reinhardt.
Opened at Deutsches Theater October 12 and ran for 38
performances. Lubitsch played Peto.

213 KÖNIG HEINRICH IV, II ("King Henry IV, Part II") by Shakespeare. Directed by Max Reinhardt.
Opened at Deutsches Theater October 18 and ran for 35
performances. Lubitsch played Peto.

214 DER BLAUE VOGEL ("The Blue Bird") by Maurice Maeterlinck.
German by Epstein. Directed by Max Reinhardt.
Opened at Deutsches Theater December 23 and ran for 41
performances. Lubitsch played two roles, The Poplar and A
Cold.

1913

215 KAISERLICHE HOHEIT ("His Imperial Highness") by J. A. Simons-
Mees. German by E. Otten and R. Lothar. Directed by Felix
Holländer.
Opened at Kammerspiele June 4 and ran for 12 perform-
ances. Lubitsch played a journalist.

216 FRANZISKA ("Francisca") by Frank Wedekind. Directed by Frank
Wedekind.
Opened at Kammerspiele September 5 and ran for 24 per-
formances. Lubitsch played two roles, Kullman and William
Fahrstuhl.

217 SOMMERNACHTSTRAUM ("A Midsummer Night's Dream") by Shakespeare.
Directed by Max Reinhardt.
Opened at Deutsches Theater November 14 and ran for 31
performances. Lubitsch's role is unknown.

218 VIEL LÄRM UM NICHTS ("Much Ado about Nothing") by Shakespeare. Directed by Max Reinhardt.
Opened at Deutsches Theater November 21 and ran for 20 performances. Lubitsch played "Ein Schreiber"; this could be the Town Clerk in IV.2.

219 HAMLET by Shakespeare. Directed by Max Reinhardt.
Opened at Deutsches Theater December 1 and ran for 20 performances. Lubitsch played the second gravedigger.

1914

220 ROMEO UND JULIA ("Romeo and Juliet") by Shakespeare. Directed by Max Reinhardt.
Opened at Deutsches Theater January 28 and ran for 15 performances. Lubitsch played Simson (Sampson), Capulet's servant.

221 KÖNIG HEINRICH IV, I ("King Henry IV, Part I") by Shakespeare. Directed by Max Reinhardt.
Opened at Deutsches Theater February 11 and ran for five performances. Lubitsch's role is unknown.

222 KÖNIG HEINRICH IV, II ("King Henry IV, Part II") by Shakespeare. Directed by Max Reinhardt.
Opened at Deutsches Theater February 20 and ran for five performances. Lubitsch's role is unknown.

223 WAS IHR WOLLT ("Twelfth Night") by Shakespeare. Directed by Max Reinhardt.
Opened at Deutsches Theater March 13 and ran for 47 performances. Lubitsch played Fabian, servant to Olivia.

1915

224 DAS JAHRMARKTSFEST ZU PLUNDERSWEILERN ("The Fair at Plundersweilern") by Goethe, with the original music of Ettersburger. Directed by Max Reinhardt.
Opened at Deutsches Theater May 21 and ran for nine performances. Lubitsch's role is unknown.

225 DIE RÄUBER ("The Robbers") by Schiller. Directed by Max Reinhardt.
Opened at Volksbühne September 1 and ran for 23 performances. Lubitsch played Schufterle, a bandit.

226 TRAUMULUS by Arno Holz and Oskar Jerschke. Directed by Berthold Held.
Opened at Volksbühne November 29 and ran for 19 performances. Lubitsch played Goldbaum.

227   <u>DER STERN VON BETHLEHEM</u> ("The Star of Bethlehem") by Otto
      Falckenberg, music by B. Stavenhagen. Directed by Max
      Reinhardt.
         Opened at Deutsches Theater December 27 and ran for nine
      performances. Lubitsch's role is unknown.

1916

228   <u>VIEL LÄRM UM NICHTS</u> ("Much Ado about Nothing") by Shakespeare.
      Directed by Max Reinhardt.
         Opened at Volksbühne January 25 and ran for 15 perform-
      ances. Lubitsch played "Ein Schreiber"; this could be the
      Town Clerk in IV.2.

229   <u>FUHRMANN HENSCHEL</u> ("Coachman Henschel") by Gerhart Hauptmann.
      Directed by Felix Holländer.
         Opened at Volksbühne February 21 and ran for 30 perform-
      ances. Lubitsch's role is unknown.

230   <u>BALLET NACH RAMEAU</u>; also called <u>DIE SCHÄFERINNEN</u> ("The Shep-
      herdesses"). Directed by Max Reinhardt.
         Opened at Kammerspiele March 16 and ran for 68 perform-
      ances. Lubitsch played "Wilder," a wild man.

231   <u>DIE GRÜNE FLÖTE</u> ("The Green Flute"), ballet by Hugo von Hof-
      mannsthal, with music by Mozart and Nilson. Directed by
      Max Reinhardt.
         Opened at Deutsches Theater April 26 and ran for 30 per-
      formances. Lubitsch played Ho, the Sorcerer's sister.

232   <u>DAS WINTERMÄRCHEN</u> ("The Winter's Tale") by Shakespeare. Di-
      rected by Max Reinhardt.
         Opened September. Theater and number of performances
      are unknown. Lubitsch played Autolycus, a rogue.

233   <u>NACHTASYL</u> ("The Lower Depths") by Maxim Gorki. Adapted by
      Richard Vallentin. Newly staged by Eduard von Winterstein
      from a plan for an earlier production directed by Max Rein-
      hardt.
         Opened at Volksbühne October 7 and ran for 42 perform-
      ances. Lubitsch played Kostylew.

1917

234   <u>DER GEIZIGE</u> ("The Miser") by Molière. Adapted by Carl Stern-
      heim. Directed by Max Reinhardt.
         Opened at Deutsches Theater April 16 and ran for 28 per-
      formances. Lubitsch played Gensbourger, a moneychanger
      (Maître Simon).

235 DER LEBENDE LEICHNAM ("The Living Corpse") by Leo Tolstoi.
Directed by Max Reinhardt.
    Opened at Deutsches Theater September 25 and ran for 32
    performances. Lubitsch played Petrushin, Fedia's lawyer.

2. Productions for Max Reinhardt (Unverified)

     Various sources mention Reinhardt stage productions in
     which Lubitsch is supposed to have appeared, but these have
     not been verified. They are listed below, in alphabetical
     order, under the title of the work in its original language.

236 FAUST, PARTS I AND II by Goethe. Photographs after page 70 in
     Max Reinhardt and His Theater, ed. Oliver M. Sayler (New
     York: Brentano's, 1924) show Lubitsch as Wagner in Faust
     I, Deutsches Theater, March 1909, and as Famulus in Faust
     II, Deutsches Theater, February 1911. The Max-Reinhardt-
     Forschungs und Gedenkstätte informed the authors that the
     date in the caption to Faust I must be wrong and that Lu-
     bitsch probably played Wagner in a later Faust I. As for
     Faust II, Tully (1926) says " [Victor] Arnold secured for
     Lubitsch the role of Famulus in Max Reinhardt's production...
     at the Deutsches Theater in Berlin. Lubitsch was nineteen
     years of age at the time [that is, 1911]. The future di-
     rector toured Europe for a season in the Goethe play."

237 JEDERMANN ("Everyman") by Hugo von Hofmannsthal. See Nur ein
     Traum (entry 243).

238 JUDITH by Friedrich Hebbel. Salka Viertel in The Kindness of
     Strangers (New York: Holt, Rinehart and Winston, 1969,
     pp. 54-55) describes performances for Reinhardt's company
     of Judith in which she played Judith and Paul Wegener
     played Holofernes in the evening, with Wegener's understudy,
     Lubitsch, replacing him for the matinee performances.

239 KING LEAR by Shakespeare. According to Photoplay (February
     1935, p. 92) Lubitsch "played everything [for Reinhardt]
     from the fool in King Lear to the grave-digger in Hamlet."

240 THE MERCHANT OF VENICE by Shakespeare. Deutsches Theater-
     Lexikon: Biographisches und Bibliographisches Handbuch
     (Klagenfurt: F. Kleinmayr, 1960) lists Lubitsch as Tubal
     in this play. Also see Nur ein Traum (entry 243).

241 A MIDSUMMER NIGHT'S DREAM by Shakespeare. Deutsches Theater-
     Lexikon: Biographisches und Bibliographisches Handbuch
     (Klagenfurt: F. Kleinmayr, 1960) lists Lubitsch as Schnauz
     (Snout) in this play. An obituary in the German-language

newspaper <u>Aufbau</u> (December 5, 1947) lists Lubitsch as having appeared as one of the rude mechanicals (this could also be Snout in this play.

242 DAS MIRAKEL ("The Miracle") by Karl Vollmöller, music by Engelbert Humperdinck. Oliver M. Sayler in <u>Max Reinhardt and His Theatre</u> (New York: Brentano's, 1924, p. 12) says Lubitsch made his stage debut as one of the two thousand 'supers' in the London production of <u>The Miracle</u>. Huff (1947) also includes this credit. <u>The Miracle</u> opened at Olympia Hall on December 23, 1912. If Lubitsch did appear in the London production, it was not his acting debut, as he had already appeared in several Reinhardt productions in Berlin.

243 NUR EIN TRAUM ("Only a Dream") by Lothar Schmidt [Goldschmidt]. Grover Jones (1935, p. 26) quotes Lubitsch: "Reinhardt gave me the part of a little professor in a play called <u>Only a Dream</u>. My acting didn't draw any critical raves but it was good enough to win for me a place in his stock company, and I was with him for seven years, playing everything from Lancelot, in <u>The Mercant of Venice</u>, to The Devil, in <u>Everyman</u>. It was a valuable experience." <u>Nur ein Traum</u> was the source play for Lubitsch's films <u>The Marriage Circle</u> and <u>One Hour with You</u>.

244 SUMURÛN by Friedrich Freksa, music by Victor Holländer. At some point in his association with Reinhardt Lubitsch appeared in <u>Sumurûn</u>, though in which production(s) is not known. Pola Negri (1924) says Lubitsch "played an old woman, a grotesque character, in the pantomime." She may be thinking of his role in <u>Die grüne Flöte</u>, however. Weinberg (1968) says Lubitsch appeared in the version at the London Coliseum in February 1911. Alfred Hitchcock in the Lubitsch tribute in <u>Action</u>! (1967) says he saw Lubitsch in the role of the hunchback clown in this production. But programs for the production in the Theatre Collection at Lincoln Center for the Performing Arts list Ernst Matray in this role. According to Matray (1969) Lubitsch played the role only when Reinhardt was no longer interested. "I took it over and set it to rhythm, and then put Lubitsch in it." Lubitsch played the hunchback clown in his film adaptation of the play (1920).

245 DER VERLORENE SOHN ("The Prodigal Son") by Wilhelm Schmidtbonn. A program for <u>The Shop around the Corner</u> in the Margaret Herrick Library at the Academy of Motion Picture Arts and Sciences states that Lubitsch and Joseph Schildkraut appeared together for Reinhardt in <u>The Prodigal Son</u> in 1913. A production of <u>Der Verlorene Sohn</u>, directed by Reinhardt, opened on October 23, 1913, and played 27 performances.

3. <u>Miscellaneous Stage Performances</u>

246   Hans Kraly was reported in the New York <u>Daily News</u> (July 15,
      1934, p. 52) to have had "many reminiscences of himself and
      Lubitsch in the early days when as a pair of blackface com-
      edians they toured Germany in a small time vaudeville
      show."

247   In his 1947 letter to Herman G. Weinberg (<u>see</u> entry 269) Lu-
      bitsch wrote: "My last stage appearance was in 1918 in a
      revue, <u>Die Welt Geht Unter</u> at the Apollo Theatre in Berlin."
      According to Huff (1947) this was a "variety show," with
      Senta Söneland and Lucie Blattner also billed, which ran
      from October 1 to November 30, 1918.

WRITINGS

1921

*248   Reprint of Letter to a Berlin Newspaper. <u>Der Film</u>, no. 37, p. 31.
       Citation as provided by Jay Leyda from unpublished re-
       search materials.

1922

249   "Lubitsch Praises Griffith." <u>Film Daily</u>, January 5, p. 1.
         Lubitsch writes a public letter of congratulations to
      Griffith for <u>Orphans of the Storm</u>, which he has just seen.
      "Mr. Griffith's artistic direction of <u>Broken Blossoms</u> had
      previously made a deep impression on me, and his new film
      has immensely strengthened my profound admiration. I was
      not only interested in the scenic construction, his flaw-
      less handling of masses and the big, highly effective
      scenes, but also in his smaller, more delicate details,
      which as a film director, I can appreciate. Griffith pos-
      sesses an extraordinary personality which does not travel
      the trodden path of conventionality, and it is this quality
      that I admire most in his art."

1923

250   "American Cinematographers Superior Artists." <u>American Cine-</u>
      <u>matographer</u>, December, pp. 4, 18-19.
         Having completed two films in America, Lubitsch has high
      praise for the work of American cinematographers. He also
      says that the role of the cinematographer is much more im-
      portant in America than in Germany, where cinematographers
      "haven't had the time nor technical equipment to develop

their art to so high a degree." It is interesting to compare Lubitsch's remarks in this article to remarks he made
on the same topic to an interviewer for the same magazine
in 1938 (entry 132).

251   "Comparing European and American Methods." Film Daily, May 6,
       p. 25.
           The one fundamental "technical" difference Lubitsch
       singles out lies in the structuring of scripts: "In the
       American theaters the film is usually shown without inter-
       missions, and never with more than one. In Germany every
       picture is divided in from five to seven parts and after
       each part the lights go on. The reason is twofold: the
       eyes are given a rest--and certain lapses of time are
       bridged. The American manner of showing pictures has the
       result that the American script has a continuous line with
       climax at the end, while the German script has from five
       to seven climaxes, one at the end of each part." He also
       observes that American films usually have to have happy
       endings while European filmmakers are not bound by the same
       restriction, and he concedes the technical superiority of
       the American industry.

252   "Film-Internationalität," in Das Deutsche Lichtbild Buch:
       Filmprobleme von Gestern und Heute. Ed. by Heinrich
       Pfeiffer. Berlin: A. Scherl, n.d., pp. 13-14.
           Lubitsch makes the point that international hegemony in
       film ought to be an artistic rather than a commercial con-
       sideration. Only by imposing the highest artistic stand-
       ards on their work, he says, will the filmmakers of Germany
       or any other nation produce films that will be generally
       deserving of worldwide attention.

                              1924

253   "My Two Years in America." Motion Picture. December, pp. 24-
       25, 104.
           Lubitsch relates his anxieties over coming to work in
       America, gives his first impressions of Hollywood, de-
       scribes his first working days at the Pickford-Fairbanks
       Studio, and talks about his current film with Pola Negri,
       Forbidden Paradise. He says he has found only one funda-
       mental difference making films in America, the absence of a
       "social caste between the players," which gives the tal-
       ented greater opportunities than they would ever have in
       Europe.

*254   "Unsere chance in Amerika." Licht-Bild-Bühne, no. 56, pp. 9-
       12.
           Citation as provided by Jay Leyda from unpublished re-
       search materials.

255 "Wie mein erster Grossfilm entstand," in Licht-Bild-Bühne, Luxusnummer, 30 Jahre Film. Berlin: "Lichtbildbühne," pp. 13-14.

Lubitsch traces the steps of his transition from short comedies to the massive costume epics that made him internationally famous, but confesses that his real preference is for small, intimate dramas (Kammerspiele) like Rausch, Die Flamme, and The Marriage Circle.

1927

*256 LUBITSCH, ERNST, and E[WALD] A[NDRÉ] DUPONT. Hollywood, das Filmparadies. Berlin: Verlag d. "Lichtbildbühne" Gebr. Wolffsohn, 24 pp.

Not located. Listed in Deutsches Bücherverzeichnis, 1926-30.

1928

*257 "Ich über mich," in Wir über uns selbst: autobiographische Sammlung. Berlin: Sibyllen Verlag. (As cited and reprinted in Retrospektive, 1967, pp. 3, 34; see entry 351.)

Brief memoir in which Lubitsch relates some highlights of his youth and early career.

1929

258 "Concerning Cinematography...as Told to William Stull." American Cinematographer, November, pp. 5, 21.

Lubitsch describes how the coming of sound has changed the role of the American cinematographer. The practice in sound pictures of shooting a scene simultaneously with three or four cameras places an intolerable strain on the cinematographer and everyone else, he says, but it has also had a positive effect by freeing the principal cinematographer from the mechanical routine of running his camera. He also contrasts the specialization of function in the American studio system with European practice (he uses art direction as an example) and comments on color and on the future of talking pictures.

1932

259 Letter to Columnist Julia Shawell. New York Evening Graphic, February 27, II:M-17.

Lubitsch sidesteps a question from the columnist for this famous tabloid about who is the most beautiful actress he has worked with, but goes on to give high praise to

Jeanette MacDonald. He also singles out Lionel Barrymore
as the foremost American character actor, gives some of his
reactions to New York, and mentions that he hopes to produce a play on Broadway later in the year (see Unrealized
Projects, entry 288).

1933

260   "Film Directing," in The World Film Encyclopedia. Ed. by
      Clarence Winchester. London: Amalgamated Press, pp. 442-
      44.
          Lubitsch writes about his scripting and shooting methods
      and explains why he spends a great deal of time on prepara-
      tion before the shooting begins. Reprinted in Hollywood
      Directors 1914-1940, ed. Richard Koszarski (New York: Ox-
      ford, 1976, pp. 270-74), and (in French) in the Cahiers du
      Cinéma special Lubitsch issue (1968).

1935

261   "La pantomima moderna." Schermo (Milan), Vol. 1, 27-28.
          Lubitsch writes to congratulate the organizers of the
      Venice Film Festival. The title of the article comes from
      his remark, "For years I have maintained the 'internation-
      alism' of films and also that good films can, through the
      universal language of pantomime, be the most important
      factor in international understanding." (Lubitsch also
      praises Il Duce in such a way that our translator remarked,
      "This article may have been tampered with by Fascist cen-
      sors.")

1936

262   "Two Hundred Million of Them." Boxoffice, October 10, p. 14.
          Lightweight piece on the continuing give-and-take be-
      tween a film director and his mass audience.

1937

263   "Gli attori che ho diretto in America." Cinema (Rome), no.
      28, August 25, pp. 124-25.
          Lubitsch gives thumbnail characterizations of the major
      performers he has directed in American films. It's high
      praise for all except Pickford, whose compliment might seem
      backhanded to some. Reprinted (in French) in Verdone
      (1964).

264　"Lubitsch Demands Beauties." New York <u>World-Telegram</u>, October 13, p. 42.
　　　"Regardless of how good an actress she might be, I will never direct a star who is not beautiful.... I want my stars to be good actresses also. But if I have to give a little, I would prefer that it be in acting ability rather than beauty." He says Marlene Dietrich especially has the qualities of beauty he looks for in a screen actress.

1939

265　"Garbo, as Seen by Her Director." <u>New York Times</u>, October 22, IX.4.
　　　Lubitsch writes about his experiences directing Garbo in <u>Ninotchka</u>. "Garbo is probably the most inhibited person I have ever worked with...but when finally you break through this and she really feels a scene, she's wonderful. But if you don't succeed in making her feel it, she can't do it cold-bloodedly on technique."

1940

266　"What Do Film Audiences Want?" New York <u>Herald Tribune</u>, September 16, p. 25.
　　　"A good picture which is based on a simple story of basic human values and emotions, or one which gets its entertainment value from genuine humor, will always make its way. That is my only prediction [about the future of motion picture trends]."

1942

267　"Mr. Lubitsch Takes the Floor for Rebuttal." <u>New York Times</u>, March 29, VIII.3.
　　　Lubitsch replies to the critics on <u>To Be or Not To Be</u>. He defends himself against three accusations--that the film is an unsuccessful mutation of melodrama and comedy-satire, that it treats the Nazi menace too lightly, and that it shows bad taste in having Nazi-occupied Warsaw as a setting for comedy.

1951

268　WEINBERG, HERMAN G. "A Tribute to Lubitsch, with a Letter in Which Lubitsch Appraises His Own Career." <u>Films in Review</u>, August/September, pp. 3-12.

The earliest of four printings of Lubitsch's very important letter of July 10, 1947 to Weinberg in which he gives a thumbnail sketch of his career and says what he thinks are his most important films. The letter has been "edited" for this article; <u>see</u> the 1962 <u>Film Culture</u> photo-reproduction of it for the definitive text. Also reprinted in Weinberg (1968), pp. 264-67, and, in French, in Verdone (1964).

1962

269   Letter to Herman G. Weinberg (July 10, 1947). <u>Film Culture</u>, Summer, pp. 37-40, 45.
      Probably the most important general statement by Lubitsch on his films. He is reacting to Theodore Huff's index, which was published earlier in the year. He recalls his early days in pictures, then gives a critical survey of his career. He says that <u>Die Austernprinzessin</u>, <u>Die Puppe</u>, and <u>Kohlhiesels Töchter</u> are his best German comedies, <u>Carmen</u>, <u>Madame Dubarry</u>, and <u>Anna Boleyn</u> his best costume epics. He thinks <u>Rausch</u> and <u>Die Flamme</u> were insufficiently appreciated. Of his American silent films he prefers <u>The Marriage Circle</u>, <u>Lady Windermere's Fan</u>, <u>The Patriot</u>, and <u>Kiss Me Again</u>. Of his sound films he singles out <u>Trouble in Paradise</u> ("as for pure style I think I have done nothing better"), <u>Ninotchka</u> ("as to satire, I believe I probably was never sharper"), <u>The Shop around the Corner</u> ("as for human comedy, I think I never was as good"), and <u>Heaven Can Wait</u> ("I consider it one of my major productions, because I tried to break away in several respects from the established moving picture formula").

MISCELLANEOUS FILM CREDITS

1928

270   <u>THE LAST COMMAND</u>. Directed by Josef von Sternberg. Lubitsch is said to be the source of the idea for this story. (<u>See</u> "Sidney Skolsky's Hollywood" syndicated column, dateline June 3, 1941. <u>Also see</u> Kevin Brownlow, <u>The Parade's Gone By</u>, p. 225.)

1933

271   <u>MR. BROADWAY</u>. Directed by Johnny Walker. Ed Sullivan is the master of ceremonies in this "screen travelogue" of Broadway night life. Lubitsch is shown dancing at the Central Park Casino.

1942

272   KNOW YOUR ENEMY GERMANY. During World War II, while many of
Hollywood's talents were joining the ranks of the Armed
Services, the film industry aided the war effort by producing films to be used for training and for building morale.
Many of Hollywood's directors, writers, editors, cameramen,
and producers provided their services to complete several
thousand Army training films. After Lubitsch completed To
Be or Not To Be in early 1942, he moved over to 20th Century-Fox to begin his term contract. He began preparations
for several projects, but abandoned them because (he said)
of the inappropriateness of their frivolous themes in wartime. After the script for Heaven Can Wait was written by
Samson Raphaelson in late August 1942, Lubitsch took time
out to direct an Army training film at Fox, under the supervision of Lt. Col. Frank Capra. Lubitsch started working
on the script with writers at the end of August. He shot
the film in a week, beginning on October 14 and finishing
on October 21. Animation work was then begun at the Disney
studio. The budget for this film was $37,692.85. The film
portrayed Karl Schmidt at various ages, Anna Schmidt, the
Kaiser, and Dr. Ziemer as commentator. It was originally
titled This Is Your Enemy, Germany, was changed to Know
Your Enemy Germany, but was never released. The film was
reassigned to different personnel in the Capra unit several
years later and became Your Job in Germany. Except for the
subject matter, the latter film that was released in the
autumn of 1945 had little to do with the Lubitsch project.
Although Lubitsch told a reporter for the New York Post in
1943 (July 31, p. 11) he had directed a series of training
films for the Army, Know Your Enemy Germany is the only one
the authors have been able to determine was definitely directed by Lubitsch. Also see Hollywood Reporter, Sept. 2,
p. 4, Oct. 16, p. 1, Oct. 19, p. 4.

1943

273   THE MEANEST MAN IN THE WORLD. Directed by Sidney Lanfield.
Lubitsch directed the re-takes for this Jack Benny comedy.
"Twentieth Century-Fox has called in Morris Ryskind to
write material for 10 days of retakes.... Ryskind is working on the set with the new director, devising additional
key laugh situations for scenes involving Benny, Priscilla
Lane and Eddie Anderson" (Hollywood Reporter, Nov. 2, 1942,
p. 4).

Also see:
Hollywood Reporter, Nov. 11, 1942, p. 2 and Variety,
Oct. 14, 1942, p. 6 and Nov. 4, 1942, p. 23.

UNREALIZED PROJECTS

1919

274   MEDEA. An adaptation of Austrian dramatist Franz Grillparz-
er's 1821 trilogy, scenario by Hans Kraly, to star Pola
Negri, Harry Liedtke, and Paul Wegener (Horak, 1975,
p. 80).

1921

275   MACBETH. "Berlin, Feb. 15. Several new Pola Negri films are
soon to be begun. The first will be a massive spectacular
production of Macbeth, with Pola...as Lady Macbeth and Emil
Jannings as Macbeth. Ernst Lubitsch will direct from a
scenario by Norbert Falk and Hans Kraly. Ernst Stern will
design special scenery. In sight also is The Mountain
People (Die Bergkopfe), by Lubitsch and Kraly..." (Variety, Mar. 4, p. 45).

1922

276   DOROTHY VERNON OF HADDON HALL. Mary Pickford invited Lubitsch
to come from Berlin and direct her in this film. When he
arrived they were unable to agree on the story, and the
project was postponed. Dorothy Vernon was later directed
by Marshall Neilan (1924). See the following entry.

1923

277   FAUST. When Lubitsch and Mary Pickford were unable to agree
on Dorothy Vernon of Haddon Hall, Lubitsch proposed to direct her as Marguerite in Faust. The project was announced
in New York Times Jan. 14 (VII.2) and in Moving Picture
World Jan. 20 (p. 219). Mitchell Leisen did costume
sketches for Pickford and Lubitsch shot a test scene. Then
the New York Times reported on Feb. 25 (VII.3) that Faust
had been postponed. Conflicting reasons have been given
why Faust was abandoned. Also see Film Daily, Jan. 9,
p. 1 and Feb. 21, p. 1; Variety, Jan. 12, p. 38; David
Chierichetti, Hollywood Director: The Career of Mitchell
Leisen (New York: Curtis, 1973), pp. 33, 319.

278   Mary Pickford/Douglas Fairbanks films. It was announced in
Photoplay (February, p. 90) that Lubitsch would direct
Fairbanks in a pirate picture, not yet written; the project
never materialized. Despite his differences with Pickford
over Rosita and their other projects that never came to

fruition, Lubitsch signed a contract with her in the summer
of 1923 (before the release of Rosita) to direct her in one
film a year. Their first picture together under the new
contract was to be Romeo and Juliet, possibly with Fairbanks as Romeo; this too never materialized. (See Film
Daily, Aug. 14, p. 1 and Aug. 29, p. 1; Photoplay, Nov.,
p. 90.) In 1926, Photoplay announced yet another Pickford/
Fairbanks film with Lubitsch which never came about, this
one to be co-directed by Lubitsch and Max Reinhardt from a
script by Karl Vollmöller, subject unspecified (July,
p. 76).

279 DEBURAU. "Among the number of classics to be directed by Mr.
Lubitsch is the picturization of David Belasco's play,
Deburau, the French drama by Sacha Guitry, in which Lionel
Atwill starred last year on Broadway" (Moving Picture
World, June 30, p. 746). Also see Film Daily, June 19,
p. 1. See Best Plays 1920-21, pp. 19-62, 414, for sum-
mary of play and cast list. The film was made in 1924 as
The Lover of Camille, directed by Harry Beaumont.

1925

280 A WALTZ DREAM. Lubitsch's next project after Kiss Me Again
was to be a film of Oscar Straus's operetta. Picture
rights were negotiated for and preparations were under way
when Ufa claimed the rights and Warner Brothers called off
the project. The Ufa version, directed by Ludwig Berger,
was released by MGM in the U.S. in 1926 as The Waltz Dream.
Lubitsch had contemplated making a film from this Straus
work as early as 1922 (see *Licht-Bild-Bühne, no. 39,
p. 26), and it was the source work for The Smiling Lieutenant. (Moving Picture World, Apr. 18, p. 712, Apr. 25,
p. 803, June 27, p. 992; Variety, Jan. 21, 1931, p. 6.)

281 Warner Brothers spectacles. Warner Brothers repeatedly announced in the trade papers in this year and into the first
half of 1926 that Lubitsch would make two historical spectacles on the order and scale of Madame Dubarry. In Moving
Picture World of Nov. 14 (p. 125), H. M. Warner was quoted
as saying that the first would be "a great American spectacle on a gigantic scale...the most elaborate ever made in
America." The article went on to say that Lubitsch had
been eager to make such a film ever since he had been in
this country. It was announced on June 19, 1926, after So
This Is Paris had been completed, that preparations were
underway on the spectacles (Moving Picture World, p. 633),
but shortly afterwards Warner Brothers sold the balance of
Lubitsch's contract (Moving Picture World, Sept. 4, 1926,
Supp., p. 3).

1926

282 THE DOOR MAT. An adaptation of a play by Ethel Clifton and
     Brenda Fowler, seen in Los Angeles and elsewhere in 1925
     (not to be confused with The Doormat, by H. S. Sheldon,
     which opened on Broadway Dec. 7, 1922). "This will be the
     director's first attempt to interpret Fifth Avenue, Broad-
     way and their environs. Heretofore, all of Mr. Lubitsch's
     stories have been laid in Continental atmosphere with the
     exception of Three Women, which was an American story with
     the locale not mentioned. But The Door Mat is a Simon
     pure, American, domestic comedy-drama with scenes in Madi-
     son Avenue homes, Broadway beauty shops, the studios of
     Washington Square and other colorful trimmings of Manhat-
     tan" (Moving Picture World, Mar. 6, p. 24; also see
     Jan. 30, p. 441). It was announced that Irene Rich had been
     signed to play the lead. The film was eventually directed
     by James Flood and released by Warner Brothers in August
     1926 as Honeymoon Express.

283 THE JAZZ SINGER. Lubitsch initiated the Warner Brothers pur-
     chase of Samson Raphaelson's play in a telegram May 20.
     According to Charles Higham (Warner Brothers, 1975, pp. 27-
     28) it was cameraman Charles Van Enger who got Lubitsch in-
     terested in the project. Raphaelson says Lubitsch later
     told him of his great interest in filming The Jazz Singer
     (Unpublished Raphaelson Transcript and copy of telegram in
     University of Illinois Archives). Alan Crosland made the
     film after Lubitsch had left Warner Brothers. Also see:
     Variety, July 14, p. 11; Louella Parsons syndicated column,
     Aug. 4.

284 THE MELTING POT. From Israel Zangwill's story; one of the two
     films scheduled for Lubitsch to make for Warner Brothers
     (the other was The Jazz Singer) just before his contract
     with them was sold. See Variety, July 14, p. 11.

285 THE LAST OF MRS. CHEYNEY. "Late in '26 Paramount's plans to
     film The Last of Mrs. Cheyney, starring [Florence] Vidor
     and Menjou, and with [Mal] St. Clair directing, were aban-
     doned. St. Clair had begun to drink; he quarrelled with
     Menjou; he had to be replaced (by Lubitsch). The delay in-
     terfered with Menjou's other commitments. Miss Vidor fell
     ill. Paramount decided to put Mrs. Cheyney on the shelf"
     (Harold Dunham, Films in Review, Jan. 1970, p. 31). In 1928
     it was reported that Paramount was lending Lubitsch to
     United Artists to direct John Barrymore in Mrs. Cheyney as
     Barrymore's last picture under his United Artists contract.
     Lubitsch and Hans Kraly prepared the scenario. Constance

222

Talmadge was signed for the title role. Shooting was to begin on June 20. (Variety, Jan. 18, 1928, p. 11, Apr. 11, 1928, p. 16, Apr. 25, 1928, p. 10, May 9, 1928, pp. 47-48, May 30, 1928, p. 11.) However, Variety announced on July 11, 1928 (p. 11) that through an arrangement with United Artists, MGM would produce Mrs. Cheyney as a starring vehicle for Norma Shearer.

1928

286 RASPUTIN. Variety reported on August 15 (p. 2) that Lubitsch would direct Emil Jannings in this picture, and on September 12 (p. 5) that Jesse Lasky had given permission to Jannings for him to make one picture a year with Lubitsch. Early the following year, however, Jannings obtained cancellation of his Paramount contract, reportedly out of dissatisfaction over a double speaking his lines in The Patriot (Variety, Apr. 24, 1929, p. 6).

1931

287 LOVE ME TONIGHT. "Alfred Savoir's play, Love Me Tonight, has been bought by Paramount for the second Maurice Chevalier-Jeanette MacDonald picture under Ernst Lubitsch's direction" (Variety, Oct. 20, p. 2). "Paramount has decided on Ernst Lubitsch to direct Maurice Chevalier in Love Me Tonight" (Film Daily, Oct. 23, p. 7). Also see Variety, May 31, 1932, p. 4.

1932

288 Stage project. There were several reports during this year that Lubitsch was about to undertake his first Broadway directorial project. Film Daily reported February 24 that Lubitsch was reading musical comedy scripts and that Walter Wanger was interested in the project (p. 2). New York Times (Feb. 28, VIII.6) and Film Daily (Mar. 25, p. 1) both reported that Lubitsch was actually at work on preliminary production matters with Albertina Rasch and Dmitri Tiomkin. Variety reported on Mar. 1 (p. 1) that Lubitsch was considering an operetta version of The Czarina (the source play for Forbidden Paradise and A Royal Scandal) to star Maria Jeritza. Late in October a Los Angeles newspaper (clipping of unknown origin in file of Theatre Collection, New York Public Library at Lincoln Center) reported that Lubitsch would stage a new Gershwin musical comedy produced by Aarons and Freedley and starring Jack Buchanan and Lyda

Roberti. (The Gershwins' Pardon My English, with Lyda
Roberti, produced by Aarons and Freedley, opened on Broadway Jan. 20, 1933.)

1933

289 Jeanette MacDonald picture, to be shot in Paris. "Arrangements are being made for Ernst Lubitsch to make one film
for Paramount in Paris. Robert Kane, head of the Joinville
(France) studios discussed the matter with h.o. execs in
New York last week. No date set due to insistence of New
York on a complete story okay before the director is allowed to leave Hollywood. Understanding is the idea would
be to make the picture with Jeanette MacDonald starring in
French and English versions" (Variety, Jan. 10, p. 2).

290 THERE WERE FOUR WOMEN. Announced by the Los Angeles Times
(June 27) as an "all-star" picture "cover[ing] various his-
toric periods as well as the present" to be written and
directed by Lubitsch. Mentioned for the cast were Miriam
Hopkins, Sylvia Sidney, Fredric March, Gary Cooper, Claudette Colbert, Cary Grant, Dorothea Wieck, and Carole Lombard. Also see Film Daily, June 27, p. 6.

291 MARIE ANTOINETTE. "It has been reported that the Irving
Thalberg-Ernst Lubitsch deal for the director to handle
the megaphone on Marie Antoinette, the Stefan Zweig novel,
which will be Norma Shearer's second starring vehicle for
MGM, is very hot and will likely come to a head very soon"
Hollywood Reporter, Sept. 9, p. 1). A version of Marie
Antoinette starring Norma Shearer was made by W. S. Van
Dyke in 1938.

292 Alexander Korda picture. Hollywood Reporter said on Nov. 9
(p. 1) Maurice Chevalier had signed to do an unspecified
picture with Korda's London Films co-starring Charles
Laughton and directed by Lubitsch. On Nov. 10 the Los Angeles Times (II.9) reported that negotiations were on for
Lubitsch to direct Laughton in a historical spectacle to
be made in England and produced by Korda.

1934

293 CARMEN. On July 10 (p. 11) Variety reported that Carmen was
under consideration as Lubitsch's first project back at
Paramount after his loan-out to MGM for The Merry Widow.
(Also see Hollywood Reporter, July 9, p. 1 and Aug. 23,
p. 6.) Hollywood Reporter said on Sept. 26 (p. 3) that
Lubitsch still wanted to do the picture, with Claudette

Colbert, but "elaborate story and music requirements bar it from immediate production." Lubitsch discussed the <u>Carmen</u> project with the film reviewer for the New York <u>Sun</u> (Oct. 17, p. 33).

294   Toeplitz contract. It was widely reported in the press on or about Sept. 19 that Lubitsch was signing with Toeplitz Productions of London to direct a series of pictures in England after the expiration of his Paramount contract. A follow-up story in <u>Motion Picture Daily</u> on Oct. 10 (p. 1) said Lubitsch would alternate productions between Hollywood and England. On Oct. 24 (p. 7) <u>Hollywood Reporter</u> stated that Lubitsch's first picture in England would be <u>Lady Windermere's Fan</u> and that Lubitsch would go over in June. The Toeplitz arrangement never materialized; shortly afterwards Lubitsch became head of production at Paramount. <u>Also see</u> <u>Variety</u>, Jan. 22, 1935, p. 2.

295   SHOE THE WILD MARE. "Gene Fowler's <u>Shoe the Wild Mare</u> will probably be Marlene Dietrich's next at Paramount. Studio is also flirting with the idea of getting John Barrymore as co-star of the picture: Ernest [sic] Lubitsch, though he has not as yet assented, has been penciled in as the director. Tiffany Thayer is adapting the story. Production is set for around Jan. 1" (<u>Variety</u>, Nov. 6, p. 3). "Paramount took two scripts off the shelf this week. For two years it has contemplated Gene Fowler's <u>Shoe the Wild Mare</u>, but every time a treatment was prepared it was put back in the vault" (<u>New York Times</u>, June 2, 1935, IX.3).

                                1935

296   ROSE OF THE RANCHO. It was originally announced that Lubitsch would direct Marlene Dietrich in this remake of a Paramount silent film based on David Belasco's play (<u>Variety</u>, Jan. 22, p. 2 and Jan. 29, p. 2), but shortly after the announcement he became head of production. <u>Rose of the Rancho</u> was directed by Marion Gering.

297   THE CHOCOLATE PRINCESS. "The busy Ernst Lubitsch will stop being an executive long enough to personally supervise a musical of his own creation. He is calling his innovation <u>The Chocolate Princess</u>, and it is an innovation because it will be the first musical on the screen to have an all-colored cast.... Mr. Lubitsch, of course, will have a director working with him. He is negotiating with such well-known personages as Ethel Waters, Paul Robeson, Bill Robinson, Daniel Haynes, Etta Moten and others" (Louella O. Parsons syndicated column, dateline Sept. 19). <u>Also see</u> <u>Hollywood Reporter</u>, Sept. 19, p. 3; <u>Variety</u>, Sept. 25, p. 4.

                                225

1936

298   I LOVED A SOLDIER. This remake of Pola Negri's Hotel Imperial
      was before the cameras under Henry Hathaway's direction and
      Lubitsch's personal supervision when Lubitsch was replaced
      as head of production at Paramount. It had been a tempes-
      tuous project from the start, and Marlene Dietrich walked
      out, citing Lubitsch's departure as her reason. Hollywood
      Reporter stated on August 14 (pp. 1-2) that Lubitsch (now
      back from a vacation in Europe) would make an attempt to
      salvage this project on which Paramount had already spent a
      million dollars, this time as director. The film was even-
      tually made by Robert Florey as Hotel Imperial. See Vari-
      ety, Dec. 18, 1935, p. 3; Hollywood Reporter, Jan. 7, p. 1,
      Jan. 9, p. 1, Jan. 14, p. 1, Feb. 12, pp. 1, 4, Feb. 17,
      p. 1, Feb. 21, p. 1; New York Times, Mar. 1, IX.5; Florey,
      Hollywood d'hier et d'aujourd'hui (Paris: Editions Prisma,
      1948), p. 194; Homer Dickens, Films of Marlene Dietrich
      (New York: Citadel, 1968), p. 22; Charles Higham, Marlene
      (New York: Norton, 1977), pp. 168-72.

299   THE PATRIOT. Lubitsch told a reporter for the New York Times
      he wanted his next project to be a sound remake of The Pa-
      triot with Charles Laughton (Mar. 1, IX.5). He later men-
      tioned The Patriot and Laughton to an interviewer for Liv-
      ing Age (June, p. 327).

300   DER ROSENKAVALIER. According to Walter Reisch, Lubitsch long
      wanted to make a film of Richard Strauss's operetta. He
      was making preliminary arrangements for the project when he
      saw Reisch in Vienna in this year, but there were complica-
      tions over the rights. See detailed account in Weinberg
      (1968), pp. 215-20.

1937

301   THE BUCCANEER. It was reported in the New York press May 13
      that Lubitsch might be cast as Napoleon in this Cecil B.
      DeMille swashbuckler (New York World Telegram, p. 33;
      New York Times, p. 31). The World Telegram quoted Lubitsch
      as saying he had always wanted to play Napoleon and added
      he "bears a striking resemblance to the French Emperor."
      According to Charles Higham in his Cecil B. DeMille, De
      Mille wanted Lubitsch for the role but "the plan fell
      through when Lubitsch proved camera-shy" (Dell paperback
      edition, 1976, p. 188).

1938

302   Independent production deal with Myron Selznick. In the sum-
       mer of this year Hollywood's top agent launched an ambi-
       tious scheme whereby he and some of the industry's top stars,
       directors and writers would form independent production
       companies and make their own films on a profit-sharing
       basis. The first company formed was Ernst Lubitsch Produc-
       tions. The first Lubitsch-Selznick picture was to have
       been The Shop around the Corner, with German actress Dolly
       Haas, who had been brought to Hollywood the year before by
       Columbia, in the lead role. (Janet Gaynor was indicated
       as a possible replacement once Miss Haas was out.) A sec-
       ond unnamed Lubitsch-Selznick project to follow Shop and to
       star Carole Lombard and William Powell was also announced.
       MGM took over Shop around the Corner as part of its deal
       with Lubitsch after the Selznick venture folded. See Vari-
       ety, July 27, p. 3, Aug. 3, p. 4, Aug. 10, p. 7, Sept. 28,
       p. 3, Nov. 16, p. 3, Dec. 28, p. 4, Mar. 1, 1939, p. 2;
       New York Times, July 25, p. 18, July 31, IX.3.

303   THE WOMEN. Lubitsch was originally set to direct Norma Shear-
       er in Clare Boothe's play (Variety, June 8, p. 7). Later
       in the summer he was replaced on this project by Clarence
       Brown. George Cukor eventually made The Women.

1939

304   MADAME CURIE. Lubitsch was originally scheduled to direct
       Greta Garbo in a screen biography of the famous scientist
       as his first assignment at MGM (Variety, Jan. 11, p. 2).
       Madame Curie was eventually made in 1943 by Mervyn LeRoy.

1941

305   A SELF-MADE CINDERELLA. This was to be Lubitsch's first pic-
       ture for 20th Century-Fox. It was to star Ginger Rogers
       (her RKO contract allowed her one outside commitment).
       See Film Daily, July 17, p. 17, also pp. 1, 20, Sept. 8,
       p. 2, Sept. 17, p. 6; Variety, July 23, p. 7, Feb. 18,
       1942, p. 6. Variety reported (Feb. 25, 1942, p. 5) that
       Lubitsch called off the project because he felt "the friv-
       olous theme is not desirable in wartime."

306   MARGIN FOR ERROR. Lubitsch was originally scheduled to do an
       adaptation of Clare Boothe's play as one of his first as-
       signments at 20th Century-Fox, but the project never mate-
       rialized. Margin for Error was eventually made by Otto
       Preminger, who also recreated his original role in the play.

See <u>New York Times</u>, Apr. 4, 1940, p. 26, Apr. 22, p. 26;
<u>Film Daily</u>, Sept. 8, p. 2; <u>Variety</u>, Sept. 10, p. 7.

1943

307   ALL-OUT ARLENE. Lubitsch postponed <u>The Lady in Ermine</u> (being
      planned at this time to star Irene Dunne) in order to un-
      dertake a more suitable wartime project, a comedy on the
      WACs, based on a story by New York <u>Sun</u> columnist H. I.
      Phillips. He spent several weeks in Washington conferring
      with Colonel Oveta Cupp Hobby, head of the WACs. When ill-
      ness forced him to give up directing for a time, the proj-
      ect was reassigned to Otto Preminger. Lubitsch talked at
      length about preparations for <u>All-Out Arlene</u> to New York
      interviewers; <u>see</u> New York <u>Post</u>, July 31, p. 11 and New
      York <u>Sun</u>, Aug. 2, pp. 15, 17. <u>Also see Hollywood Reporter</u>,
      July 19, p. 1, July 22, p. 1, July 27, p. 1, Aug. 18, p. 2,
      Sept. 28, p. 3, Oct. 1, p. 4; Ephron (1977).

308   QUO VADIS. Orson Welles and Lubitsch were among those MGM ap-
      proached about directing this superspectacle. (Welles was
      also to play Nero.) <u>Quo Vadis</u> was eventually made by Mer-
      vyn LeRoy. See <u>Hollywood Reporter</u>, Feb. 16, p. 6, May 5,
      p. 1.

1944

309   TYPHOON. An adaptation of Melchior Lengyel's play dealing
      with the elaborate spy network set up by the Japanese at
      the time of the Russo-Japanese war. Lubitsch was set to
      produce for 20th Century-Fox, Charles Boyer was approached
      to play the leading role--that of Tokeramo, a Japanese--
      and Melchior and Thomas Lengyel were assigned to write the
      screenplay. The play was produced on Broadway in 1912.
      See <u>Hollywood Reporter</u>, Mar. 16, p. 3, May 22, pp. 1, 4,
      May 7, 1945, p. 3, Jan. 9, 1946, p. 1; <u>Daily Variety</u>,
      Sept. 25, p. 10.

310   JACOBOWSKY AND THE COLONEL. Two studios, 20th Century-Fox and
      Columbia, were in the final bidding for the screen rights
      to Franz Werfel's Broadway hit. "The Fox plan, if the
      property is bought by them, is to have Ernst Lubitsch play
      the role of Jacobowsky. Lubitsch, according to his own
      statement, is anxious to do this one movie role...and feels
      the part of the Polish scapegoat is worth donning grease
      paint for again. Also, if the Fox purchase is cinched,
      Elia Kazan, who directed the play, will direct the film"
      (<u>Hollywood Reporter</u>, Apr. 17, p. 3). Columbia eventually won
      out in the bidding and the film was finally made at Columbia

in 1958 as <u>Me and the Colonel</u>; it was directed by Peter
Glenville and featured Danny Kaye as Jacobowsky. <u>Also see</u>
<u>Hollywood Reporter</u>, Apr. 25, p. 12, May 1, p. 4.

Undated

311   <u>MISS LIBERTY</u>. "Mae West...and Chevalier wanted to make [a
      film] with Lubitsch directing. It was a very slight story
      outline but many years later, much revamped, it became an
      Irving Berlin stage musical called <u>Miss Liberty</u>. The West-
      Chevalier film was supposed to have been a comedy about
      West being the model for the Statue of Liberty and Cheval-
      ier the man who designed it. All of which was supposed to
      be a rather risque joke because if [you] happen to have a
      photo of the Statue of Liberty and you cover the upper part
      of the torch and just show the upraised hand with the lower
      portion of the torch grasped in the fist, you'll get the
      idea" (Gene Ringgold, letter to the authors, July 16,
      1976.

312   Other reported unrealized projects. The following projects
      are mentioned briefly in secondary sources without attribu-
      tion or corroborating details and no further information on
      them has been found, or else there are references to them
      in sources the authors have not seen: <u>Mania</u>, ca. 1918,
      with Pola Negri (Weinberg, 1968, p. 303; also *<u>Der Film</u>,
      no. 45, 1918, p. 58; *<u>Licht-Bild-Bühne</u>, no. 11, 1919, p.
      30); <u>Mephistopheles</u>, 1920, scenario by Hans Kraly (*<u>Film</u>
      <u>und Presse</u>, issue of July 1); <u>Salome</u>, ca. 1920, with Pola
      Negri (Weinberg, 1968, p. 309); <u>The Merry Wives of Windsor</u>,
      1921, with Emil Jannings (*<u>Film und Presse</u>, no. 17/18,
      p. 162); a film on the life of Johann Strauss, 1922 (<u>Photo-</u>
      <u>play</u>, Dec., p. 99); <u>Carnival in Toledo</u>, ca. 1923 (Weinberg,
      1968, p. 312); <u>Compromise</u>, 1924, a film version of Suder-
      mann's "Song of Songs" (<u>Vanity Fair</u>, July, p. 26); <u>The</u>
      <u>Tempest</u>, ca. 1929, with John Barrymore (Weinberg, 1968,
      p. 321); <u>Alexanderplatz</u>, 1930, from Alfred Doeblin's story,
      to be made in Berlin with Emil Jannings (<u>Variety</u>, June 18,
      p. 6); <u>An American Tragedy</u>, ca. 1930 (Weinberg, 1968,
      p. 321); <u>Morals and Marriage</u>, 1931, with Fredric March (<u>Mo-</u>
      <u>tion Picture Herald</u>, May 2, sec. 2, product announcement
      advertisement; <u>Film Daily</u>, May 7, p. 12); a costume pic-
      ture, 1933, to be made after <u>Design for Living</u> (Los Angeles
      <u>Times</u>, Mar. 21, II.7); <u>One Sunday Afternoon</u>, 1933, James
      Hagan's comedy then playing on Broadway (New York <u>Sun</u>,
      Apr. 25, p. 16); "musical revue" with the Four Marx Broth-
      ers, 1933 (<u>Film Daily</u>, Dec. 8, p. 6); <u>All the King's Horses</u>
      or <u>Carnival</u>, 1934 ("Director has already okayed both yarns
      and will make decision on first to go when he gets back to
      Paramount the end of this month"--<u>Variety</u>, Aug. 7, p. 5);

a film with Marlene Dietrich as Napoleon's Josephine, 1935 ("it now goes to another piloter on Lubitsch's announcement that he won't direct any pictures while holding his current exec berth at the studio"--Variety, Mar. 6, p. 3); a remake of La Chienne, ca. 1937, made in 1931 by Jean Renoir and as Scarlet Street in 1945 by Fritz Lang (Weinberg, 1968, pp. 330-31); Papa, n.d., with Maurice Chevalier, from a boulevard farce by De Flers and Caillavet (Weinberg, 1968, p. 327).

APOCRYPHAL OR UNVERIFIED FILM CREDITS

1912

313   DAS MIRAKEL ("The Miracle"). A filmization of Max Reinhardt's London production of Karl Vollmöller's stage spectacle. Lubitsch may have been one of the two thousand 'supers' in this production (see entry 242) and therefore he may also appear in the film.

1913

314   LE CLUB DES INVISIBLES ("Club of the Invisibles"). Listed in Georges Sadoul, Dictionnaire des Cinéastes (Paris: Editions du Seuil, 1965) as a film directed by Lubitsch for Decla-Pommer, Vienna.

315   EINE VENEZIANISCHE NACHT ("A Venetian Night"). Directed by Max Reinhardt. Listed by Werner Dütsch and Peter B. Schumann; (see entry 351); Weinberg (1968) and Felix Bucher, Germany, Screen Series (New York: A. S. Barnes, 1970) as a film Lubitsch appeared in.

1914

316   RUND UM DIE EHE ("The Marriage-Go-Round"). Listed as starring Lubitsch in Weinberg (1968).

317   SERENISSIMUS LERNT TANGO ("Serenissimus Learns the Tango"). Directed by Stellan Rye. Listed by Felix Bucher, Germany, Screen Series (New York: A. S. Barnes, 1970) as a film Lubitsch appeared in.

1915

318   MARIONETTEN ("Marionettes"). Directed by Richard Löwenbein. Georges Sadoul, Dictionary of Filmmakers, ed. Peter Morris

(Berkeley: University of California Press, 1972); Weinberg (1968); and Kosmorama (1976) list as directed by Lubitsch, all giving date as 1918.

1916

319   DER ERSTE PATIENT ("The First Patient"). Listed by Dütsch and Schumann (see entry 351); Felix Bucher, Germany, Screen Series (New York: A. S. Barnes, 1970); and Georges Sadoul, Dictionary of Filmmakers, ed. Peter Morris (Berkeley: University of California Press, 1972) as a film Lubitsch directed and appeared in.

1917

320   DIE EHE DER LUISE ROHRBACH ("The Marriage of Luise Rohrbach"). Directed by Rudolf Biebrach. At one place in Histoire général du cinéma (Paris: Denoel, 1947-   ), Georges Sadoul lists this as a film directed by Lubitsch (vol. 3, pt. 2, plate 118, no. 360), but elsewhere in the same volume he correctly attributes direction to Biebrach (p. 389).

321   FAMA DER LASTERGRUBE ("The Renown of the Den of Vice"). Listed in Enciclopedia dello Spettacolo as a film directed by Lubitsch.

322   DER LETZTE ANZUG ("The Last Suit"). Listed by Dütsch and Schumann (see entry 351); Felix Bucher, Germany, Screen Series (New York: A. S. Barnes, 1970) and Georges Sadoul, Dictionary of Filmmakers, ed. Peter Morris (Berkeley: University of California Press, 1972) as a film Lubitsch directed and appeared in.

1918

323   FUHRMANN HENSCHEL ("Coachman Henschel"). Several filmographies--including Mitry (1948), Verdone (1964), and Brion (1968)--attribute such a film to Lubitsch, but this has not been established and further information is lacking. (Lubitsch did appear in a stage version of the play by Gerhard Hauptmann in 1916; see Stage Appearances, entry 229.)

1919

324   COMTESSE DODDY ("Countess Doddy"). Directed by Georg Jacoby. Mitry (1948) listed this film as Komtesse Doddy, attributed direction to Lubitsch, and dated it 1915-16.

325 VENDETTA. Directed by Georg Jacoby. A young Corsican nobleman is killed in a duel; his sister (Pola Negri) vows to
avenge his death but falls in love with and marries the
young English officer who killed him without knowing who he
is. Released in the United States on the heels of Pola
Negri's Lubitsch films and at the height of her popularity
as a foreign actress. Although American reviewers identified the director as Georg Jacoby (New York Times, Dec. 19,
1921, p. 13; Variety, Dec. 23, 1921, p. 35), Vendetta was
registered with the U.S. Copyright Office as directed by
Lubitsch, and this attribution has been repeated in several
filmographies and in the autobiography of Emil Jannings
(1951), who had a role in the film. Pola Negri wrote the
authors (Aug. 24, 1976) she did not remember who directed
her in Vendetta but she was sure it wasn't Lubitsch.

1920

326 DER GOLEM. Directed by Paul Wegener. Mitry (1948) and Eisenschitz (1968) say that Lubitsch supervised the direction of
this film.

327 MEDEA. Listed by Felix Bucher, Germany, Screen Series (New
York: A. S. Barnes, 1970) as a film directed by Lubitsch.
(See Unrealized Projects, entry 274.)

328 DIE TOLLE RISCHKA ("Crazy Rischka"). Listed by Dütsch and
Schumann (see entry 351) and (as Die tolle Rikscha) by
Felix Bucher, Germany, Screen Series (New York: A. S.
Barnes, 1970) and Georges Sadoul, Dictionary of Filmmakers,
ed. Peter Morris (Berkeley: University of California
Press, 1972) as a film Lubitsch directed. (Could this be
an early title for Die Bergkatze, in which Pola Negri stars
as a crazy character named Rischka?)

329 DIE WOHNUNGSNOT ("The Housing Shortage"). According to Weinberg (1968), Lubitsch and Hans Kraly wrote a sketch that
was used in this Ossi Oswalda film (p. 309). Also see
*Licht-Bild-Bühne, no. 5, p. 27.

1921

330 FRÄULEIN JULIE. Directed by Felix Basch. Mitry (1948) lists
this as a film directed by Lubitsch, from Hans Kraly's
adaptation of the Strindberg play. Enciclopedia dello
Spettacolo repeats the attribution but dates it 1922.

1923

331 DAS MILLIARDENSOUPER ("The Billion Dollar Dinner"). Directed by Victor Janson. Listed by Mitry (1948) and by Enciclopedia dello Spettacolo as a film directed by Lubitsch.

332 SOULS FOR SALE. Directed by Rupert Hughes. Several directors and numerous stars appear in this sensationalistic behind-the-scenes view of Hollywood life. Roger Holman, Chief Cataloguer of the National Film Archive, British Film Institute, wrote the authors (August 9, 1976): "Lubitsch visited the Goldwyn Studios and was persuaded to put on make-up and appear in several scenes of the picture." A photograph in the Lubitsch file in the Museum of Modern Art Stills Collection shows Lubitsch with several of the stars on the elaborate ballroom set. A person who looks like Lubitsch appears in some of the scenes.

1935

333 HANDS ACROSS THE TABLE. Directed by Mitchell Leisen. Romantic comedy with Carole Lombard as a golddigging manicurist who snags a down-on-his-luck millionaire (Fred MacMurray). Variety hailed this as the "first 100% Lubitsch picture [as production head at Paramount] from story to final editing" (Nov. 20, p. 6), a theme which was also sounded by the reviewer for New York Times (Nov. 2, p. 13). The extent of Lubitsch's involvement in it has yet to be determined.

1939

334 TEMPÊTE SUR PARIS ("Storm Over Paris"). Directed by Bernard Deschamps. Kosmorama (1976) says Lubitsch appeared in this film; perhaps the author misread a statement in Weinberg (1968) that von Stroheim appeared in the film (p. 300).

1945

335 WHERE DO WE GO FROM HERE? Directed by Gregory Ratoff. Lubitsch was originally scheduled to play himself (Hollywood Reporter, May 26, 1944, p. 1) in this comedy about a man who travels backward into American history, but this role does not appear in the film. Eisenschitz (1968) reports that Lubitsch plays one of the sailors who mutiny against Christopher Columbus; Weinberg (1968) prints a photograph of Lubitsch on the set in costume (third ed., p. 186). The authors have screened the picture and cannot verify that Lubitsch appears in it.

VI. Archival Sources

CALIFORNIA

336   MARGARET HERRICK LIBRARY
Academy of Motion Picture Arts and Sciences
8949 Wilshire Boulevard
Beverly Hills, California 90211
Mildred Simpson, Librarian
(213) 278-4313

9 a.m. to 5 p.m.   Monday, Tuesday, Thursday, Friday
Open to public
Photograph duplication services available

Scripts:
The Love Parade (scene continuity 10/25/29; scene and dialogue continuity 10/28/29; scene continuity of silent version
12/23/29, all Paramount Collection), Paramount on Parade
(scene and dialogue continuity 4/3/30, Paramount Collection),
Monte Carlo (scene and dialogue continuity 8/21/30; synchronized foreign version scene and dialogue continuity 11/11/30,
Paramount Collection), The Smiling Lieutenant (scene and dialogue continuity 7/6/31, Paramount Collection), The Man I
Killed (scene and dialogue continuity 1/14/32, Paramount Collection), One Hour with You (scene and dialogue continuity
2/19/32, Paramount Collection), Une heure près de toi (French
version of One Hour with You by Léopold Marchand, production
script 12/28/31; also, in Paramount Collection, scene and dialogue continuity 3/23/32), Trouble in Paradise (scene and dialogue continuity 10/15/32, Paramount Collection), If I Had a
Million (production scripts, episodes variously dated, Lubitsch episode not included), Desire (production script,
11/4/35; also, in Paramount Collection, production script "final" 11/4/35 with revised ending 11/20/35), Angel (scene and
dialogue continuity 9/2/37, Paramount Collection), Bluebeard's
Eighth Wife (scene and dialogue continuity 3/14/38, Paramount
Collection), To Be or Not To Be (production script "revised

final" 10/27/41), <u>Heaven Can Wait</u> (<u>Birthday</u>, production script
"final" 12/14/42), <u>Dragonwyck</u> (production script "final"
2/8/45 revisions and retakes to 12/11/45), <u>Cluny Brown</u> (production script "first draft continuity" 5/10/45).

Stills:
    Paramount Collection contains bound stillbooks (some with
items missing) for <u>Forbidden Paradise</u>, <u>One Hour with You</u>, and
<u>Paramount on Parade</u> (3 vols.) and loose stills for most other
Lubitsch Paramount films, including <u>Smiling Lieutenant</u> (35)
and <u>Bluebeard's Eighth Wife</u> (60). Production files (alphabetical by film title) contain loose stills on most Lubitsch
American films, including <u>The Patriot</u> (27), <u>The Love Parade</u>
(22), and <u>Cluny Brown</u> (28). Lubitsch biography file contains
numerous photographs and sketches of Lubitsch.

Other:
    Production files (alphabetical by title) for most Lubitsch
American films. For the films into the early thirties, these
typically contain a few reviews and articles from trade journals and West Coast papers and magazines; from <u>The Merry Widow</u>
on they also contain such materials as studio cast and credit
sheets, press releases, news clippings, and programs. The Lubitsch biography file is of special interest for its many
clippings from trade journals and West Coast papers and magazines. The Paramount Collection contains press sheets or
pressbooks for all the Lubitsch Paramount pictures except <u>For-</u>
<u>bidden Paradise</u>. The Paramount Collection contains a story
file on <u>Divorçons</u>, the source play for <u>Kiss Me Again</u> and <u>That</u>
<u>Uncertain Feeling</u>; included are synopses of several versions
(including one by Laura and S. J. Perelman) and script drafts
by Norman Krasna and Jacques Thery (12/18/35) and Benn Levy
(7/2/36). The file for <u>The Patriot</u> in the Paramount Collection contains materials on the source play by Alfred Neumann,
including a typescript of an English-language translation.
Ernst Matray Gift file contains rare stills of Lubitsch and
Matray from the early German period, including several from
<u>Zucker und Zimt</u>, and a 1975 letter from Matray telling about
his early association with Lubitsch in the Max Reinhardt Theater and in films. (Some of the photographs were printed in
Luft [1976].) Irene Scrapbooks contain two pages of annotated
wardrobe descriptions for Carole Lombard's costumes for <u>To Be</u>
<u>or Not to Be</u>. The Harold Grieve Collection contains a large
scrapbook with photographs of the interior of Lubitsch's home
in Bel Air for which Grieve, Lubitsch's art director on two
Warners films, did the interior decoration.

337 CHARLES K. FELDMAN LIBRARY
     The American Film Institute
     501 Doheny Road
     Beverly Hills, California 90210
     Anne G. Schlosser, Librarian
     (213) 278-8777

     9 a.m. to 5:30 p.m. Monday through Friday. Open to scholars,
     historians, writers, educators, and advanced graduate students,
     as well as members of the entertainment industry.

     Scripts:
     Monte Carlo (scene and dialogue continuity 8/21/30),
     Trouble in Paradise (35 pages of excerpts from a production
     script), The Shop around the Corner (production script
     10/20/39), Heaven Can Wait (Birthday, production script "fi-
     nal" 12/14/42), Cluny Brown (production script "first draft
     continuity" 5/10/45, annotated [by Zanuck?], letter from
     Joseph Breen stating two objections inserted at end).

     Other:
     Transcripts of American Film Institute Seminars; with Jack
     Benny, June 4, 1971 (Transcript 111); with Walter Reisch,
     November 28, 1973 (Transcript 178).

338 SPECIAL COLLECTIONS LIBRARY
     University of California at Los Angeles
     405 Hilgard Avenue
     Los Angeles, California 90024
     Brooke Whiting, Curator
     (213) 825-4988 and 825-4879

     Arrangements should be made in advance.

     Jeanette MacDonald Scrapbooks: Book I contains extensive
     clippings from French (and occasionally other European) news-
     papers during Miss MacDonald's visit to Paris in August 1931,
     when mass publicity accompanied her every move. Also includes
     many items on Chevalier, whose new $1 million contract to work
     with Lubitsch and Miss MacDonald was announced at the time,
     and numerous French-language reviews of Monte Carlo, which
     played simultaneously with her visit.

     Charles Ruggles Collection contains many stills of Ruggles
     in Lubitsch films.

339 THEATER ARTS LIBRARY
University of California at Los Angeles
405 Hilgard Avenue
Los Angeles, California 90024
Audree Malkin, Librarian
(213) 825-4880

9 a.m. to 6 p.m. Monday through Friday, 12 noon to 4 p.m.
Saturday

Scripts:
The Merry Widow (production script undated but 3/24 on some
pages), Ninotchka (production script, incomplete, ends at shot
118, official refusing Leon visa), The Shop around the Corner
(production script 10/20/39).

Stills:
Very few Lubitsch stills in collection except for Cluny
Brown (30).

Other:
Suggested music guides for Das Weib des Pharao, Lady Win-
dermere's Fan, and So This Is Paris. Music cue sheets for
Madame Dubarry, The Marriage Circle, and Three Women.

340 UCLA FILM ARCHIVE
University of California at Los Angeles
1438 Melnitz Hall
Los Angeles, California 90024
Robert Rosen, Director
(213) 825-4142

Arrangements should be made in advance.

Prints:
Lady Windermere's Fan (excerpt), The Love Parade, Paramount
on Parade (incomplete), Monte Carlo, The Smiling Lieutenant,
The Man I Killed, One Hour with You, Trouble in Paradise, If
I Had a Million (excerpt; includes Lubitsch-Charles Laughton
sequence), Design for Living, Desire, Angel, Bluebeard's
Eighth Wife, Heaven Can Wait, Cluny Brown, That Lady in Ermine.
These are 35mm in-house prints on deposit from the studios.

341 CINEMA LIBRARY
Department of Special Collections
Doheny Library
University of Southern California
Los Angeles, California 90007
Robert Knutson, Head
(213) 746-6058

Arrangements should be made in advance.

Scripts:
   The Marriage Circle (scene continuity, undated), The Student Prince (see below), The Merry Widow (see below), Cluny
Brown (production script "first draft continuity" 5/10/45),
That Lady in Ermine (The Lady in Ermine, production script
9/12/47 revisions to 10/22/47 with addendum of lyrics including songs not in the film).

Stills:
   Scattered loose stills of many Lubitsch films from Madame
Dubarry on. The 20th Century-Fox Set-Stills Collection includes complete books of photographs of each individual set
used in Dragonwyck and That Lady in Ermine; each set photograph indicates the setting, scene number in the shooting
script, and the director, and therefore in the Lady in Ermine
book the scenes that were directed by Preminger are indicated.

Other:
   Clipping files and pressbooks for many Lubitsch films from
Madame Dubarry on; typically the clipping files include ad-
vertisements and reviews from Los Angeles newspapers, photographs from fan magazines, press sheets, and publicity. The
Student Prince file in the MGM Script Collection contains a
production script (11/6/26), a scene continuity (8/20/27), an
intertitles list (8/20/27), synopses, outlines, reader reports, research materials, a typed version of the Meyer-
Förster book, and other documents pertaining to the various
source works. The Merry Widow file in the MGM Script Collection contains four folders of documents on this production
dating back to 1929; included are two script drafts by Vajda
and Raphaelson (2/28/34 and 3/24/34), five pages of rewrites
by Anita Loos (12/28/33), a scene and dialogue continuity
(10/4/34), an earlier script by Vajda (2/3/30), various scripts
and trailer continuities for the French, Belgian, and British
versions, and earlier treatments by Hans Kraly (10/9/33), Dr.
Fleishman (3/30/33), Rowland Leigh (9/26/33 and 10/16/33), and
Vicki Baum (six drafts from 11/3/33 to 12/7/33); also many
production schedules, including shooting, wardrobe, and music,
and a 107-page advertising approach book by Howard Dietz.

ILLINOIS

342   UNIVERSITY ARCHIVES
      University of Illinois
      Urbana, Illinois 61801
      Maynard Brichford, Archivist
      (217) 333-0798

8 a.m. to 12 noon, 1 p.m. to 5 p.m. Monday through Friday
Advance approval must be secured for use of the Samson Raphaelson autobiographical transcripts and tapes.

Samson Raphaelson Collection:

<u>Scripts:</u>
   <u>The Smiling Lieutenant</u> (production script "first white
script" 1/27/31), <u>The Man I Killed</u> (production script "first
script" 8/4/31), <u>One Hour with You</u> (production script "final"
12/24/31 with rewritten last scene), <u>Trouble in Paradise</u> (production script "first script" 7/15/32 and scene and dialogue
continuity 10/15/32), <u>The Merry Widow</u> (production script
3/24/34), <u>Angel</u> (production script, undated, some individual
pages dated 1/28/37 to 2/1/37), <u>The Shop around the Corner</u>
(production script 10/20/39), <u>Heaven Can Wait</u> (production
script, undated, inserted revision pages dated 1/20/43), <u>That
Lady in Ermine</u> (scene and dialogue continuity 7/28/48).

<u>Other:</u>
   Raphaelson autobiographical transcripts and tapes, with extended commentaries on his work with Lubitsch. Communications
between Lubitsch and Raphaelson (5 items) and through their
agents (6 pieces). Letters to Raphaelson giving details of
Lubitsch's death by Mary Loos, Walter Reisch, and Lubitsch's
secretary Steffie Trondle, the last two with precise details
of the state of <u>That Lady in Ermine</u>. Raphaelson's financial
records, with studio dealings. English-language typescript of
<u>Parfumerie</u>, the source play for <u>The Shop around the Corner</u>.

<u>NEW YORK</u>

343   FILM STUDY CENTER
       Museum of Modern Art
       11 West 53rd Street
       New York, New York 10019
       Charles Silver, Supervisor
       (212) 956-4212

   Materials in the Film Study Center are made available only
to qualified scholars working on specific research projects.
Students who wish to view films must present a letter from
their instructor requesting permission, stating the nature and
validity of the project and listing the films required. Writers who present a similar letter from their editor or publish-
er may also obtain permission to view films. The Department
of Film retains the right of approving all requests. Due to
the limited facilities available, no projects requiring exten-
sively detailed analysis (i.e. shot analysis) of individual
films can be permitted. An appointment is necessary. The

hours are from 1 p.m. to 5 p.m. Monday through Friday. Appointments for viewing films must be made at least one week in advance. Film books and older bound periodicals are located in the Museum Library. Those who anticipate using these materials should make a separate appointment with the library (212) 956-7236. Film stills are available through appointment with the Stills Archivist only (212) 956-4209.

Prints:
    Carmen (excerpt), Die Austernprinzessin, Madame Dubarry, Die Puppe, Romeo und Julia im Schnee, Anna Boleyn, Die Bergkatze, The Marriage Circle, Lady Windermere's Fan, So This Is Paris (French intertitles), The Student Prince in Old Heidelberg, The Love Parade, The Smiling Lieutenant (Danish subtitles), The Man I Killed, Trouble in Paradise, Desire, That Uncertain Feeling.

Stills:
    Extensive stills collection, with files on Lubitsch and on practically all of his films that were released in the United States. Samples: 37 loose stills from Angel, 17 from The Merry Widow, 22 from The Smiling Lieutenant. (The original basis of the collection was the stills archive of Photoplay magazine.)

Other:
    Extensive clipping files (some on microfiche), arranged alphabetically by persons and film titles. The Lubitsch file contains many articles and interviews from magazines, trade papers, and New York newspapers. The files for Lubitsch films contain such materials as reviews (mainly from New York papers), magazine articles, pressbooks, programs, and program notes (many unpublished) by Eileen Bowser, William K. Everson, Miles Kreuger, Herman G. Weinberg, and others. (The newspaper materials usually give source and date but no page citation.) The Weinberg Scrapbooks of Film Reviews (in the Museum's Library, 80.78/W431), compiled by Herman G. Weinberg, 3 vols., 1925-1928 (unpublished), contain many articles and reviews for the Lubitsch films of these years, especially So This Is Paris, The Student Prince in Old Heidelberg, and The Patriot. (The sources are not identified, but presumably the materials are clipped mainly from New York papers.) The Museum's library also has some of the rare foreign language titles listed in the bibliography, such as the 1927 Russian monograph on Lubitsch by Nedobrovo and the 1924 special issue of Licht-Bild-Bühne.

344   THEATRE COLLECTION
    Library of the Performing Arts at Lincoln Center
    New York Public Library

111 Amsterdam Avenue
New York, New York 10023
Paul Myers, Curator
(212) 799-2200 ext. 213 or 214

12 noon to 8 p.m. Monday and Thursday; 12 noon to 6 p.m.
Tuesday, Wednesday, Friday and Saturday
Photographic Service is available Monday through Saturday,
12:15 to 6 p.m.

Scripts:
  Design for Living (scene and dialogue continuity 11/24/33),
The Merry Widow (scene and dialogue continuity 10/4/34), To Be
or Not To Be (production script 10/6/41 with changes 10/7/41),
Cluny Brown (production script "first draft continuity"
5/10/45.

Other:
  The Theatre Collection at Lincoln Center contains an im-
mense treasure of specialized materials for research on Lubitsch's films. The cataloguing system is complex, and materials on Lubitsch and his associates are to be found under several different classifications. There is a file for virtually
every Lubitsch film released in the United States. For the
silent era, the files typically contain a few photographs,
clippings (largely New York area newspaper reviews), a program, and a press sheet or pressbook. For the sound films
there are clippings, a pressbook, and usually a larger number
of photographs. The Lubitsch file contains a large number of
clippings of press interviews with Lubitsch from New York area
newspapers. There are also files on many Lubitsch associates,
especially writers and performers. (The clippings at Lincoln
Center usually indicate source and date but not page number.)
There are Paramount Studios publicity bulletins for the 1930s
such as Paramount International News, Paramount Sales News,
and Paramount around the World, which contain much information
on Lubitsch films. Scrapbooks of Monte Blue, Rod La Rocque,
Ronald Colman, and Jeanette MacDonald (among others) contain
Lubitsch material. Scrapbooks for the Capitol Theatre (New
York) contain newspaper clippings for Lubitsch films that
played there. Script collection contains unpublished English-
language typescripts of: Only a Dream, the source play for
The Marriage Circle and One Hour with You; the source play for
Angel; and Reginald Berkeley's stage adaption of Maurice Rostand's The Man I Killed. Edwin Justus Mayer Collection contains clipping service folder of over 200 American newspaper
reviews of To Be or Not To Be. Cluny Brown folder contains
several dozen production stills. Lincoln Center also has an
extensive collection of film trade papers and fan magazines.

345 FILM DEPARTMENT
     International Museum of Photography
     George Eastman House
     900 East Avenue
     Rochester, New York 14607
     Marshall Deutelbaum, Assistant to the Director
     (716) 271-3361

Arrangements should be made well in advance.

Declined to provide information about holdings for this survey.

   Reported to hold a print of the German short <u>Ich möchte kein</u>
<u>Mann sein</u>; several of the German features; a few of the rare
American silent features; and several of the American sound
features. Also holds the Warner Brothers New York City stills
library (1,000,000 pieces), which includes material on the Lubitsch Warners films.

WASHINGTON, D.C.

346 MOTION PICTURE SECTION
     Prints and Photographs Division
     Library of Congress
     1046 Thomas Jefferson Building
     Washington, D.C. 20540
     Barbara Humphrys, Reference Librarian
     (202) 426-5840

8:30 a.m. to 4:30 p.m. Monday through Friday

   The Motion Picture Section maintains the Library's film
collections for scholarly study and research. Public projec-
tion, preview, and loan services are not available. The Section staff answers written and telephone inquiries about the
holdings and makes appointments for the use of the reference
facilities by individual scholars. The viewing facilities
may be used free of charge by serious researchers only; viewing times must be scheduled in advance. The facilities may
not be used by high school students; undergraduate college
students must provide a letter from their professor endorsing
their project. The Section maintains a reading room with extensive card files describing the Library's motion picture
holdings. The files include a shelflist, a dictionary catalog, a nitrate film file, a directors file, and chronological
and production company files for silent films. Copies of film
footage not restricted by copyright, by provisions of gift or
transfer, or by physical condition may be ordered through the
Section. The requester is responsible for a search, either in
person or by mail, of Copyright Office records to determine
the copyright status of specific works.

Prints:
    Sumurun, So This Is Paris, Trouble in Paradise, Desire,
Heaven Can Wait (b/w), Dragonwyck, Cluny Brown.

Scripts:
    The Marriage Circle (scene continuity, undated), Kiss Me
Again (scene continuity, undated, 121 shots), The Student
Prince (scene continuity, undated), The Merry Widow (scene
and dialogue continuity 10/4/34), Ninotchka (scene and dialogue continuity 9/26/39), The Shop around The Corner (scene
and dialogue continuity 12/30/39), That Uncertain Feeling
(scene continuity, undated), To Be or Not To Be (scene continuity 2/11/42), Heaven Can Wait (dialogue continuity 11/4/43),
A Royal Scandal (dialogue continuity, undated), Dragonwyck
(dialogue continuity 1/14/46), Cluny Brown (dialogue continuity
4/4/46).

Other:
    For each motion picture registered for U.S. copyright, the
copyright file contains some sort of descriptive material,
usually a single item such as a script or a pressbook. The
scripts listed above are in the copyright files. The copyright
files for the other Lubitsch films contain plot synopses,
press sheets, or pressbooks.

WISCONSIN

347   WISCONSIN CENTER FOR FILM AND THEATRE RESEARCH
       816 State Street
       Madison, Wisconsin 53706
       Susan Dalton, Film Archivist
       Steve Masar, Manuscripts Archivist
       (608) 262-0585, 262-8975

       8:30 a.m. to 4:30 p.m. Monday through Friday

       Prints:
           Sumurun (incomplete), So This Is Paris.

       Scripts:
           S. N. Behrman Collection contains a script draft of Ninotch-
       ka by Behrman (11/9/38 revisions to 11/28/38, 130 pp. type-
       script), plus working notes and subsequent revisions of the
       Ninotchka script.

       Stills:
           Eternal Love (about 150), To Be or Not To Be (about 300),
       plus loose stills from six other films. Melvyn Douglas Col-
       lection contains a few loose stills with Douglas in Angel and
       Ninotchka.

Other:
United Artists Collection contains extensive files covering the legal arrangements, financial details, and tax case on To Be or Not To Be. United Artists Collection also contains: story rights file on Three Women (includes an English translation of the source novel, Lillis Ehe); file of title registration dispute over Eternal Love; and contracts and legal papers of Lubitsch arrangement with Sol Lesser under which That Uncertain Feeling was made.

OUTSIDE OF UNITED STATES

CZECHOSLOVAKIA

348 THE CZECHOSLOVAK FILM ARCHIVES
Czechoslovak Film Institute
Národní 40
110 00 Praha 1
Slavoj Ondroušek, Director
Telephone: 26 00 87

Prints:
Schuhpalast Pinkus, Die Augen der Mumie Mâ, Die Puppe, Die Austernprinzessin, Madame Dubarry, Anna Boleyn, Romeo und Julia im Schnee, Sumurun, Die Bergkatze, Rosita, Three Women, Lady Windermere's Fan, So This Is Paris, Eternal Love, The Love Parade, Trouble in Paradise, One Hour with You, The Man I Killed (German dubbed version), If I Had a Million, Design for Living, The Merry Widow, Angel, Bluebeard's Eighth Wife, To Be or Not To Be, Heaven Can Wait.

Stills:
Sizeable collection, mainly from the period 1930 to 1940.

DENMARK

349 DET DANSKE FILMMUSEUM
St. Søndervoldstraede
1419 København K
Ib Monty, Director
Telephone: Asta 6500

Prints:
Madame Dubarry, Die Puppe, Kohlhiesels Töchter, Sumurun, The Smiling Lieutenant, Trouble in Paradise, Design for Living, Angel, Bluebeard's Eighth Wife, That Uncertain Feeling, To Be or Not To Be.

Stills:
Files on most Lubitsch films, with concentration on the
sound films. Also 200 photographs (including some private
photographs) donated by Nicola Lubitsch; some of these are
reproduced in the special Lubitsch feature in Kosmorama
(1976).

FRANCE

350   LA CINEMATHÈQUE FRANÇAISE
      82 Rue de Courcelles
      Paris 8e

      Did not respond to a request for information.

      Said to hold a number of Lubitsch films, including some of
      those made in French-language versions. Also holds a collec-
      tion of Ernst Stern set design materials for Die Bergkatze,
      Das Weib des Pharao, and Die Flamme.

GERMANY (BRD)

351   STIFTUNG DEUTSCHE KINEMATHEK
      Pommernallee 1
      1000 Berlin 19 (West)
      Heinz Rathsack, Director
      Telephone: 3036-212 and 234

      Prints:
      Fräulein Piccolo, Hans Trutz im Schlaraffenland, Carmen,
      Die Augen der Mumie Mâ, Die Austernprinzessin, Madame Dubarry,
      Die Puppe, Anna Boleyn, Kohlhiesels Töchter (Danish interti-
      tles), Die Bergkatze, Trouble in Paradise, Ninotchka.

      Stills:
      About 260 in collection, including materials on Carmen,
      Madame Dubarry, Die Puppe, Kohlhiesels Töchter, Anna Boleyn,
      Das Weib des Pharao.

      Other:
      Four posters by Josef Fenne-ker to the following films of
      1918: Die Augen der Mumie Mâ, Carmen, Der Fall Rosentopf,
      and Das Mädel vom Ballett. Material concerning Ernst Lubitsch
      collected by the authors for their booklets on the 1967 and
      1968 Berlin Lubitsch retrospectives: Peter B. Schumann, Ret-
      rospektive (Filmhistorische Vorführungen der Internationalen
      Filmfestspiele: Berlin, 1967), pp. 1-34, and Peter B. Schu-
      mann and Werner Dütsch, Retrospektive (Filmhistorische Vor-
      führungen der Internationalen Filmfestspiele: Berlin, 1968),
      pp. 1-35. Some of the material is reproduced in these book-
      lets.

Note:
   At the time this volume went to press, Mikrofilmarchiv der deutschsprachigen Presse e.V. (46 Dortmund, Hansaplatz, 3 West Germany), had just concluded arrangements, in cooperation with Stiftung Deutsche Kinemathek, to microfilm a series of early German film trade periodicals. The first titles to be available are: Der Film, 1916-1943; Kinematograph, 1907-1935; and Licht-Bild-Bühne, 1924-1939. These will provide invaluable information about Lubitsch's German years.

351a   PHOTO- UND FILMMUSEUM
       Münchner Stadtmuseum
       St. Jakobs-Platz 1
       D 8 München 2
       Enno Patalas, Curator

       Prints:
          Ein fideles Gefängnis, Die Austernprinzessin, Ich möchte kein Mann sein!, Romeo und Julia im Schnee, Sumurun, Die Bergkatze, Das Weib des Pharao (about 3/4 complete), Die Flamme (30-minute fragment).

       Note:
          Some of the above are unique, specially-restored prints (see entry 206a).

352   FILMARCHIV
       Deutsches Institut für Filmkunde
       Schloss
       6202 Wiesbaden-Biebrich
       Eberhard Spiess, Director
       Telephone: 69074-75

       Prints:
          Der Stolz der Firma, Schuhpalast Pinkus, Die Augen der Mumie Mâ, Carmen, Die Austernprinzessin, Madame Dubarry, Die Puppe, Kohlhiesels Töchter, Anna Boleyn, Sumurun, Die Bergkatze.

       Other:
          Gigantic collection of newspaper clippings, photographs, posters, press sheets, and censorship records. Also virtually complete runs of the following rare German trade periodicals for the periods indicated: Der Film (late 1918 to 1926), Kinematograph (1908 to 1935).

GERMANY (DDR)

353 STÄATLICHES FILMARCHIV DER D.D.R.
Hausvogteiplatz 3-4
108 Berlin (East)
Wolfgang Klaue, Director
Telephone: 21 243 24

Prints:
Schuhpalast Pinkus, Wenn vier dasselbe tun, Die Augen der
Mumie Mâ, Carmen, Die Austernprinzessin, Madame Dubarry, Die
Puppe, Kohlhiesels Töchter, Romeo und Julia im Schnee, Sumu-
run, Anna Boleyn, Die Bergkatze.

Other:
Materials (stills or programs) on ten of Lubitsch's German
films, including Rausch, Das Weib des Pharao, and Die Flamme.

GREAT BRITAIN

354 BRITISH FILM INSTITUTE
National Film Archive
81 Dean Street
London W1V 6AA
David Francis, Curator
Telephone: 01-437 4355

Prints:
So This Is Paris, Paramount on Parade (excerpts), Monte
Carlo, The Man I Killed, One Hour with You, If I Had a Million,
Design for Living, Angel, That Uncertain Feeling, To Be or Not
To Be.

Stills:
Sizeable stills collection, including materials on twelve
of Lubitsch's German films and most of the American ones.

ITALY

355 CINETECA NAZIONALE
Centro Sperimentale di Cinematografia
Via Tuscolana 1524
00173 Roma
Leonardo Fioravanti, Director
Telephone: 740046

Prints:
Die Austernprinzessin, Madame Dubarry, Die Puppe, Die Bergkatze, The Marriage Circle, The Love Parade.

356   GOSFILMOFOND
       Stancia Bielye Stolby
       Moskovskaia Oblast
       Victor Privato, Director
       Telephone: 136.10.18

       "As for Lubitsch films, we do have a few prints..., but,
      as a rule, they are not complete, of bad photo quality and
      cannot be of interest to you."

VII. Film Distributors

357   Below is a list of Lubitsch films currently available for non-theatrical rental in the United States, arranged alphabetically, with an abbreviation opposite indicating the rental source. Following the list of films is an alphabetical list identifying the rental sources and giving contact information. A few titles are also listed as available for purchase and are so indicated.

Film	Source
Angel (1937)	UNI
Bluebeard's Eighth Wife (1938)	UNI
Broken Lullaby (The Man I Killed) (1932)	MMA, UNI
Carmen. See Gypsy Blood.	
Cluny Brown (1946)	FNC
Design for Living (1933)	UNI
Desire (1936)	MMA, UNI
Dragonwyck (1946)	FNC
Gypsy Blood (Carmen) (1918)	EMG, FCE (also sale)
If I Had a Million (1932)	UNI
The Lady Dances (The Merry Widow) (1934)	FNC
Lady Windermere's Fan (1925)	CIE (sale), EMG, FCE, SEL (sale), WIL
The Love Parade (1929)	MMA, UNI
Madame Dubarry. See Passion.	
The Man I Killed. See Broken Lullaby.	

The Marriage Circle (1924)	CIE (sale), EMG, KP, MMA, RI (sale)
The Merry Widow. See The Lady Dances.	
Monte Carlo (1930)	UNI
Ninotchka (1939)	FNC
One Hour with You (1932)	UNI
Paramount on Parade (1930)	UNI
Passion (Madame Dubarry) (1919)	CIE (sale), EMG, KP, MMA
A Royal Scandal (1945)	FNC
The Shop around the Corner (1940)	FNC
So This Is Paris (1926)	EMG, UAS
The Student Prince in Old Heidelberg (1927)	FNC
That Uncertain Feeling (1941)	SEL, WIL
To Be or Not To Be (1942)	CIE (sale), FNC, KP, MAB, RI (sale), SEL (sale)
Trouble in Paradise (1932)	MMA, UNI

Sources:

CIE	Cinema Eight 91 Main Street Chester, CT 06412 (203) 526-9513
EMG	Em Gee Film Library 16024 Ventura Boulevard Suite 211 Encino, CA 91436 (213) 981-5506
FCE	Film Classic Exchange 1914 South Vermont Avenue Los Angeles, CA 90007 (213) 731-3854

FNC	Films Incorporated 733 Greenbay Road Wilmette, IL 60091 (312) 256-6600 and regional offices in Atlanta, Hollywood, Honolulu, and New York City
KP	Kit Parker Films Carmel Valley, CA 93924 (408) 659-3474/659-4131
MAB	Macmillan Audio Brandon 34 MacQuesten Parkway South Mount Vernon, NY 10550 (914) 664-5051 and regional offices in Brookfield, (IL), Dallas, Los Angeles, and Oak- land
MMA	Museum of Modern Art Department of Film 11 West 53rd Street New York, NY 10019 (212) 245-8900

RI	Reel Images
	East of Mississippi:
	  456 Monroe Turnpike
	  Monroe, CT 06468
	  (203) 261-5022
	
	West of Mississippi:
	  10523 Burbank Boulevard No. 104
	  North Hollywood, CA 91601
	  (213) 762-5341

SEL	Select Film Library 115 West 31st Street New York, NY 10001 (212) 594-4450
UAS	United Artists 16 729 Seventh Avenue New York, NY 10019 (212) 575-4715

UNI   Universal 16
                   445 Park Avenue
                   New York, NY 10022
                   (212) 759-7500
                   and regional offices in Atlanta,
                   Chicago, Dallas, and Los Angeles

WIL   Willoughby-Peerless
                   110 West 32nd Street
                   New York, NY 10011
                   (212) 564-1600

                     and

                   415 Lexington Avenue
                   New York, NY 10017
                   (212) 687-1000

Author Index to
Sections III through VI

Film Title Index to
Sections III through VII